The **Beatles Memorabilia**
Price Guide

BY

JEFF AUGSBURGER

MARTY ECK

AND

RICK RANN

Third Edition

Antique Trader Books

A division of Landmark Specialty Publications

ISBN: 0-930625-68-4
Library of Congress Catalog Card Number: 97-72622

Editor: *Elizabeth Stephan*
Art Director & Cover Design: *Jaro Sebek*
Designer: *Judy Ludowitz*
Design Assistants: *Lynn Bradshaw, Aaron Wilbers*

Cover photo credits:

Front Cover: *Top row (left to right)*—item #288,
13" Overnight Case, mfd. by Air Flight; item #116,
13"-tall Inflatable Dolls; item #253, Lunchbox, mfd.
by Aladdin Industries.

Middle Row (left to right)—item #284, Paint by Number (Paul),
mfd. by Artistic Creations; item #351, Four-Speed Record Player;
item #296, Pencil by Number Kit, mfd. by Kitfix (U.K.).

Bottom Row (left to right)—item #121, 8"-tall Bobbin' Head Dolls,
mfd. by Carmascot; Promotional Poster for *Yellow Submarine*
paperback, written by Max Wilk; item #555, $5^1/_4$"-long die-cast
Yellow Submarine, mfd. by Corgi.

Printed in the United States of America

To order additional copies of this
book ar a catalog please contact:

Antique Trader Books
P.O. Box 1050
Dubuque, Iowa 52004
1-800-334-7165

Antique Trader Books
A division of Landmark Specialty Publications

Dedications

To Barbara, Bradley, and Laurel, and all the good friends I've made through this hobby.

- Jeff Augsburger

With love to my wife Debbie, my son Michael, and my parents.
Thanks for putting up with all this for so many years.

- Marty Eck

To my wife Eileen, my children Tim and Claire, and my parents for all their love,
support and patience over the years.

- Rick Rann

With our thanks to the four young men who took the world by storm.

Acknowledgments

We would like to thank the following people who provided information and photographs for this book. Their contributions have made this a better guide.

Jim Acker
Stephen Bailey
Diana Barbee
Pat Bender
Jay Benjamin
John Beznik
Phil Biebl
Uwe Blaschke
Eric Block
Tyler-Travis Bolden
Stephen Braitman
Presley Cheshire
Stefanie Childs
Mike Cobern
Perry Cox
Jim Cunningham
Kevin Curran
Cliff DeManty
Ed Dieckmann
Tom Eringer
Marty Feier
Laurie Fidler
Mel Floss
Tom & Mary Fontaine
Tony Fornaro
Pat Fosarelli
Steve Freedman
Randy French
Michael Gervais
Mario Giannella
Rick Glover
Bob Gottuso
Joe Greco
Steve Green
Benjy Greenberg
Tom Haack
Trevor Halliday
David Harper
Gary Hein
Hi-De-Ho Collectibles
Joe Hilton

Jackie Holmes
Pete Howard
Don Hunter
Lauren Kane
Seth Kaplan
Cynthia Kimble
Thomas Komorowski
Fred Koogler
Marty Krim
Ray Labrolia
Jeff Leve
Gregory Linder Photography
Janet Macoska
Peter Madlock
Chris Maddock
Waide Maguire
Jerry Marasco
Kent Melton
Peter Mildren
Mark Naboshek
Peter Nash
Chris Ridges
Gib Robbie
Rockaway Records
Wayne Rogers
Ralph Rophie
Mike Runyan
Ed Schreiber
Craig Smith
Ron Taub
Chris Tessitore
Herb van Vliet
Paul van Winsum
Paul Wane
Bill Weaver
Kelly Wesson
Jonathan White
Mike White
Suzanne Wiencek
Paul Wultz
Cliff Yamasaki
Joe Zabel

We would also like to thank all our friends and customers with whom we have dealt over the last twenty years. The majority of items illustrated in this book are from the collections of Jeff Augsburger and Marty Eck

CONTENTS

INTRODUCTION

THE GROUP

Four young musicians from Liverpool, England, John Lennon, Paul McCartney, George Harrison, and Ringo Starr, collectively known as the Beatles are arguably the most influential rock music group of all time. Their domination of the English music scene in 1963 and the rest of the world the following year, tells only a small part of the story. On a musical level, the Beatles' records changed the way rock albums were made. No longer was an LP merely a vehicle for a hit record, with a collection of "fillers" completing the package. Each track became important. (At least in England, where the Beatles had more control over the way music was handled.) Records designated as "singles" were not included on the Beatles' British album releases.

As time went on, the Beatles took more control over both the music and its packaging, with major accomplishments such as "Sgt. Pepper's Lonely Hearts Club Band" and the "White Album." The Beatles set trends that others attempted to follow. The Beatles also changed the way studios were used. Musicians, including the Beatles, used to visit the studio to record the music they had rehearsed. The Beatles began using the studio as the place where music was developed and refined. All-day and all-night sessions became commonplace, with the tape machines running almost continuously.

In the live music arena, the Beatles did more than establish all-time attendance marks for both concerts and tours. The screaming, pushing crowds characteristic of Beatlemania, coupled with the primitive equipment of the times, nullified any musical interaction with the crowds. Going to a Beatle concert became a musical event where the music was a minor facet of the experience.

In many other ways, the Beatles mirrored societal changes. Many of their original fans lost interest when the group began speaking out on subjects ranging from religion and meditation to drugs. At the same time they attracted new listeners as their music reflected their changing concerns and values.

THE MEMORABILIA

The earliest Beatles memorabilia available to the average collector would date from 1962, when the group began to attract a significant following. This resulted in a Liverpool-based fan club, a recording contract and more media attention. This publicity was due in a large part to the efforts of their manager, Brian Epstein.

The year 1963 brought a national following in the United Kingdom, with merchandising depicting the "fab four" available to every fan. The Beatles' relentless schedule of live appearances in this and the following three years kept interest in the group at a high level, although the flow of memorabilia ebbed considerably after their worldwide rise to fame in 1964. That year saw American companies produce a flood of items. When the Beatles first appeared in the U.S. in February 1964 there were limited amounts of memorabilia to purchase. By the time the Beatles returned for their first U.S. concert tour in August of 1964 the marketplace was saturated with every imaginable item from Beatle shampoo to tennis shoes. Some items were simply converted from the companies' standard product with the addition of a Beatles picture, such as record cases, scrapbooks and sweatshirts. Other items were more creative, such as the Beatle models, dolls, and games. The initial wave of memorabilia concentrated on the young girls who constituted the group's most vocal and intense following. Magazines, posters, and jewelry were big sellers, along with more utilitarian items such as nylons, handbags, and hair spray. For the boys there were toy drums, guitars, models, and Beatle boots. The Beatle wig was a popular gag item among adults for a brief time, with reported sales of several million in 1964.

Despite the abundance of Beatle products, the Beatles themselves saw little money from these items. Poor licensing deals, a flood of unlicensed merchandise and the inability to effectively collect royalties all added to the problem. Companies avoided paying licensing royalties to the Beatles by producing items which cashed in on their "image." No doubt the fifteen-year-old fan buying the "Swingers" nodder dolls on the card, thought they were the Beatles. Long-haired lads, collarless suits, left-handed guitarist, violin bass, bugs (beetles), "Yeah Yeah Yeah," etc. would convey the proper image which the teen would buy. We have concentrated on items that invoke the name of "the Beatles" or are unmistakably the Beatles and not any other 1960s British invasion group. Most companies looked upon the Beatles as a fad to use to gain a quick profit. Many outfits set up their box numbers, sold all the items they could, and were out of business a year later. Many of the fans were just as fickle. Other British groups, such as the Dave Clark Five and Herman's Hermits, followed the Beatles and quickly gained their own fans, often at the expense of the Beatles. Although the Beatles' musical abilities insured that they would remain popular, the initial fervor of 1963 and 1964 soon subsided, along with the flood of merchandise. Throughout 1965, 1966, and 1967, there were few new items produced.

In 1968, the release of *Yellow Submarine* brought a new wave of merchandise connected to the movie. Many of these items were aimed at a new younger audience. This effort was probably largely unsuccessful, as warehouse stocks of many of these items have appeared from time to time. Though several of the items, such as the Goebel figurines and the wrist watch, appear to have been quickly suspended as they are quite hard to locate today. After 1968 production of new Beatle memorabilia was primarily limited to fan club items and items associated with their company, Apple.

The value of items in this guide reflect what we feel to be the average market value at the present time. Prices often vary from one section of the country to another. Over time the general trend in prices has been upward for all but the most common items. In the last five years the highest increases in value has been for these categories of items: the rarer items and items in original packaging in the General Memorabilia and Yellow Submarine chapters; Record promotion items; and Concert tickets and programs. Recent collecting booms in other collectibles such as lunchboxes or cereal boxes have driven up the price for

the Beatle collector of that Beatle related item. The ultimate judge of value should be the individual collector himself.

Occasionally there are legitimate "warehouse finds" of original memorabilia. These will often cause a drop in the price of an item, which will last until the quantities of the "find" have been depleted. Many times these "warehouse finds" can also turn out to be reproductions or counterfeits. Please refer to the Reproductions and Counterfeits chapter for more information. If you see a ★ *Repro Alert* marked below a listing, then a known reproduction exists. Be sure to check the Reproductions and Counterfeits chapter for tips on how to determine if that item is original.

The value of memorabilia is based on three factors: rarity, desirability, and condition.

Rarity: How many of an item were produced and how many have survived? Some items were not produced by major companies and/or were not nationally distributed. Many items that were produced were of a disposable nature such as hair spray, shampoo, talcum powder, food or candy products, etc. These items are less likely to have survived than dolls or trading cards which many people have held onto over the years. The original price of an item is also a contributing factor to rarity. The $29.95 record player (item #351) or the $24.95 headphones (item #227) sold far fewer units than did the $2.50 Remco doll (items #123 to 136).

Desirability: Prices are not always based on rarity. An example is the belt (item #28) which is much more difficult to find than a set of the Beatle Remco dolls (items #123 to 126) out of the boxes. Yet the doll set is valued higher than the belt. A collector may be attracted to an item that he remembers from his youth, while other collectors may prefer certain categories of memorabilia. A die-hard collector or "completist" may try to obtain all variations (color, size, etc.) of a certain item.

Condition: Condition is another important factor in determining price. A perfect piece of memorabilia will bring top dollar. The same item in poor condition will bring a fraction of the perfect price. In most cases a "good" condition item will be valued at half the price of a "near mint" condition item.

It is important to grade items properly when using this guide to value items. Don't just look at the highest (near mint) value! It is important to understand that an item in good condtion is generally valued at one-half the near mint value. We have listed general guidelines for each grade. It is hard to list exact guidelines given the large variety of Beatle memorabilia available (everything from beach towels to record players!) As in other hobbies, experience will help develop your grading expertise.

Grading Guidelines

(In all grades items must be complete.)

(NM) Near mint condition: Item must be near perfect with no defects.

(VG) Very good condition: Item has few signs of wear. Wear should not detract from the appearance of the item.

(G) Good condition: Item shows wear. Wear should not detract greatly from overall appearance.

Defects such as tears, tape, cracks, ink marks or writing, missing pieces, etc. should be noted in addition to grade. For example (VG, writing on cover). A plus (+) or minus (-) can also be used to better describe a grade. Additional guidelines are listed at the beginnings of some of the chapters.

REPRODUCTIONS AND COUNTERFEITS

The increase in Beatle memorabilia prices has led to an increase in Beatle memorabilia reproductions and counterfeits. For collecting purposes we define reproductions as copies or fakes of original 1960s memorabilia. Reproductions were made in the mid-1970s up to today. An example of a reproduction is the Beatle metal serving tray. The original 1964 edition has "Made in Great Britain" on the front. The reproduction has "Made in England" on the front. Those original items which have known copies are marked with ★ *Repro Alert* following their entry in the guide. A corresponding entry will be found in the list of reproductions. If you see ★ *Repro Alert* when checking the value of an item, be sure to check the list of reproductions for some tips to determine authenticity.

USING THIS BOOK

This book contains nearly all known Beatles memorabilia items produced between 1962 and 1970 (the year of the group's breakup). If you were a Beatles fan during those years, you're certain to remember some of the items pictured and listed in the book. Photographs are provided for about two-thirds of the items, and every item listed is described completely enough to allow for easy identification by the collector. Items photographed are usually listed in the text on the same or facing page.

Most items we have listed in this book were products officially licensed by the Beatles. Many of the items were marked "Nems Ent. Ltd." or "Seltaeb." "NEMS" was an acronym for North End Music Stores which was Brian Epstein's company. (Brian Epstein was the Beatles' manager.) "Seltaeb" (Beatles spelled backwards) was the Beatles' American licensing company's name. Unfortunately, since the mid-1970s memorabilia counterfeiters have marked items with "NEMS" or "SELTAEB" and dated them "1964," so the collector must beware.

This book reflects the combined efforts of three longtime Beatle fans. Many of the items in this book are quite rare and have never been photographed for a publication before. Others, although somewhat common, are quite popular among collectors.

THE BASIC BEATLE MEMORABILIA COLLECTION

Many beginning collectors of Beatles memorabilia are overwhelmed by the variety and prices of the pieces offered for sale. Getting started in building a collection can therefore be somewhat intimidating. Eventually collectors tailor their collections to suit personal interests, budget, and space limitations. But there are certain items that almost every collector aspires to own. With this in mind we have attempted to build a model of a basic Beatles memorabilia collection. We have limited the collection to items that can be bought for $400 or less in at least very good condition. We have included a variety of pieces, all of which have proven to be quite popular for many years.

1. Set of Remco Dolls (items #123-126)
2. 1965 (blue) Lunchbox (item #253)
3. Flip Your Wig Game (item #144)
4. Pillow (item #307, 308, or 309)
5. Wallet or Pencil Case (item #430 or 298)
6. Record Case, Disk-Go-Case (item #349)
7. Binder (item #31 or 32)
8. Paul or Ringo Bubble Bath (item #53 or 54)
9. Dell Poster (item #765 or 766)
10. Yellow Submarine Corgi Toy (item #555)
11. Model Kit (item #261, 262, 263, or 264)
12. Yellow Submarine Lunchbox (item #504)
13. In His Own Write book by John Lennon (item #789)
14. One set of Trading Cards (item #1207-1209, 1216, 1217 or 1223)

15. Movie Poster (item #997, 1017, 1028, or 1038)
16. *Life, Look,* or *Post* magazine with the Beatles on the cover (item #953, 954, 960, 964, 965, or 967)
17. Yellow Submarine Bank (item #444, 445, 446, or 447)
18. Yellow Submarine Puzzle (item #528-541)
19. Wig, in package (item #442)
20. Concert Ticket (see Chapter 14)

THE LISTINGS

Most items in the book appear as listings. Each numbered listing provides descriptive information about the item. At the very least, the listing includes a checkbox, an item number, the name of the item, and the prices for the item in various conditions.

THE CHECKBOX

The circles to the left of the item numbers are provided so that collectors can check off each item as it is added to their collection. These checkboxes do not imply that the numbered list in this book is exhaustive. Instead, the circles are meant to provide a convenient way for collectors to inventory their collection

ITEM NUMBER

Items listed in the book are numbered consecutively from #1 to #1306. These numbers do not necessarily agree with those in the first or second editions. For a few of the collecting categories, such as sheet music (see Chapter 8) and newspaper supplements (see Chapter 7), a representative sampling or description is provided rather than a numbered list. Items that originally were sold separately, such as the dolls by Remco (items #123-126), have been given separate numbers. If there are several versions of a given item, these are usually listed separately (versions representing each of the Beatles are listed in the order familiar to most Beatle fans—John, Paul, George, and Ringo—rather than alphabetically).

ITEM NAME

The item name is listed next to the number. In most cases, a generic name is given rather then a brand name. Although, in some cases, such as the Flip Your Wig Game and the Kaboodle Kit, the brand name is more descriptive, so it is used. When possible, the generic name of the item is taken directly from the packaging or from other advertising for the product. For example, item #1, the airbed, could also be referred to as an air mattress. It is called an airbed here because that's the name under which it was advertised.

Items that were used for point-of-use (i.e., retail) advertising (such as a display board for pinback buttons) are listed under the name of the item they displayed (e.g., item #95, which is called the Coloring Book Display because it is the store display for item #94, the Coloring Book.) Similarly, product offers, such as toys or gifts available in soap or cereal boxes or by mail-order offers are listed under the name of the toy or gift offered rather than under the name of the sponsoring product (e.g., item #119 is the Nestlés Quik can that advertised item #116, the inflatable dolls).

OTHER INFORMATION

With each piece of memorabilia listed we have tried to list the manufacturer, size, country of production (if other than U.S.), year of manufacture (if other than 1964) and description. We have also tried to list the original packaging (referred to as "OP" in the guide).

REPRO ALERT

In some listings, the phrase ★ *Repro Alert* appears just after the description. This is an important warning. It means that a known reproduction of the item exists. All items that have a "★ *Repro Alert*" warning in their listing also appear in Chapter 16 under the List of Known Reproductions under the same number with an "RA" prefix. Be sure to consult that list to determine how to tell the authentic item from the reproduction. (For more information, see the "Reproductions and Counterfeits" section earlier in this introduction.

VALUES

Values (in dollars) appear at the end of each listing. These values reflect the current average market value of the item and are based on the three condition grades already discussed: near mint (NM), very good (VG), and good (G).

In some cases, a variation in the style or packaging of an item leads to a further variation in value. When such variations occur, they are described in the listing as an addition to or deduction from the values listed. Thus, according to the listing for item #53, if the Paul Bubble Bath in VG condition is in the original packaging (OP), 100% should be added to the value. Knowing the price for the Paul Bubble Bath in VG condition is $110, the collector should do the following equations:

To calculate 100% of $110, multiply $110 by 1.00
$110 x 1.00 = $110

Then add this amount to the original price
$110 + $110 = $220

So the price for the item in its original packaging (OP) is $220.

While no book on collectibles with this variety can be complete, we have tried to be as comprehensive as possible. The discovery of previously uncataloged items is always one of the most enjoyable parts of any collecting venture, and Beatles memorabilia collecting affords that opportunity. We appreciate any and all contributions of information.

We welcome your opinions and suggestions. If you have information on an item we have not listed or additional information on an item we have listed we would appreciate your input. We can use your help in compiling a revised edition. We will also be happy to answer your questions about Beatles memorabilia. Catalogues are available by request.

As authors, columnists, and collectors, we are actively looking to add to our inventory of original Beatles memorabilia. We will buy one item or an entire collection, and we will travel anywhere for quality accumulations. We have a reputation for buying "warehouse finds" and would like to purchase significant quantities of good merchandise. We pay finder fees for good leads. Please contact us if you feel you have any items of interest.
Happy Collecting!

Jeff Augsburger   Marty Eck   Rick Rann

Please send all inquiries to the authors at:

JMR
P.O. Box 5311
River Forest, IL 60305

or

E-Mail to: fabfour@dave-world.net

or call

(309) 452-9376 or (630) 365-5468

General Memorabilia

"General Memorabilia" is the term we use to describe all items that do not fit into the other thirteen chapters. The other thirteen chapters deal with distinct categories of memorabilia. In this chapter the listings are alphabetically arranged by the item name. We have tried to list an item by the type of product it is, rather than the brand name. For example, the Disk-Go-Case is listed under Record Case. All items are from 1964 and were made in the U.S. unless otherwise noted.

○ **1.   Airbed;** Mfd. by Li-Lo (U.K.); 6' x 3'; vinyl inflatable bed with "The Beatles" and their faces and first names printed on top; available in red and yellow vinyl or blue and yellow vinyl.
G $350   VG $525   NM $700

○ **2.   Apron;** white paper with repeating pattern of Beatles' pictures, names and song titles in black.
G $200   VG $300   NM $400

○ **3.   Arcade Cards;** $3^3/_8$" x $5^3/_8$"; B&W cards with printed info on the Beatles on the back; various cards of each Beatle and group photos; sold in vending machines. ★ *Repro Alert*
G $2   VG $3   NM $5

1

2

4. **Armband;** 8" wide x 4" tall; oval-shaped red felt armband with elastic back; "Paul Lives Radio WRIT" printed in black; 1969 Milwaukee radio station item.
   G $60   VG $90   NM $120

5. **Ashtray (U.K.);** 3³/₄" square; white plastic ashtray with round clear glass insert; early B&W photo between glass and plastic.
   G $150   VG $225   NM $300

6. **Assignment Book;** Mfd. by Select-O-Pack; 4" x 6 ¹/₂"; vinyl notebook; pad of lined paper with drawing of the Beatles at top of each page; available in various colors.
   G $100   VG $160   NM $200

7. **Autograph Book;** Mfd. by Seagull Ent. (U.K.); 6" x 4³/₄"; blue, red or white vinyl autograph book has paper Beatle photo under clear plastic on front; plain white pages inside.
   G $150   VG $225   NM $300

8. **Bag (Japan);** 1966; vinyl bag with vinyl cord strap or drawstrings; various images, including drawings or photos; originally sold with a hang tag.
   G $75   VG $110   NM $150

9. **Ball;** Mfd. by Shenstone Creations; 9" diameter; black rubber inflatable ball; drawing of Beatles and signatures in 5¹/₂" white oval on side.
   G $300   VG $450   NM $600

10. **Ball (U.K.);** 8" diameter; white rubber inflatable ball; B&W picture of each Beatle with autograph on ball; "The Beatles" written on two sides.
    G $300   VG $450   NM $600

11. **Ball;** 14" diameter; inflatable "Playball" has faces in oval; ball has ring protrusion on side for grasping; OP: clear bag with header card; add 100% if packaging is present.
    G $200   VG $300   NM $400

12. **Balloon;** Mfd. by United Industries; 5 ¹/₂" x 6" (packaged size); balloon has B&W photo of the group; various colors of balloons; OP: sealed plastic bag with group photo printed on bag; value is for sealed item.
    G $60   VG $90   NM $125

13. **Bamboo Plate;** Mfd. by Bamboo Tray Specialist; 12" diameter; bamboo plate with Beatles pictured in director's chairs from *A Hard Day's Night*.
    G $60   VG $90   NM $125

14. **Bamboo Plate;** (same as above); 11¹/₂" diameter

15. **Bamboo Plate;** (same as above); 6" diameter

16. **Banjo;** Mfd. by Mastro; 22" long; plastic four-string banjo which has Beatle faces on skin and top of neck; sold with instruction booklet; OP: sealed in plastic with backer board; add 50% to value if in OP; price for instruction book only in NM is $200.
    G $1,000   VG $1,500   NM $2,000

5   6   7

4

11

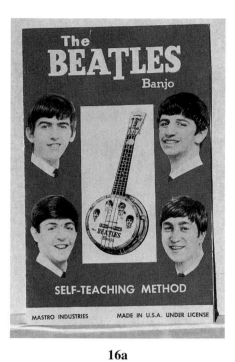

16a

8

12

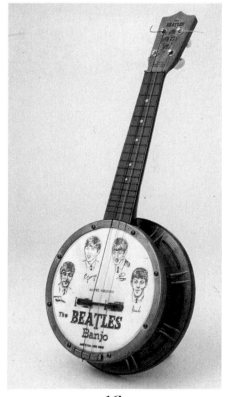

16b

10

13

○ **17. Bank (U.K.);** 10" tall; white plastic molded sculpture of group with sticker on front; reads "The Beatle Bank."
G $450   VG $675   NM $900

○ **18. Beach Hat;** Mfd. by Lamron Co.; 9" diameter; red and white or blue and white with faces and autographs on front.
G $50   VG $75   NM $100

○ **19. Beach Towel;** Mfd. by Towel Decorators for Cannon; 35" x 65"; drawing of the Beatles in old fashioned swim suits with "The Beatles" across top.
G $80   VG $120   NM $160

○ **20. Beat Seat;** Mfd. by Unitrend, Ltd. (U.K.); 14" diameter, 4" thick; vinyl-covered cushion in the design of a record; individual Beatle pictured with autograph in center "label" area; label on bottom has drawing of group.
G $350   VG $525   NM $700

○ **21. Bedsheets (Boston);** 1" square swatch stapled to a 4" x 8 1/2" certificate; bedsheets from the Beatles stay at the Hotel Madison in Boston on September 12, 1964; sold by the Massachusetts Chapter of the National Multiple Sclerosis Society to benefit charity.
G $40   VG $60   NM $80

○ **22. Bedsheets (Detroit);** 1" square on a 6" x 9" certificate; bedsheets that the Beatles slept on at the Whittier Hotel in Detroit on September 6, 1964; these squares were glued on a certificate of authenticity; one certificate for each Beatle; value is for each. ★ *Repro Alert*
G $15   VG $25   NM $35

○ **23. Bedsheets (Riviera);** 1 1/2" square on a 8 1/2" x 11" certificate; small piece of a bedsheet used by the Beatles during their stay at the Idlewood Hotel in Riviera, New York on September 20 & 21, 1964; sold with photo and affidavit; value is for each.
G $25   VG $35   NM $50

○ **24. Bedsheets (San Francisco);** 1 1/2" x 2 1/2" swatch encased in a 2 1/2" x 4" clear plastic sleeve; with a small photo of the group and a Junior Achievement sticker; reverse side has a letter of authenticity from the general manager of the San Francisco Hilton stating the Beatles stayed on these bedsheets on August 18 and 19th, 1964.
G $50   VG $75   NM $100

18

19

21

○ **25. Bedspread (U.K.);** 72" long x 100" wide; pleated white or yellow cotton with the group playing instruments; "The Beatles" and "Yeah Yeah Yeah" embroidered on it; embroidery is done in six colors.

G $250   **VG $375**   **NM $500**

○ **26. Bedspread (U.K.);** red cotton with the Beatles grouped around drum; drum has "The Beatles" in circular print on face.

G $250   **VG $375**   **NM $500**

○ **27. Belt;** black cord belt with $1^1/_2$"-round B&W vinyl fob on one end and $1^1/_2$" metal medallion with Beatle faces; another variation came with two metal medallions and did not have a vinyl fob; metal medallion showed faces with first names on one side, "The Beatles MCMLXIV" on other.

G $60   **VG $90**   **NM $125**

○ **28. Belt;** Mfd. by Tradewinds Unlimited; $1^1/_4$" wide; black leather belt with Beatle pictures under plastic on $3^1/_4$" x 2" brass colored buckle; "Official Beatles Belt" printed on the inside of the belt.

G $75   **VG $110**   **NM $150**

○ **29. Belt Buckle (U.K.);** 2" x 3"; gold colored metal buckle with B&W group picture under clear plastic.

G $35   **VG $50**   **NM $75**

25

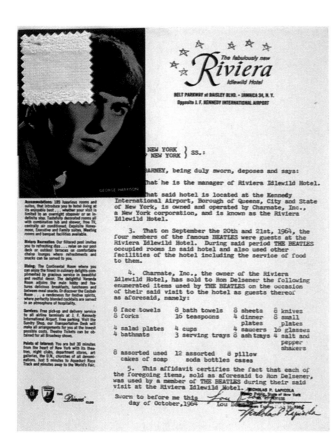

23

27

28

○ **30.   Binder;** Mfd. by Beat Publications. (U.K.); 6¹/₂" x 9"; grey cloth covered binder which held twelve issues of the *Beatles Book Monthly;* Beatles' faces on cover; "The Beatles Book" printed on spine.

G $100   **VG $150**   **NM $200**

○ **31.   Binder;** Mfd. by New York Looseleaf Corp.; 10¹/₂" x 11³/₄"; white 3-ring binder with group photo and autographs on front.

G $55   **VG $80**   **NM $110**

○ **32.   Binder;** Mfd. by Standard Plastic Products (SPP); 10¹/₂" x 11³/₄"; 3- or 2-ring binder; group photo and autographs on front; value depends on color:

Off white

G $60   **VG $90**   **NM $120**

Red, blue or yellow

G $80   **VG $120**   **NM $160**

Pink or lavender

G $90   **VG $135**   **NM $180**

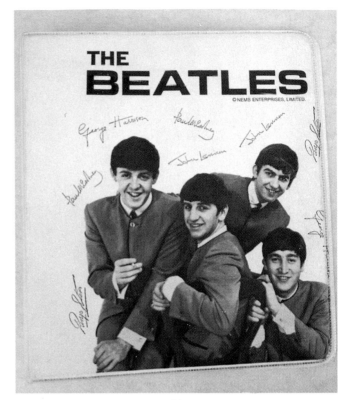

31

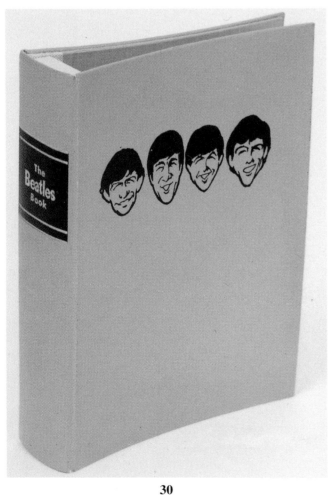

30

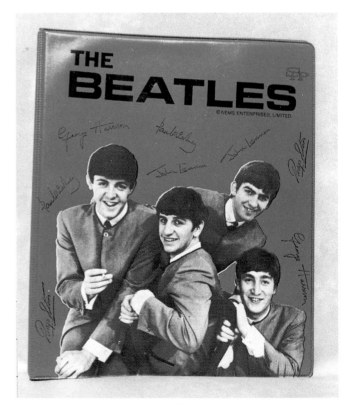

32

33

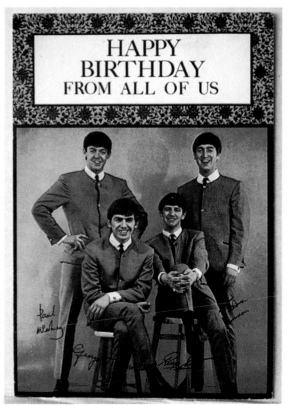

35

39

○ **33. Binder Box;** Mfd. by Fleer Corp.; 10" x 12" x 4$^1/_2$" deep; cardboard shipping box for Dubble Bubble Gum which was sent to retailer; box held 480 one-cent pieces of gum and included a free Beatles Binder (see also item #32—2-ring variation); value is for empty box.
G $250   VG $375   NM $500

○ **34. Bingo Game;** Mfd. by Toy Works. (U.K.); colorful boxed game with spinner.
G $400   VG $600   NM $800

○ **35. Birth Certificates;** Mfd. by Davidson's Authentic Documents (D.A.D.); 5" x 11"; exact reprints of the original documents; one for each Beatle; value is for set of four in the original envelope.
G $40   VG $60   NM $80

○ **36. Birthday Card;** Mfd. by American Greetings (Hi Brows HBB-1); 5$^1/_4$" x 14$^1/_4$"; "Look and feel at least 10 years younger on your birthday" on cover; unfolds into 21" x 28$^1/_2$" color poster of the Beatles.
G $30   VG $45   NM $60

○ **37. Birthday Card;** Mfd. by American Greetings (Hi Brows HBB-2); 5$^1/_4$" x 14"; "A gift straight from the heart to a wonderful friend..." on cover; unfolds into a 21" x 28$^1/_2$" color poster of the Beatles.
G $30   VG $45   NM $60

○ **38. Birthday Card;** Mfd. by American Greetings (Hi Brows HBB-3); 8$^1/_2$" x 12$^1/_4$"; cover has a color picture of the Beatles; "Happy birthday from the Beatles" on bottom section of cover.
G $25   VG $35   NM $50

○ **39. Birthday Card;** Mfd. by American Greetings (Hi Brows HBB-4); 8$^1/_2$" x 12$^1/_4$"; cover has a color picture of the Beatles; "Happy birthday from all of us" on top section of cover; Beatle autographs on the inside.
G $25   VG $35   NM $50

○ **40. Birthday Card;** Mfd. by American Greetings (Hi Brows HBB-5); 8$^1/_4$" x 12$^1/_4$"; "I think you're the greatest..." on cover; color Beatle photo inside.
G $25   VG $35   NM $50

○ **41. Birthday Card;** Mfd. by American Greetings (Hi Brows HBB-6); 8$^1/_4$" x 8$^1/_4$"; Beatle picture on cover. "...got a really good buy on this new Beatle record..." printed on cover; a 1" plastic "record" is glued to inside of card.
G $25   VG $35   NM $50

○ **42. Birthday Card;** Mfd. by Barker Greeting Card Co. (Longfellow Cards); 4" x 9"; drawing of group on cover; "To Celebrate Your Birthday why not do as the Beatles do" on cover; "Let Your hair Down! Happy Birthday" inside.
G $20   **VG $30**   **NM $40**

○ **43. Blanket;** Mfd. by Witney (U.K.); 62" wide x 80" long; tan wool fiber blend blanket; "The Beatles" printed in center, with black and red head and shoulder shots of each Beatle and instrument.
G $175   **VG $260**   **NM $350**

Board Game; see Flip Your Wig Game (item #144)

○ **44. Bongos;** Mfd. by Mastro (Beat Bongo); $5^{1}/_{4}$" tall, 5" head & $5^{3}/_{4}$" head; red plastic body with white skin; Beatle group sticker on each drum and Mastro decal on center bridge; two different styles of group stickers were used; OP: cardboard box with Beatles pictured (model number 360 on box); add 50% to value if box is present.
G $1,000   **VG $1,500**   **NM $2,000**

○ **45. Bongos;** Mfd. by Mastro (Big Beat Bongo); $6^{1}/_{4}$" tall, $6^{1}/_{4}$" head & $7^{1}/_{4}$" head; red plastic body with white skin; Beatle group sticker on each drum and Mastro decal on center bridge; two different styles of group stickers were used; OP: cardboard box with Beatles pictured (model number 370 on box); add 50% to value if box is present.
G $1,000   **VG $1,500**   **NM $2,000**

○ **46. Book Covers;** Mfd. by Book Covers Inc.; 10" x 13"; paper covers with B&W photos on edges; OP: seven covers and paper insert with Beatle photo sealed in plastic; value is for sealed package of seven; individual covers are valued at $8 each in NM shape. ★ *Repro Alert*
G $40   **VG $60**   **NM $80**

43

45

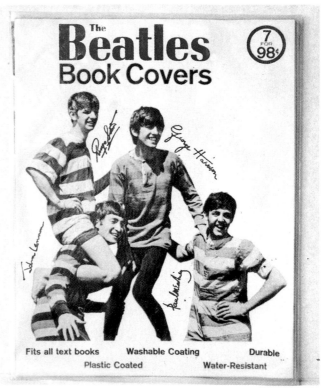

46

○ **47. Book Cover;** Mfd. by Sears & Capitol Records; 10" x 12½"; paper cover with color photo of Beatles on front; "Back to Cool!" on front; Capitol Record albums printed on the inside, including Beatle LPs; an August 1967 back-to-school promotion.

    G $12   **VG $18**   **NM $25**

○ **48. Boots (Canada);** 7" high with 1" heels; black leather boots; marked "RINGO" on the inside.

    G $75   **VG $110**   **NM $150**

○ **49. Booty Bag;** 10" x 15"; clear heavy plastic bag with cord handle; Beatles in blue suits pictured on front; yellow paper insert describes uses; add 50% for insert.

    G $50   **VG $75**   **NM $100**

○ **50. Bowl;** Mfd. by Washington Pottery (U.K.); 6" diameter; pottery bowl with fired blue and black decal of the group in the center.

    ★ *Repro Alert*

    G $75   **VG $110**   **NM $150**

○ **51. Brief Cover;** Mfd. by Select-O-Pak (Hi Craft); 9" x 11½"; grey vinyl folder with inside pockets; I.D. card and photo card fit in cover; value is for item with both cards.

    G $125   **VG $180**   **NM $250**

○ **52. Brunch Bag;** Mfd. by Alladin; 1965; 8" tall; blue vinyl case with zipper around top and black plastic strap; group pictured on front; sold with blue thermos (item #403); value is for bag alone.

    G $300   **VG $450**   **NM $600**

50

51

49

52

○ **53. Bubble Bath (Paul);** Mfd. by Colgate; 1965; 9" tall; red plastic container which held eleven ounces of bubble bath; head unscrewed to remove contents; OP: wrap-around cardboard box that covered bottom half of figure with B&W Beatle photos on back; add 100% to price if in the original box. ★ *Repro Alert*

    G $75　　　**VG $110**　　　**NM $150**

○ **54. Bubble Bath (Ringo);** same as above except in blue plastic container. ★ *Repro Alert*

○ **55. Bubble Bath Display Board;** Mfd. by Colgate; 1965; $12^7/_8$" x $19^1/_2$"; drawing on Ringo and Paul containers on cardboard; four slots on bottom for attaching to box or stand.

    G $300　　　**VG $450**　　　**NM $600**

○ **56. Bumper Sticker;** Mfd. by Aldine Co.; $7^1/_2$" x 4"; "Vote for Ringo" in orange on black background.

    G $20　　　**VG $30**　　　**NM $40**

○ **57. Bust (Ringo);** Mfd. by Starfans; $6^1/_4$" tall; hard rubber bust of Ringo with gold finish.

    G $100　　　**VG $150**　　　**NM $200**

○ **58. Cake Decorations;** Mfd. by Katat (Hong Kong); $4^1/_2$" tall; plastic figures with moveable heads; looks like scaled down version of 8" tall Nodder dolls (Item #121); set of four sold on a $7^1/_8$" x $7^1/_2$" card marked "The Swingers Music Set"; add 100% to value if sealed on card; also supplied to bakeries in sealed clear plastic bag. Two variations exist: one set is well painted and has dark brown hair (set on card is first variation); second set is not as carefully painted with light brown hair. ★ *Repro Alert*

    G $20　　　**VG $30**　　　**NM $40**

○ **59. Cake Decoration;** $4^1/_2$" wide; plastic group picture of the Beatles with autographs; this is made to place on top of a cake; the faces are pressed out and are 3-D.

    G $40　　　**VG $60**　　　**NM $80**

53　　　**54**

55

57

58

○ **60.** **Cake Decoration;** $1^3/_4$" long; plastic pin which has a $1^1/_4$" heart-shaped flasher attached; image changes from picture of George and John to image of Paul and Ringo; found in three colors: green, orange, and purple.

G $10 **VG $15** **NM $20**

○ **61.** **Calendar (U.K.);** 5"; eight-sided white plastic calendar; has knobs on back to set day, date, and month; red front has B&W picture of the group and "Make a date with the Beatles"; there is an easel on the back. ★ *Repro Alert*

G $150 **VG $225** **NM $300**

○ **62.** **Calendar;** $11^1/_4$" x $19^3/_4$"; glossy paper backing with color photo of the Beatles in a doorway; tear-off page for each month from March 1964 to December 1964.

G $50 **VG $75** **NM $100**

61

122
121
58

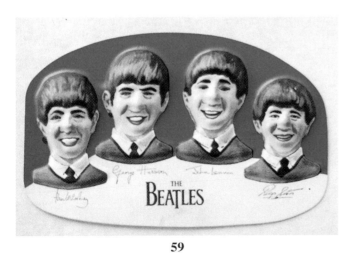

59

62

○ **63.** **Calendar;** Mfd. by Beat Publications (U.K.); 9" x 11"; "The Beatles Book"; 1964 calendar with a color or B&W photo of the Beatles each month; calendar is spiral bound on the top.
G $80   **VG $120**   **NM $160**

○ **64.** **Calendar;** Mfd. by Blackpool Pub. (U.K.); 1965; 5" x 10"; six page 1965 calendar; two months per page with color pictures of the group or individuals on each.
G $25   **VG $35**   **NM $50**

○ **65.** **Calendar;** 10" x 12"; color picture of group with tear-off page for each month in center (photo has orange background); calendar was a giveaway item; store name is at top; calendar pages run from mid-1964 to December 1965.
G $50   **VG $75**   **NM $100**

○ **66.** **Calendar Sales Kit;** Mfd. by Fine Arts Calendar; $14\frac{1}{2}$" x $19\frac{1}{2}$"; envelope included six sizes of calendars and price and order sheets.
G $400   **VG $600**   **NM $800**

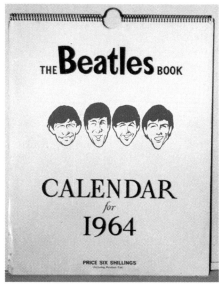

63

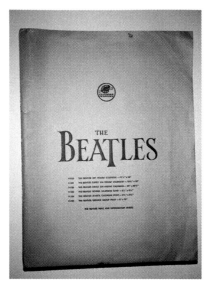

66

64

65

○ **67. Calendar Cards;** Mfd. by Louis F. Dow Co.; 3$\frac{1}{2}$" x 2$\frac{1}{4}$"; plastic cards with color photo on one side and September 1964 through June 1965 calendar on the other; six different photos—two group and one of each Beatle; value is per card.

G $10   **VG $15**   **NM $20**

○ **68. Candy Sticks Box;** Mfd. by World Candies Inc.; 1" x 2$\frac{1}{2}$" x $\frac{3}{8}$"; box held two candy sticks; boxes have a cartoon drawing of one of the Beatles; six different variations: John (green or red), Paul (orange or pink), George (yellow), Ringo (blue); color variations: The John box with both eyes showing is green, box with one eye showing is red, the Paul box with him looking to his right is pink, the Paul box with him looking to his left is orange; candy

sticks boxes were sold from a larger box (item #69) which contained a plastic Ringo hand puppet (see also item #207).

G $50   **VG $75**   **NM $100**

○ **69. Candy Sticks Display Box;** Mfd. by World Candies Inc.; 8" x 4$\frac{1}{4}$" x 2"; box which held 50 "sugar delights" (25 boxes—2 per box); colorful cello wrap on box shows cartoon Beatles and has offer for Ringo puppet (see also item #207).

G $400   **VG $600**   **NM $800**

○ **70. Cap;** cap with small bill has "The Ringo Cap" printed inside; various colors (black, loden green, and camel) and various fabrics (wool and cord) were used; available in small, medium, or large; add 20% to value if it has the original cardboard tag.

G $75   **VG $110**   **NM $150**

67

68

69

70

○ **71.** **Carpet;** 1" square on $3\frac{1}{4}$" x $5\frac{1}{2}$" card; swatch from the group's August 26, 1964 visit to Denver, Colorado.
G $40   **VG $60**   **NM $80**

○ **72.** **Carrying Case;** Mfd. by Air Flite; 6" x 9" x 4"; rectangular vinyl case with plastic handle; group pictured on front, brass closure on top; found in red, brown, light blue or black.
G $300   **VG $450**   **NM $600**

○ **73.** **Cartoon Fabric;** 1966; colorful material depicting the Beatles from their Saturday morning cartoon show; material could be used to make most anything; value is per square yard.
G $100   **VG $150**   **NM $200**

○ **74.** **Cel, Cartoon Beatles:** Original animation art from the Beatles Cartoon Show (1965-68) painted on celluloid. Beatle Cartoon cels are very hard to find because they were never sold to the public, whereas cels from Yellow Submarine were sold in art galleries in the early 1970s. No price is listed for these because original ones are seldom seen for sale. They are much more difficult to find than Yellow Submarine cels and would command a higher price depending on quality and content. Imitation Beatle cartoon cels have been sold at recent conventions. See item #469 for a more in depth description of cels and their markings.

○ **75.** **Cellophane Tape;** Mfd. by Starlight (Philippines); roll of tape in clear plastic wrapper with color picture of group on paper insert (three yards of $\frac{1}{2}$" wide cellophane tape on each roll).
G $50   **VG $75**   **NM $100**

72

74a

73

74b

76. Cellophane Tape Display Card; Mfd. by Starlight (Philippines); 8" x 10¼"; yellow, green and red card that held twelve rolls of #75; each attached to card by a staple; value is for empty card.
G $200   **VG $300**   **NM $400**

77. Chocolate Wrapper; Mfd. by Mac Robertson (Australia); 3⅜" x 2¼"; milk chocolate wrapper; blue with Beatles' faces on front.
G $40   **VG $60**   **NM $80**

78. Christmas Card; Mfd. by Star Pics; 2½" x 5½"; B&W photo on cover; "From Me To You Wishing You a Very Merry Christmas" inside.
G $20   **VG $30**   **NM $40**

79. Christmas Card; Mfd. by Oxfam Cards (U.K.); 4" x 5"; Lennon drawing "The Fat Budgie" on the cover; "With Best Wishes for Christmas and the New Year" inside.
G $30   **VG $45**   **NM $60**

80. Christmas Card (U.K.); 3¼" x 5¾"; Lennon drawing of a couple under mistletoe on cover; "With Best Wishes for Christmas and the New Year" inside; to fund the Fund For Crippling Diseases.
G $30   **VG $45**   **NM $60**

81. Christmas Seals; Mfd. by Hallmark Merchandisers Inc.; 4" x 7¼"; a repackaging of item #383 (Beatle Stamps) with a green cover; contains 100 color stamps.
G $40   **VG $60**   **NM $80**

82. Cigar Bands (Holland); various size paper labels; each has a B&W photo of one Beatle; various Brands such as Old Dutch or Jamayca; available in various colors; price is per set of four—one of each Beatle.
G $15   **VG $22**   **NM $30**

83. Clothing Tags; Mfd. by Ninth St. Limited; 8" x 8½"; cardboard clothes tags reads "The Beatles Authentic Mod Fashions"; red or blue variation; most times found with 1" x 2" cloth label; value is for one cardboard tag and one cloth label.
G $7   **VG $10**   **NM $15**

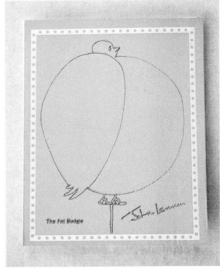

79

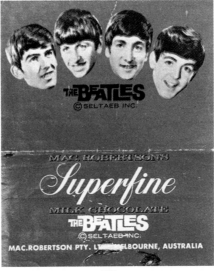

75 & 76   77   81

84. Clutch Purse; Mfd. by Dame; 5¹/₂" x 9¹/₂"; white or blue cloth purse with faces and autographs in black over entire surface; 5¹/₂" black strap handle on zippered top; add 20% to value if it has the original tag.

| G $130 | VG $200 | NM $260 |

85. Clutch Purse; 6" x 9¹/₂"; vinyl purse with zippered top and strap handle; has head and shoulder picture of group with autographs on front; various colors. ★ *Repro Alert*

| G $80 | VG $120 | NM $160 |

86. Coasters (Canada); 2¹/₂" diameter, set of four color cardboard "drink mats," one of each Beatle; given out as a premium with cans of Tango and Top Deck Shandy soft drinks; price is for set of four.

| G $50 | VG $75 | NM $100 |

87. Coin; 1¹/₄" diameter; brass coin; one side shows the Beatles' faces and names; the other side reads "Commemorating the 1964 Beatles' visit to the United States"

| G $5 | VG $7 | NM $10 |

88. Coin (Canada); 1¹/₄" diameter; brass coin; similar to above coin, except one side reads "Commemorating the 1964 Beatles' visit to Canada"; see also Medal (item #258) and Medallion (item #259)

| G $25 | VG $35 | NM $50 |

89. Coin Holder; 2" x 3"; red or black plastic coin purse which you squeeze to open; Beatles' faces and names on front. ★ *Repro Alert*

| G $25 | VG $35 | NM $50 |

90. Coin Holder Display Card; 9¹/₂" x 12¹/₂"; card which held twelve coin holders (item #89) in notched slots; hole on top of card for hanging on rack and stand-up easel on back; value is for empty card.

| G $175 | VG $260 | NM $350 |

84

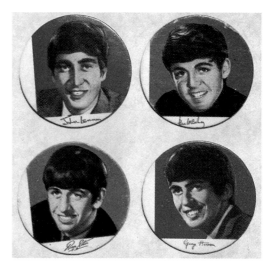

86

85

89 & 90

91. **Coin Purse (U.K.);** $2^1/_2$" x 5"; top zippered purse pictures the group with instruments; "I Should Have Known Better" printed across top on front and back.
G $50   **VG $75**   **NM $100**

92. **Coin Purse (U.K.);** $2^5/_8$" x $4^3/_8$"; similar to above item, except marked "A Hard Day's Night."
G $50   **VG $75**   **NM $100**

93. **Colorforms;** Mfd. by Colorforms; 1966; 8" x $12^1/_2$"; two trays of vinyl colorforms (Beatles, instruments, etc.) to arrange on a cardboard stage; also includes a colorful instruction booklet; value is for complete set.
G $375   **VG $560**   **NM $750**

94. **Coloring Book;** Mfd. by Saalfield; $8^1/_2$" x 11"; drawings of the group inside for coloring; there are also several B&W photos inside; value is for uncolored copy.
G $40   **VG $60**   **NM $80**

95. **Coloring Book Display;** Mfd. by Saalfield; 27" tall x 18"; wide shipping box for 36 coloring books (item #94); box converts to store display; header card pictures the group.
G $350   **VG $525**   **NM $700**

96. **Coloring Book Proof Sheet;** Mfd. by Saalfield; $17^1/_2$" x $11^1/_2$"
G $100   **VG $150**   **NM $200**

97. **Comb;** Mfd. by Lido Toys; $3^1/_4$" x $14^1/_2$"; plastic over-sized comb with Beatles and logo on sticker across top; several colors were sold including blue and yellow. ★ *Repro Alert*
G $85   **VG $130**   **NM $175**

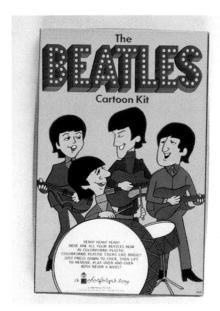

93

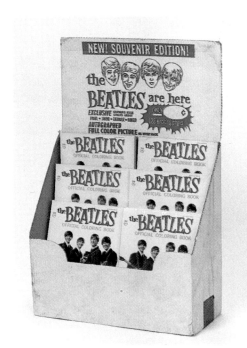

94 & 95

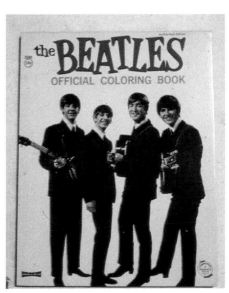

94

97

○ **98. Comb Slipcase (U.K.);** 6¼" long; off-white plastic comb sleeve with Beatles' heads and autographs below each on front side.
G $30   **VG $45**   **NM $60**

○ **99. Combo Set;** Mfd. by Selcol (U.K.); box measures 21" x 32½"; New Beat Guitar (item #188) and New Beat Drum (item #137) sold as a set in one box; box has stickers for each piece on top and a cardboard insert to hold pieces in place; value is for box and both instruments.
G $900   **VG $1,200**   **NM $1,800**

○ **100. Compact (U.K.);** 3" diameter; brass makeup compact with B&W Beatle picture on lid and mirror inside.
G $150   **VG $225**   **NM $300**

○ **101. Corkstopper;** John (West Germany); 4½" tall, carved wooden head of John with brown finish, attached to cork.
G $150   **VG $225**   **NM $300**

○ **102. Corkstopper, Paul;** (same as above)

○ **103. Corkstopper, George;** (same as above)

○ **104. Corkstopper, Ringo;** (same as above)

○ **105. Cup;** Mfd. by Washington Pottery. (U.K.); 4" tall; pottery cup with blue and black decal of group fired on side of cup; several different handles and minor variations; bottom of cup marked "England" or "Broadhurst Bros."
★ *Repro Alert*
G $60   **VG $90**   **NM $125**

○ **106. Curtains (Holland);** cotton cloth with various B&W poses of group, song titles and autographs in a repeating pattern; available in several background colors; material could be used to make other items; value is for a pair of curtains at least 48" long.
G $350   **VG $525**   **NM $700**

105

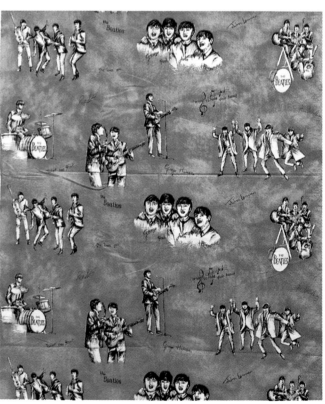

106

102

○ 107. **Curtains (Holland);** cotton cloth with various group and individual poses, names and song titles in a repeating pattern; B&W images on two-color background; sold in various colors including: light brown with yellow and aqua, blue with orange, and red with blue; value is for a pair of curtains at least 48" long.
G $350   **VG $525**   **NM $700**

○ 108. **Decals (Germany);** 4" x 7$\frac{1}{2}$"; sheet of color decals of the Beatles' faces.
G $40   **VG $60**   **NM $80**

○ 109. **Diary Booklet;** Mfd. by H.B. Langman Co. (Scotland); 3" x 4"; vinyl daily diary booklet for 1965 with some B&W Beatle photos on the inside.
G $20   **VG $30**   **NM $40**

○ 110. **Diary Booklet Display Box;** Mfd. by H.B. Langman Co. (Scotland); 8$\frac{3}{4}$" x 4$\frac{1}{4}$" x 2$\frac{1}{4}$"; orange, white and black display box for the Diary Booklet (see also item #109).
G $100   **VG $150**   **NM $200**

○ 111. **Dish, Candy, John;** Mfd. by Washington Pottery (U.K.); 4$\frac{1}{2}$" diameter; candy dish with scalloped edges and gold trim; fired decal of John in blue suit.
G $50   **VG $75**   **NM $100**

○ 112. **Dish, Candy, Paul;** (same as above)

○ 113. **Dish, Candy, George;** (same as above)

○ 114. **Dish, Candy, Ringo;** (same as above)

107

108

110

111   112
113   114

Disk-Go-Case; see also Record Case (item #349)

○ **115.   Doll, Mascot;** Mfd. by Remco Ind.; 29" tall; black cloth covered doll with cloth face and hands; sold with cardboard guitar (10 1/2" long) and a fold-open picture tag (4 3/4" square); "Official Mascot Doll" is written on tag with Beatle photo on cover and inside; value is for doll complete with guitar and tag; deduct $200 if guitar is missing; deduct $100 if tag is missing.

G $225   VG $335   NM $450

○ **116.   Dolls, Inflatable;** 1966; 13" tall; purple blow-up cartoon dolls of the Beatles with instruments; value is for set of four.

G $65   VG $100   NM $130

○ **117.   Dolls offer on Lux Soap Box;** Mfd. by Lux Soap; 1967; 4" x 2 1/2" x 2 1/2"; box with a bar of soap; box has ad with photo of Inflatable Cartoon dolls (item #116) on side; mail-in coupon for the dolls was inside box; boxes (& soap) available in five different colors: blue, green, pink, yellow, or white.

G $165   VG $250   NM $325

○ **118.   Dolls Soap Box Offer Motion Display;** Mfd. by Lux; 1967; 7' tall; colorful display bin which held Lifebuoy, Lux, and Dove bars of soap (item #117); display offers the set of Inflatable Cartoon Dolls (item #116) for $2.00 and two soap wrappers; pad of coupons for this offer attached to display bin.

G $1,500   VG $2,250   NM $3,000

117

115

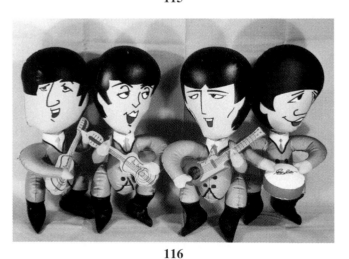

116

118

○ **119.** **Dolls Offer on Nestlés Quik Can;** Mfd. by Nestles; 1966; 5³/₈" tall; chocolate drink mix can has ad for the Inflatable Cartoon Dolls (item #116) on back.

G $350   **VG $525**   **NM $700**

○ **120.** **Dolls Offer on Nestlés Quik Can;** Mfd. by Nestles; 1966 5³/₈" x 3³/₄" x 2¹/₂"; strawberry flavor; with ad for the Inflatable Cartoon Dolls (item #116) on back.

G $350   **VG $525**   **NM $700**

Dolls; 4"-tall Nodders; see Cake Decorations (item #58)

○ **121.** **Dolls;** Bobbin' Head Dolls; Mfd. by Carmascot; 8" tall; composition doll with head that moves on a spring; sold as a set of four in a box with cellophane windows and a small instruction sheet; value for complete set in box.

★ *Repro Alert*

G $400   **VG $600**   **NM $800**

Value for individual dolls:

G $55   **VG $80**   **NM $110**

○ **122.** **Dolls, Bobbin' Head Dolls Display Set;** Mfd. by Carmascot; 14" tall; set of four composition dolls used for display in stores to promote the sale of the Bobbin' Head Dolls (item #121); value is for each doll.

G $1,000   **VG $1,500**   **NM $2,000**

119

120

122

○ **123. Doll, John;** Mfd. by Remco; 5" tall; rubber doll with rooted hair and black suit; doll comes with either hard or soft body, with instrument strapped around the neck; subtract 60% from value if instrument is missing.

| G $70 | VG $105 | NM $140 |

○ **124. Doll, George;** (same as above)

○ **125. Doll, Paul;** (same description as above)

| G $40 | VG $65 | NM $85 |

○ **126. Doll, Ringo;** (same description and value as #125—Paul)

○ **127. Doll, Promotional;** Mfd. by Remco; these dolls are quite similar to the regular set (items #123-126); the instruments are quite different, white rubber with black signatures; there are strap attachments on both sides of the drum; (these dolls are shown on the promotional poster, see also item #130); value is for each doll.

| G $150 | VG $225 | NM $300 |

○ **128. Doll box;** Mfd. by Remco; 6½" x 3¾" x 2"; interchangeable box for a single Beatle doll (item #123-126); box has Beatle photos on front and cellophane window; cardboard inner insert holds doll in place. ★ *Repro Alert*

| G $60 | VG $90 | NM $120 |

○ **129. Doll Box Set;** Mfd. by Remco; 5" square; cardboard box which held set of Remco dolls; this box was used for catalogue sales of item #123-126.

| G $150 | VG $225 | NM $300 |

○ **130. Doll Poster;** Mfd. by Remco; 18" x 7"; orange, black and white poster pictures set of dolls; the dolls are shown with reverse-painted instruments (promotional set, see also item #127); advertising for items #123-126.

| G $225 | VG $335 | NM $450 |

125   124   126   123

129

128

130

◯ **131.** **Doll, Bendy;** Mfd. by Newfeld, Ltd. (U.K.); 10" tall; soft rubber figure with collarless suit, resembles Paul; OP: Clear plastic bag with cardboard base; add 80% to value if the doll is in the original package.

    G $75   **VG $100**   **NM $150**

◯ **132.** **Dress (Holland);** fabric has stripes of color at top and bottom; Beatles pictured horizontally with their autographs below; music notes and lyrics at bottom.

    G $350   **VG $525**   **NM $700**

◯ **133.** **Dress (Holland);** fabric has polka dots; Beatles pictured vertically next to guitar; guitar has their autographs inside.

    G $350   **VG $525**   **NM $700**

◯ **134.** **Dress (Holland);** white fabric with olive green printing and pink stripes; three bars of music and two guitars (necks crossed); faces of the Beatles and autographs inside guitars.

    G $350   **VG $525**   **NM $700**

133

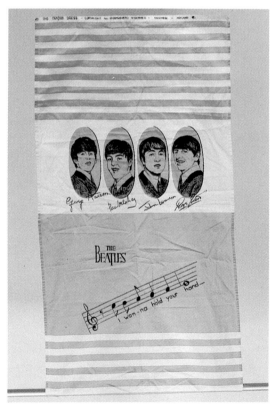

132

134

○ **135.** **Dress (Holland);** tan fabric features large blue music notes with Beatle faces inside; with white checkered background and black music bars with lyrics below.

G $400   **VG $600**   **NM $800**

○ **136.** **Drum;** Mfd. by Mastro; 14" diameter, 7" deep; drum has red sparkle finish and included metal stand; the skin has "The Beatles Drum" printed on it along with the Beatles' faces; sold with an instruction booklet, which is valued separately at $150 in NM shape; value is for drum that includes stand and sticks; add 100% to value if complete in the original box.

G $750   **VG $1,125**   **NM $1,500**

○ **137.** **Drum;** Mfd. by Selcol (U.K.); "New Beat Drum"; 14" diameter, 6" tall; drum is maroon with pink trim; skin pictures small Ringo face, drumming hands and autograph; side of drum has color Beatle sticker; OP: 19" x 19" x 9" box with Beatles New Beat and Ringo Starr drum kit stickers on top, accessories included three-legged stand, tuning key, drum sticks, and an instruction booklet; add 10% to value if item is boxed with accessories.

G $300   **VG $450**   **NM $600**

○ **138.** **Drum (U.K.);** 14" diameter; large drawing of Ringo on the skin; "Ringo Starr" in gold color plastic on side; cymbal has "Ringo Starr" printed on it; sold with sticks, brushes, and stand; value is for item that is complete. OP: 19" x 19" x 9" box with a white sticker which reads "Super Ringo Starr Drum Kit"; add 100% to value if in box with instructions.

G $500   **VG $750**   **NM $1,000**

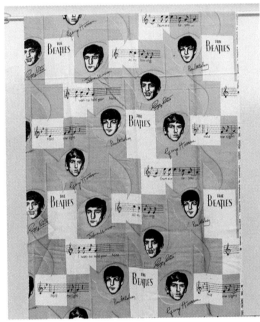

135

136

137a

137

138

⭕ **139.** **Drumsticks;** Mfd. by Ludwig; 15^1/$_4$"; wooden sticks with Ringo Starr imprint; several models were available; OP: clear plastic package with B&W photo card of Ringo inside; add 100% to value if in the original package.
G $60 **VG $90** **NM $125**

⭕ **140.** **Drumsticks;** Mfd. by Dallas Arbiter (U.K.); 15^1/$_2$"; Ringo Starr model with gold imprint; OP: several will include vinyl case with snap clasp on end; add 100% to value if in original packaging.
G $60 **VG $90** **NM $125**

⭕ **141.** **Figurine, Paul (Mexico);** 1966; 6" tall; white hard rubber figure of cartoon show Paul; black and white highlights.
G $250 **VG $375** **NM $500**

⭕ **142.** **Figurine, Ringo;** (same as above)

⭕ **143.** **Figurines;** Mfd. by Subuteo Ltd. (U.K.); 2" tall; hand-painted figures playing instruments; these authorized figures are well detailed; OP: box measures 11^1/$_2$" x 4" x 1^1/$_2$"; add 200% to value if the figures are in the box.
G $50 **VG $75** **NM $100**

⭕ **144.** **Flip Your Wig Game;** Mfd. by Milton Bradley; box size is 19" x 9^1/$_2$" x 1^3/$_4$"; game had 48 cards (three of each Beatles' face, autograph, instrument and 12 Hit Record cards); a die, four player pieces, game board, and instruction filler tray complete the package; value is for a complete game.
G $100 **VG $150** **NM $200**

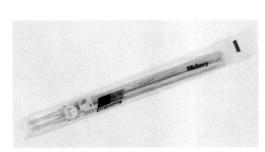

139

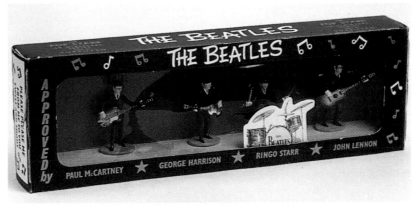

143

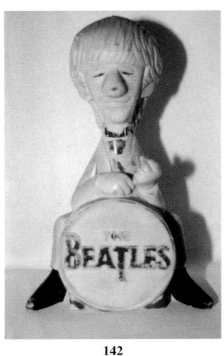

142

144

○ **145. Garter;** Mfd. by Leonard Page & Co., Ltd. (U.K.); garter came in various colors with a group picture disk attached.
G $40   **VG $60**   **NM $80**

○ **146. Glass, John;** 5$^1/_2$" tall; head and shoulder picture of John with name along side; around bottom are musical notes, records, and guitar; available with white or green paint; glass lip is raised.
G $60   **VG $90**   **NM $125**

○ **147. Glass, Paul;** (same as above, yellow paint)

○ **148. Glass, George;** (same as above, orange paint)

○ **149. Glass, Ringo;** (same as above, white or red paint)

○ **150. Glass, John;** 4$^3/_4$" tall; marked "Nems Ent Ltd. London"; head and shoulder picture is in black paint with musical notes, guitar, and records in red paint.
G $60   **VG $90**   **NM $125**

○ **151. Glass, Paul;** (same as item #150)

○ **152. Glass, George;** (same as item #150)

○ **153. Glass, Ringo;** (same as item #150)

○ **154. Glass, John;** Mfd. by J & L Co. Ltd. (U.K.); 4" tall; color decal of John on glass with gold top rim; OP: one of each Beatle in 15" x 6" x 3" box; add 50% to value if set is in box.
G $75   **VG $110**   **NM $150**

○ **155. Glass, Paul;** (same as item #154)

○ **156. Glass, George;** (same as item #154)

○ **157. Glass, Ringo;** (same as item #154)

○ **158. Glass, Group;** 5" tall; glass has insulating coating around middle; 3$^1/_2$" square color picture of group posed with instruments on side.
G $60   **VG $90**   **NM $125**

○ **159. Glass, John;** (similar to #158, with B&W photo of John)
G $100   **VG $150**   **NM $200**

○ **160. Glass, Paul;** (same as item #159)

○ **161. Glass, George;** (same as item #159)

145

146   147   148   149

150   151   152   153

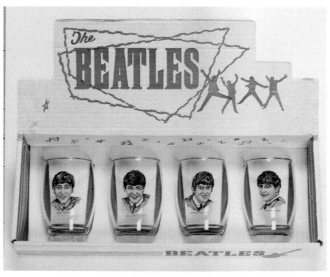

154   155   156   157

○ **162.** **Glass, Ringo;** (same as item #159)

○ **163.** **Glass, John;** 4³/₄" tall; glass with face and autograph on one side and "action" pose on the other, both in blue paint.
G $100   **VG $150**   **NM $200**

○ **164.** **Glass, Paul;** (same as item #163, with yellow paint)

○ **165.** **Glass, George;** (same as item #163, with red paint)

○ **166.** **Glass, Ringo;** (same as item #163, with green paint)

○ **167.** **Glass;** John (Holland); 5¹/₂" tall; thin glass with picture in black, white, and red; along side is his autograph; underneath picture is written "Beatle John."
G $85   **VG $130**   **NM $175**

○ **168.** **Glass, Paul;** (same as item #167)

○ **169.** **Glass, George;** (same as item #167)

○ **170.** **Glass, Ringo;** (same as item #167)

○ **171.** **Glass, John (Holland);** 5¹/₂" tall; clear glass with gold rim; color decal of John with autograph below (the Paul & John autograph are switched); there is also a variation of these glasses without autographs and the correct name of each Beatle printed beneath the photo.
G $80   **VG $120**   **NM $160**

○ **172.** **Glass, Paul;** (same as item #171)

○ **173.** **Glass, George;** (same as item #171)

○ **174.** **Glass, Ringo;** (same as item #171)

158   **176**

159   **160**   **161**   **162**

167   **168**   **169**   **170**

163   **164**   **165**

171   **172**   **173**   **174**

○ **175.** **Glass, Group;** Mfd. for Dairy Queen of Canada; $5^{1}/_{2}$" tall (or $4^{1}/_{2}$" tall variation); with B&W photo of each Beatles' face in a starburst; glass has gold rim.

G $60   **VG $90**   **NM $120**

○ **176.** **Glass, Group (Holland);** $5^{1}/_{2}$" tall; glass with black, white and flesh colored picture of group on side; "The Beatles" in Dutch flag above.

G $85   **VG $130**   **NM $175**

○ **177.** **Grow Your Own Beatle Hair;** Mfd. by A & B Ind. Inc.; 5" x $7^{1}/_{2}$"; piece of cardboard that separates into four pieces, one for each Beatle; drawing of each Beatle grows green hair when put in a glass of water; individual Beatle pieces also separated, folded, and sent to purchaser in a $4^{1}/_{2}$" x $5^{3}/_{4}$" envelope; the envelope reads "Living Beatles" and has drawing of Beatle faces on left half of envelope; envelope valued at $75.

G $200   **VG $300**   **NM $400**

Guitar; Mfd. by Mastro; $5^{1}/_{2}$"; (see also item #600)

○ **178.** **Guitar;** Mfd. by Selcol (U.K.); 14"; Junior Guitar; orange body with color paper photo of group on body; OP: sealed with backer board; add 75% to value if in the original packaging.

G $750   **VG $1,100**   **NM $1,500**

○ **179.** **Guitar;** Mfd. by Mastro; $14^{3}/_{4}$"; Junior Guitar; pink and burgundy plastic four-string guitar with Beatles pictured on body and crown; OP: sealed with backer board and instruction booklet; add 100% to value if in the original package with booklet; instruction booklet valued separately at $125 in NM shape.

G $300   **VG $450**   **NM $600**

○ **180.** **Guitar;** Mfd. by Selcol (U.K.); 21"; "Big Beat Guitar"; orange and red plastic four-string guitar with color picture sticker and autographs on front; add 100% to value if in the original packaging.

G $300   **VG $450**   **NM $600**

175

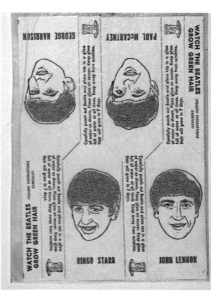

177

178

179

○ **181.** **Guitar Store Display;** Mfd. by Selcol; (U.K.); 11" x 16"; display for Big Beat Guitars (item #180) with color photo the same as the guitar sticker.

G $400   **VG $600**   **NM $800**

○ **182.** **Guitar Mfd. by Mastro;** 21"; "Four Pop Guitar"; red and pink plastic four-string guitar with Beatle faces and autographs on body; faces on crown; two variations of printing on body: One has "Four Pop," other has "FOUR POP"; OP: sealed on backer board with instruction booklet; add 100% to value if in original package with booklet; instruction booklet valued separately at $100 in NM shape.

G $300   **VG $450**   **NM $600**

○ **183.** **Guitar;** Mfd. by Mastro; 21"; "Yeah Yeah Guitar"; red and burgundy six-string guitar with faces and autographs on body; faces on crown; OP: sealed on backer board with instruction booklet; add 100% to value if in original package with booklet; instruction booklet is valued separately at $200 in NM shape; also found with faces printed over white background.

G $750   **VG $1,125**   **NM $1,500**

180

182

183

○ **184.** **Guitar;** Mfd. by Selcol (U.K.); 23"; "New Sound Guitar"; orange (or red) and cream four-string plastic guitar with faces and autographs on body; OP: sealed on backer board; add 100% to value if in original package. ★ *Repro Alert*

G $300   **VG $450**   **NM $600**

○ **185.** **Guitar;** Mfd. by Selcol (U.K.); 29"; four-string cutaway guitar, with color picture and autographs; orange body and burgundy neck; Selcol sticker inside.

G $250   **VG $375**   **NM $500**

○ **186.** **Guitar;** Mfd. by Mastro; 30"; "Beatle-ist Guitar"; pink and burgundy six-string plastic guitar with faces and autographs on body; OP: sealed on backer board with instruction booklet; add 100% to value if in original package.

G $450   **VG $675**   **NM $900**

○ **187.** **Guitar;** Mfd. by Selcol (U.K.); 31"; "Beatles Red Jet Electric"; red, orange, and white six-string electric guitar with group sticker and autographs on body; OP: coffin-shaped cardboard box with color sticker; add 100% for box.

G $500   **VG $750**   **NM $1000**

185

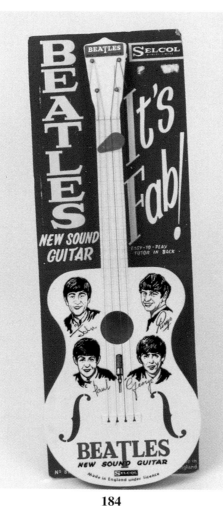

184

186

⭕ **188.** **Guitar;** Mfd. by Selcol. (U.K.); 32$\frac{1}{2}$"; "New Beat Guitar"; red and burgundy four-string plastic guitar with color group sticker and autographs on body; OP: coffin-shaped cardboard box with color sticker; add 50% for box.

G $250   **VG $375**   **NM $500**

⭕ **189.** **Guitar;** Mfd. by Selcol (U.K.); 32$\frac{1}{2}$"; "Big Six Guitar"; orange, red, and burgundy six-string plastic guitar with color group sticker and autographs on body; OP: coffin-shaped cardboard box with color sticker; add 50% for box.

G $300   **VG $450**   **NM $600**

⭕ **190.** **Guitar String;** Mfd. by Hofner, Selmer (U.K.); 3$\frac{1}{2}$" square; green-tinted paper packet with group picture on the front; contains one guitar string; six different strings available (first through sixth).

G $40   **VG $60**   **NM $80**

188

189

187a

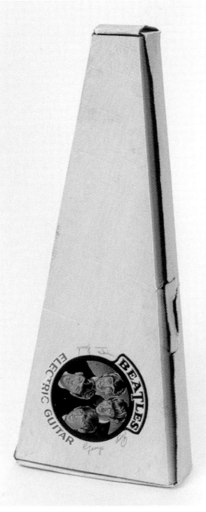

187b

○ **191.** **Gumball Figures;** 3" tall; black soft-rubber figures which were sold in capsules from gumball machines; display card measures 5¹/₂" x 6¹/₂"; price is for set of four on card; individual figures valued at $10 each in NM shape.

    G $35   **VG $55**   **NM $75**

○ **192.** **Gumball Charms;** ³/₄" diameter; plastic record with Beatle photo on one side and Capitol or VJ logo with song title on reverse.

    G $5   **VG $7**   **NM $10**

○ **193.** **Gumball Sticker;** 1" x 3"; black and gold sticker with faces and names; sold in capsules in gumball machines.

    G $5   **VG $7**   **NM $10**

○ **194.** **Hairbow;** Mfd. by Burlington; 5¹/₂" x 3¹/₂"; centered-knotted cloth hairbow in various colors with "I Love the Beatles" printed in repeating pattern; OP: original light blue card measures 6" x 7¹/₂" and has "Official Beatle Bow" printed on it; wallet photo on bottom of card; value is for bow on card; subtract 75% from value if original card is not present.

    G $175   **VG $260**   **NM $350**

○ **195.** **Hairbow;** (same as item #194, only with Beatle autographs printed in repeating pattern on bow.)

○ **196.** **Hairbrush;** Mfd. by Belliston Products; 2 x 3¹/₂"; flat pocket hairbrush with Beatles' faces embossed on back; OP: clear plastic bag with illustrated header card and wallet photo inside; brush available in solid red, white, or blue plastic; value is for item in original packaging. ★ *Repro Alert*

    G $25   **VG $35**   **NM $50**

○ **197.** **Hairbrush Promo Flyer;** 8¹/₂" x 11"; two-sided promotional flyer for item #196.

    G $60   **VG $90**   **NM $125**

190

194

196

198. **Hair Pomade;** Mfd. by H.H. Cosmetic Lab (Philippines); 2¹/₂" x 1"; packet of hair grease, with color faces on top.

G $30   VG $45   NM $60

199. **Hair Pomade Box;** box which held fifty of the above item; 5" x 6" box with color faces on top, color picture insert in box; value is for empty box with insert. ★ *Repro Alert*

G $250   VG $375   NM $500

200. **Hair Spray;** Mfd. by Bronson Products; 8" tall; can with Beatles pictured on wrap around paper label; white plastic cap ★ *Repro Alert*

G $500   VG $750   NM $1,000

201. **Hair Spray, Holding and Setting;** Mfd. by Bronson Products; 8" tall; can with paper label; drawing of girl in center of label with photos of Beatles around her.

G $500   VG $750   NM $1,000

202. **Halloween Costume, John;** Mfd. by Ben Cooper; child's costume and mask; costume comes in small, medium and large; mask is flesh colored with brown fuzzy "hair"; OP: box measures 11" x 12" and has name of costume stamped on end; add 200% to value for original box.

G $125   VG $190   NM $250

203. **Halloween Costume, Paul;** (same as above)

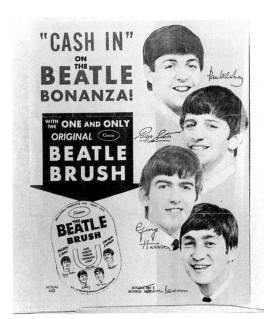

197

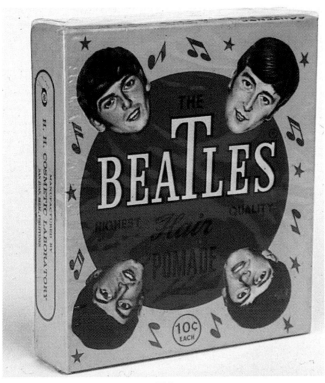

199

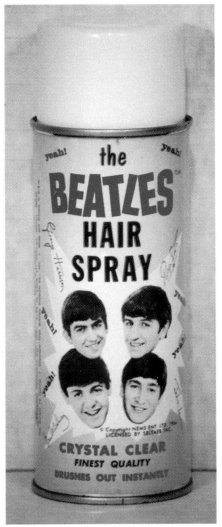

200

○ **204. Halloween Costume; George;** (same as above)

○ **205. Halloween Costume; Ringo;** (same as above)

○ **206. Halloween Costume Store Poster;** Mfd. by Ben Cooper; 22" x 8¼"; paper poster used in stores to advertise items #202-205; "We have the...authentic official Beatles Costumes" printed on poster along with photos of the Beatles.
G $250   **VG $375**   **NM $500**

○ **207. Hand Puppet, Ringo;** Mfd. by World Candies; color illustration of cartoon show Ringo on white plastic; came in store boxes of Beatles Candy Sticks (item #68 & 69); packed one per box.
G $150   **VG $225**   **NM $300**

○ **208. Handbag;** 10" x 10"; vinyl bag with built-in brass handles on top; head and shoulder pictures on front with autographs below; various colors available.
G $175   **VG $260**   **NM $350**

○ **209. Handbag;** same size and construction as above; white vinyl with individual pictures of members playing instruments, and autographs covering entire surface.
G $200   **VG $300**   **NM $400**

○ **210. Handbag;** 10" x 10"; cloth bag with built-in brass handle on top; faces, autographs, and Beatle logos covering entire surface; originally sold with 1¾" square tag; add $40 to value if tag is present.
G $175   **VG $260**   **NM $350**

○ **211. Handkerchief;** 21" x 21"; cotton; white with colored records and instruments, faces in black, and song titles under records (same design as scarf item #358); sold with a ½" x ¾" gold tag glued on which states "Mfd. exclusively for Seltaeb Inc. All cotton WPL 209."
G $25   **VG $35**   **NM $50**

204

206

207

208

209

214

216

○ **212. Handkerchief (U.K.);** $8^1/_2$" square; "With love from me to you"; Beatles pictured in the center; beetles, musical notes, names and hearts around edges.
G $20   VG $30   NM $40

○ **213. Handkerchief (U.K.);** $8^1/_2$" square; "With love from me to you"; Beatles pictured in corner; song titles, notes, musical instruments, and names around edges.
G $20   VG $30   NM $40

○ **214. Hanger, John;** Mfd. by Saunders Ent. (U.K.); B&W two-sided 16" tall die-cut bust photo with hook on top.
G $60   VG $90   NM $125

○ **215. Hanger, Paul;** (same as above)

○ **216. Hanger, George;** (same as above)

○ **217. Hanger, Ringo;** (same as above)

○ **218. Harmonica Box;** Mfd. by Hohner; 5" long; harmonica box pictures group on lid; harmonica itself has no Beatle markings; George and Paul's names are switched on most boxes; add 25% to value if names are correct on box.
G $60   VG $90   NM $125

○ **219. Harmonica Box Display Card;** Mfd. by Hohner; 7" x 11"; card pictures group; opens up to reveal songs with music; harmonica and box were attached to front; add 400% to price if card is sealed.
G $75   VG $110   NM $150

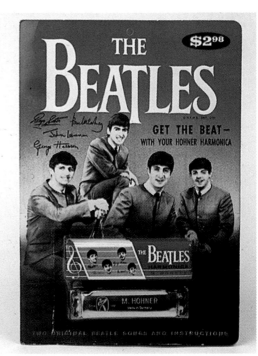

219

○ **220. Hat (Canada);** "Carnival prize" red felt hat with Beatle patch on front.
G $40   VG $60   NM $80

○ **221. Hat;** 10" x 12"; paper with the Beatles pictured twice; there are instructions along border on how to fold the paper into a hat; "Chicago Bottlers" in large letters.
G $40   VG $60   NM $80

○ **222. Headband;** Mfd. by L & C Vincent Industries (Australia); $2\frac{3}{4}$" wide; elastic headband pictures beetles and guitars; issued in various colors; OP: card reads "Official Headband" and pictures the Beatles with autographs; value is for headband on card.
G $100   VG $150   NM $200

○ **223. Headband;** Mfd. by Better Wear, Inc.; nylon stretch reversible headband came in eight different colors; reads "Love the Beatles"; OP:

package pictures each Beatle with autograph and measures $8\frac{3}{4}$" x 2"; value is for headband in package.
G $20   VG $30   NM $40

○ **224. Headband;** Mfd. by Burlington; cloth headband in various colors with repeating "I Love the Beatles" logo on entire surface; OP: package measures $8\frac{1}{2}$" x 2" includes card with B&W photos; value is for headband in package; value for headband out of package is $50.
G $200   VG $300   NM $400

222

221

223

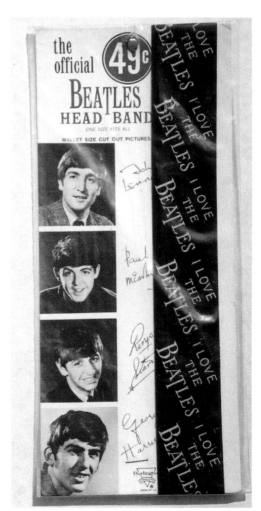

224

○ **225. Headband;** solid cloth headband with Beatle faces and autographs covering entire surface; has elastic band.
G $30   **VG $45**   **NM $60**

○ **226. Headband;** Mfd. by Park Lane; solid cloth with "The Beatles" printed in center and faces of two Beatles on each end with first name autographs below; OP: clear plastic bag (10" long) with photo and "The Beatles Official Headband" printed on top half; add 100% for packaging.
G $40   **VG $60**   **NM $80**

○ **227. Headphones;** Mfd. by Koss Electronics; 1966; blue headphones with Beatle sticker on each earphone (sticker can be paper or metal); OP: 8" x 8" illustrated box, with flyer and warranty card; value is for item in box; value is 30% for headphones, 70% for box.
G $1,100   **VG $1,650**   **NM $2,200**

○ **228. Hofner Counter Display;** Mfd. by Hofner; 17³/₄" x 13¹/₈"; cardboard display with easel back; shows B&W photo of Paul playing Hofner bass; "Paul McCartney plays a Hofner original. Why don't you?" printed on display.
G $300   **VG $450**   **NM $600**

○ **229. Hummer;** Mfd. by Louis F. Dow Co.; 11" long, ³/₄" diameter; blue cardboard tube with lithographed picture of the Beatles; plastic ends on tube produce musical tone.
G $60   **VG $90**   **NM $125**

○ **230. Hummer Display Box;** 12" x 9" x 5"; original store display box for item #229 item; white cardboard with blue print; top is die-cut and stands up in back of box.
G $200   **VG $300**   **NM $400**

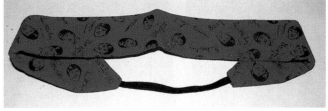

225

227

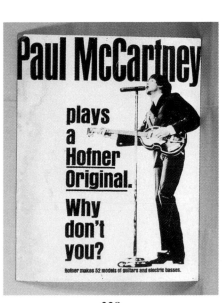

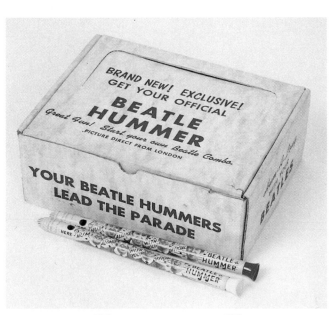

228

229   230

○ **231.** **Hummer Poster;** 20" x 11$\frac{1}{4}$"; poster for item #229; item has Beatles pictured in doorway at top; information about the hummer is on the bottom; one poster came with each box of hummers.
G $150   **VG $225**   **NM $300**

○ **232.** **Ice Cream Bar Wrapper;** paper; Mfd. by Hood (New Jersey); single panels; (unused rolls of the uncut wrapper found in quantity in recent years).
G $5   **VG $7**   **NM $10**

○ **233.** **Ice Cream Bar Wrapper, paper;** various styles and distributors.
G $45   **VG $65**   **NM $90**

○ **234.** **Ice Cream Bar Wrapper, foil;** various styles, sizes, and distributors.
G $50   **VG $75**   **NM $100**

○ **235.** **Ice Cream Bar Box;** Mfd. by Hood Ice Cream Company; 4 or 6 bar size (4 bar box measures 6$\frac{3}{4}$" x 4$\frac{1}{2}$" x 2$\frac{1}{2}$"); group is pictured on box in color.
G $200   **VG $300**   **NM $400**

○ **236.** **Ice Cream Bar Ad;** 9" x 3"; paper color advertising piece intended for store freezer point-of-sale display; pictures the group and the ice cream bar box.
G $60   **VG $90**   **NM $120**

○ **237.** **Kaboodle Kit;** Mfd. by Standard Plastic Products; vinyl case measures 9" x 7" x 3$\frac{1}{2}$"; group is pictured on front.
Tan
G $350   **VG $525**   **NM $700**

Pink, red, blue, yellow, or lavender
G $425   **VG $635**   **NM $900**

231

232

233

236

234

235

○ **238.** **Keychain (U.K.);** brass keychain with $1^1/_4$" x $^3/_4$" brass enclosed B&W photo under plastic.
G $50   **VG $75**   **NM $100**

○ **239.** **Keychain;** 1" brass disk with $^7/_8$" group ceramic B&W photo insert mounted on front; back reads "Yeh Yeh Yeh"; attached to keyring via $1^1/_2$" chain; add 50% if on original card.
G $40   **VG $60**   **NM $80**

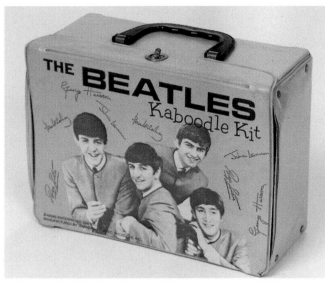

237

○ **240.** **Lamp, Table (U.K.);** lamp consists of paper shade with Beatle face photos over music background; original ceramic base is black with gold guitar in center; deduct 50% from value if base is missing.
G $500   **VG $750**   **NM $1,000**

○ **241.** **Lamp;** Table 14" tall; paper cylinder with color Beatle picture on side; two different photos were available; lamp stands on metal legs with bulb attachment in center.
G $250   **VG $375**   **NM $500**

○ **242.** **Lamp, Wall;** 14" wide; paper shade with wraparound paper picture; sides of shade attach to wall; similar construction as above item.
G $300   **VG $450**   **NM $600**

○ **243.** **Licorice Record Candy, Group;** Mfd. by Clevedon Confectionery (U.K.); $4^1/_2$" square; paper sleeve with B&W paper photo insert of the group; 4" diameter black licorice "record" inside; add 10% to price if licorice is present.
G $30   **VG $45**   **NM $60**

○ **244.** **Licorice Record Candy, John;** (same description as above)
G $25   **VG $35**   **NM $50**

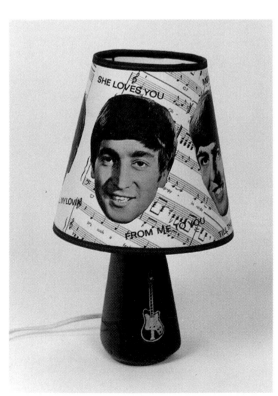

240

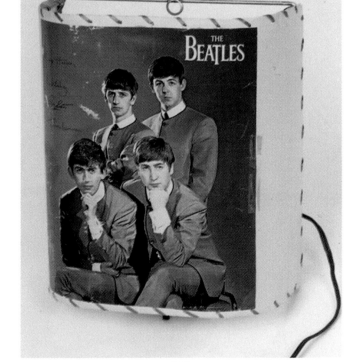

242

○ **245. Licorice Record Candy, Paul;** (same as above)

○ **246. Licorice Record Candy, George;** (same as above)

○ **247. Licorice Record Candy, Ringo;** (same as above)

○ **248. Licorice Record Candy Box;** Mfd. for Clevedon Confect (U.K.); 10" x 5$\frac{1}{2}$" x 2$\frac{3}{8}$"; orange cardboard box which held 36 licorice records (#243-247); Beatles pictured on box; price is for empty box; in the U.S. the same box was cut to 10" x 5$\frac{1}{4}$" x 1$\frac{7}{8}$" tall and held 24 licorice records; a sticker with the number "24" was affixed over the number "36" on the box.
G $300   VG $450   NM $600

○ **249. Linen;** Mfd. by Ulster (Ireland); 20" x 31"; white linen wall hanging with Beatles pictures in burgundy, black, and violet colors; various musical instruments around border.
G $60   VG $90   NM $125

○ **250. Lollipop Wrappers (Australia);** 2" x 3$\frac{1}{2}$"; waxed paper wrappers with Beatle faces and autographs; one Beatle per wrapper; available in blue or gold.
G $25   VG $35   NM $50

○ **251. Loot Tray;** Mfd. by MEA Products; 6$\frac{3}{4}$" x 9"; shallow rectangular smoked glass dish with Beatles pictured with autographs; photo heads on body drawings.
G $400   VG $600   NM $800

○ **252. Ludwig Promo Photo;** 8$\frac{1}{2}$" x 11"; B&W photo of Ringo with Ludwig drums; "Ringo Starr Plays Ludwig" printed on bottom.
G $20   VG $30   NM $40

249

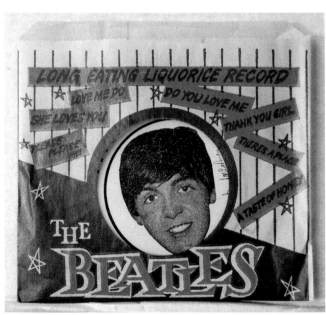
245

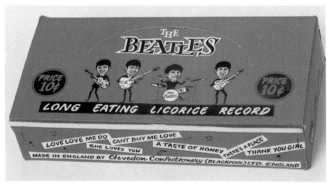
248

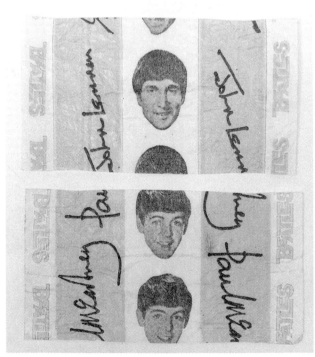
250

253. **Lunchbox;** Mfd. by Aladdin Industries; 1965; 8" x 7" x 4"; blue metal lunchbox with different poses embossed on each side; sold with blue thermos (item #403); value is for lunchbox only; lunchbox (Girl's) see also Brunch Bag (item #52).

G $200   **VG $400**   **NM $800**

254. **Magic Slate Game;** Mfd. by Merit (U.K.); 8½" x 13½", colorful board with plastic sheet which "erases" when lifted; Beatle illustrations around sides; blank back.

G $400   **VG $600**   **NM $800**

255. **Magic Trick;** Mfd. by The Supreme Magic Co. (Ireland); trick includes eight cards (four Beatles and four of a girl); paper TV folder and instruction sheet.

G $150   **VG $225**   **NM $300**

256. **Magnetic Hairstyle Game;** Mfd. by Merit. (U.K.); black, red, and white cardboard gameboard with clear plastic center section; this contains iron filings which are moved with a magnetic wand to create hair styles on the bald Beatles; instructions on back.

G $300   **VG $450**   **NM $600**

251

253

254

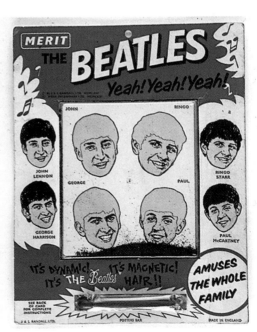

256

○ **257. Matchboxes;** Mfd. by Vlinder (Holland); 2" x 1½"; matchboxes have colorized individual photos on one side.

G $20   **VG $30**   **NM $40**

○ **258. Medal;** Mfd. by Modern Medals, Ltd. (U.K.); 1½" diameter; sterling silver coin has faces embossed on one side "The Beatles 1965-1966" and autographs on the other.

G $75   **VG $110**   **NM $150**

Medal; see also Coin (item #87)

○ **259. Medallion (Germany);** 1966; 1½"; heavy brass piece with Beatle heads and names on one side and autographs with "The Kings of Beat" and "Members of the British Empire" on other side; with or without chain.

G $50   **VG $75**   **NM $100**

○ **260. Megaphone;** Mfd. by Yell-a-Phone; 7¼" tall; cone-shaped plastic megaphone with metal mouthpiece rim and chain; Beatles pictures, names and "Beatle Bugle" printed on side; colors include orange with black print, yellow with green print, and white with red print. ★ *Repro Alert*

G $400   **VG $600**   **NM $800**

○ **261. Model Kit, John;** Mfd. by Revell; white plastic figure to assemble; box is 9" x 6" x 2" and pictures John in color; kit includes instruction sheet; value is for unassembled model in box; value for built up model without box is $75 in NM shape. ★ *Repro Alert*

G $225   **VG $375**   **NM $450**

259

257

258

260

261   262   263   264

○ **262. Model Kit, Paul;** (same description as above)
★ *Repro Alert*
G $150   **VG $225**   **NM $300**

○ **263. Model Kit, George;** (same description as above) ★ *Repro Alert*
G $225   **VG $375**   **NM $450**

○ **264. Model Kit, Ringo;** (same description as above)
★ *Repro Alert*
G $125   **VG $190**   **NM $250**

Note: All four Beatle models were also produced in England. These are marked "Revell (G.B.) Ltd." on side. The U.S. price code which is next to the model number on the end flap is missing on the U.K. versions (ie:, for U.S. John model "H-1352:150" and on the U.K. version "H-1352.") The U.K. model boxes have more vivid colors on the box and use the British spelling for "moulded." The U.K. models have the same values as their U.S. counterparts.

○ **265. Model Kit Flyer;** Mfd. by Revell; 8½" x 11"; color two-sided promotional brochure for the models; Paul on one side, Ringo on other; John and George are not pictured but described as "available at a later date."
G $100   **VG $150**   **NM $200**

○ **266. Model Kit Promotional Poster;** Mfd. by Revell; 25½" x 11"; pictures Paul and Ringo on each end, reads "Build the Beatles" in the middle.
G $300   **VG $450**   **NM $600**

○ **267. Movie, 8 mm;** 4" x 6"; on card; orange, black, and white card with 50' silent film attached to front; reel is covered by B&W photo; several titles available; value is for movie on card; value for movie alone is $15 in NM.
G $125   **VG $150**   **NM $250**

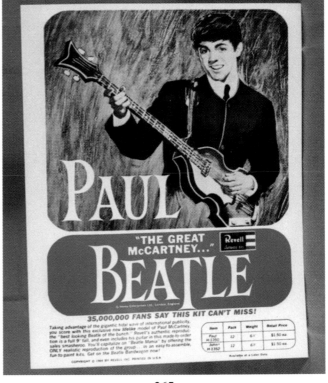

265

266

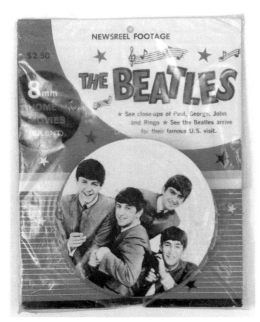

267

268

269

○ **268.** **Mug;** Mfd. by Burrite Co.; 4" tall; white plastic mug with handle has a color paper picture of each Beatle with autograph encased under clear plastic around side. ★ *Repro Alert*
G $50   **VG $75**   **NM $100**

○ **269.** **Mug;** Mfd. by Laurel Ent.; 4" tall; white pottery mug comes in thin or wide styles, with or without handle; color decal of group fired on side.
G $75   **VG $110**   **NM $150**

○ **270.** **Napkin;** Mfd. by Rolex Paper Co. (U.K.); 6½" square (folded size); white paper napkin with B&W photos of Beatles and autographs; OP: clear cello wrapper which held 50 napkins, marked "The Beatles."
G $10   **VG $15**   **NM $20**

○ **271.** **Nightshirt;** white cotton ankle-length shirt with B&W posed picture of group on front, with "The Beatles" above and autographs below; same design as the sweatshirt (item #392).
G $75   **VG $110**   **NM $150**

○ **272.** **Notebook, Group;** Mfd. by Westab; 8½" x 11" writing paper pad pictures Beatles in doorway on front; available in top bound, side bound and spiral bound.
G $30   **VG $45**   **NM $60**

272

◯ **273.** **Notebook;** John; Mfd. by Westab; 8½" x 11"; side-bound or spiral-bound paper pad featuring John on the cover.
G $75   **VG $110**   **NM $150**

◯ **274.** **Notebook, Paul;** (same as item #273)

◯ **275.** **Notebook, George;** (same as item #273)

◯ **276.** **Notebook, Ringo;** (same as item #273)

◯ **277.** **Notebook (U.K.);** Mfd. for Woolworths; 6½" x 10"; paper pad with "The Beatles Writing Pad" and group picture on front.
G $75   **VG $110**   **NM $150**

◯ **278.** **Nylons;** Mfd. by Scott-Centenaire, Ltd. (U.K.); Ballito "Shear Seamfree Micromesh" stockings have faces, guitars and autographs patterned in material; package shows Beatle heads on a record, autographs in center; value is for nylons in package.
G $100   **VG $150**   **NM $200**

◯ **279.** **Nylons;** Ballito "Textured Mesh" nylons have same design as #278; package pictures faces and autographs in yellow, blue, and black background; value is for nylons in package.
G $60   **VG $90**   **NM $125**

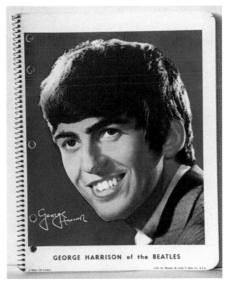

275

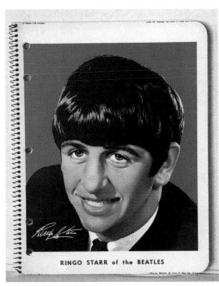

276

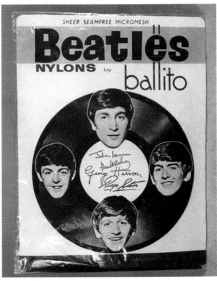

278

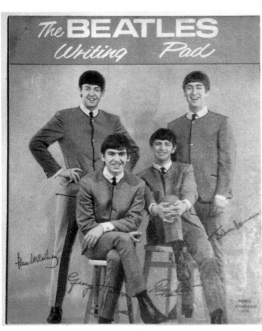

277

279

○ **280. Nylons;** "Carefree" nylons have same design as #278 and same package design as #279, with yellow, red, and black background.
   G $60   **VG $90**   **NM $125**

○ **281. Nylons Box;** 9$^1/_2$" x 5 $^1/_4$" x 1"; box which held several pairs of "Carefree" nylons (item #280); box is yellow, red, and black with B&W photos along right side.
   G $175   **VG $260**   **NM $350**

○ **282. Overnight Case;** Mfd. by Air Flite; 13" tall; round zippered vinyl case with flat bottom; strap handle attached at top; group pictured on front; available in red or black vinyl; value is for black case; add 20% to price for red case.
   G $250   **VG $375**   **NM $500**

○ **283. Paint By Number, John;** Mfd. by Artistic Creations; 14" x 19" box; contains 11" x 14" ready to paint picture, paints, thinner, brushes, and copy of finished painting.
   G $400   **VG $600**   **NM $800**

○ **284. Paint by Number, Paul;** (same as above)

○ **285. Paint by Number, George;** (same as above)

○ **286. Paint by Number, Ringo;** (same as above)

○ **287. Paint by Number Flyer;** Columbia Record Club; 6" x 8"; Ringo painting on cover; "A first for club members—Paint Your Own Beatle or other famous personality..."
   G $50   **VG $75**   **NM $100**

○ **288. Paper Clip Holder;** Mfd. for King Features; 1966; 3$^1/_2$" tall, 2$^3/_4$" diameter; black cylindrical paper-clip container pictures each cartoon show Beatle in gold around bottom, also four other cartoon figures.
   G $150   **VG $225**   **NM $300**

○ **289. Patch;** 4" diameter; circular cloth patch reads "Life Member, the Beatles Fan Club" around outside; picture of one of the Beatles in the center; red with white printing; one of each Beatle was produced; value is per patch.
   G $20   **VG $30**   **NM $40**

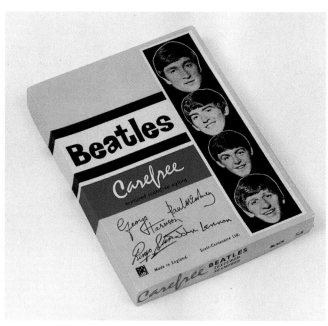

281

288

283

289   290

○ **290. Patch;** 3½"; red felt patch has guitar in center; "I like the Beatles Yea Yea" around edge in white.
G $10   VG $15   NM $20

○ **291. Patch (U.K.);** 3" x 4"; sew-on black cloth patch reads "The Beatles," also has their first names and pictures a red guitar; red and gold embroidery.
G $20   VG $30   NM $40

○ **292. Patch;** Mfd. by Newtonia (U.K.); 2" x 2½"; oval cloth patch with adhesive backing; reads "The Beatles" and has their first names with red guitar.
G $20   VG $30   NM $40

○ **293. Pen;** Mfd. by Press-Initial Corp.; 5" long; ink pen has cast Beatle heads on clip with autographs and drum on barrel; available in blue, black, tan, red, and green plastic; OP: 5" x 6" color card with perforation to hold pen, marked "The Beatles Official Ballpoint Pen." add 100% to value if original card is present; also sold on card with blister pack covering.
G $35   VG $55   NM $75

○ **294. Pen (Denmark);** 5" long; plastic ballpoint pen has photos of each Beatle under clear plastic on barrel; below is their autograph and instrument; metal band around middle reads "Made in Denmark."
G $40   VG $60   NM $80

○ **295. Pencil (U.K.);** 7"; white with black printing; marked "The Beatle pencil" and shows faces with first names below; no eraser. ★ *Repro Alert*
G $35   VG $50   NM $75

○ **296. Pencil by Number Kit;** Mfd. by Kitfix (U.K.); box measures 9" x 13¾"; includes five pencil-by-number pictures and six colored pencils.
G $400   VG $600   NM $800

291   292   293

294
295

○ **297. Pencil Case (Germany);** 10" x 3¹/₂"; vinyl covered; shows John and George on one side and Paul and Ringo on other; came with school supplies inside, which did not have any Beatle markings.

G $200   VG $300   NM $400

○ **298. Pencil Case;** Mfd. by Standard Plastic Products; 3¹/₂" x 8"; vinyl zippered pouch with picture of group and autographs on front; available in tan, blue, red, pink, and yellow; OP: sealed in plastic with header card; add 300% to value if in original packaging.

G $60   VG $90   NM $125

○ **299. Pencil Case;** Mfd. by Ramat & Co. (U.K.); beige zippered vinyl case with group picture on left, autographs on right above an additional clear snap closure with "The Beatles" on flap.

G $125   VG $190   NM $250

○ **300. Pencil Case;** 4" x 7"; vinyl top-zippered case; group pictured on front with autographs; available in various colors. ★ *Repro Alert*

G $100   VG $150   NM $200

○ **301. Perfume;** Mfd. by Olive Adair, Ltd. (U.K.); 3" tall; glass bottle with white plastic top; paper label reads "With The Beatles Perfume"; Beatles' faces on label.

G $400   VG $600   NM $800

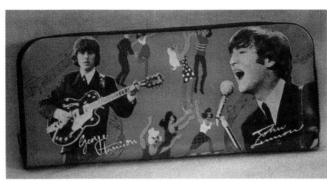

297

298

300

301

Photos

The Beatles were photographed extensively throughout their career. Copies of various photos were distributed by fan clubs and news agencies. Photos were also used for various promotional purposes as premiums and giveaways by radio stations, newspapers, and other businesses. Most of these photos were widely used shots and vary considerably in quality and size. Today's values will rarely exceed $10 each, with many in the $3-$5 range. Exceptions would be for wire service photos, which can sell for up to $20 each, depending on the photo. Wire photos or press release photos usually had a description of the photo attached to it, which makes it more desirable. Keep in mind that photos can be copied very cheaply nowadays, so dating a photo can be challenging.

○ **302.** **Photo** *Fabulous Magazine* **(U.K.);** die-cut photo on 8" x 10" card was a free insert in *Fabulous Magazine*.
  G $15   **VG $22**   **NM $30**

○ **303.** **Photos, Color;** Mfd. by J.M. Distributors; six 8" x 10" photos sealed with a header card; two group photos and four individual photos; price is for sealed package; the photos are valued individually at $6 each in NM shape.
  G $75   **VG $110**   **NM $150**

○ **304.** **Photos (U.K.);** 1963; Pixrama Foldbook; $3^{1}/_{2}$" x $4^{3}/_{4}$"; booklet contains biographies and twelve glossy photos.
  G $15   **VG $22**   **NM $30**

○ **305.** **Photos, Christmas Gift Box (Canada);** 7" x $10^{1}/_{2}$"; one plastic framed color photo ($6^{3}/_{4}$" x $5^{3}/_{16}$") of each Beatle in a Christmas Gift Box marked "4 Personally autographed & framed photos of Paul, Ringo, George, and John in living color"; value is for box with all four photos.
  G $150   **VG $225**   **NM $300**

○ **306.** **Picture;** 3-D (U.K.); $12^{3}/_{4}$" x 10" tall; colorized picture with raised images.
  G $60   **VG $90**   **NM $120**

304

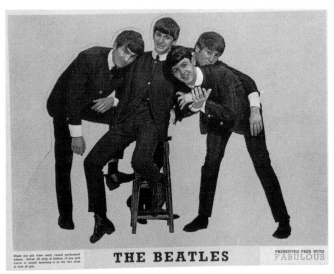

302

305

○ **307.** **Pillow;** Mfd. by Nordic House; 12" x 12"; pillow pictures group from the waist up with their autographs below each; "The Beatles" in upper left corner; white with blue or red back; came with two sewn-in tags; subtract $15 for each missing tag; a variation exists which has straps on the back; this variation features larger autographs on the front; add 100% to value for this variation.

G $75   **VG $110**   **NM $150**

○ **308.** **Pillow;** Mfd. by Nordic House; same basic design and colors as item #307; this version shows group holding red guitars; deduct $15 for each missing tag.

G $100   **VG $150**   **NM $200**

○ **309.** **Pillow;** Mfd. by Nordic House; similar construction and colors as item #307; except this version shows the group in a full-figure pose with instruments; deduct $15 for each missing tag.

G $150   **VG $225**   **NM $300**

306

307

308

309

○ **310. Pin-Up Screamers;** Mfd. by Matthews Rotary Press; 9" x 12"; package of four multi-color caricatures of the Beatles by Gordon Currie; each measures 8½" x 22"; value is for set in envelope.
G $25   **VG $35**   **NM $50**

○ **311. Plate;** Mfd. by Washington Pottery (U.K.); 7" diameter; plate with black and blue decal of group and first name autographs fired on. ★ *Repro Alert*
G $50   **VG $75**   **NM $100**

○ **312. Plate, Biscuit;** Mfd. by Washington Pottery (U.K.); 7" diameter; pottery plate with depression for cup and thumb extension on side; blue and black decal of group fired on. ★ *Repro Alert*
G $60   **VG $90**   **NM $125**

○ **313. Plate, Wall;** Mfd. by Ross of Mayfair (Margo's husband?) (U.K.); 5" diameter; china plate with full-length pose of group in B&W; autographs in blue below.
G $125   **VG $190**   **NM $250**

○ **314. Playing Cards;** deck of playing cards with color photo of group posed in doorway; box pictures same photo; cards measure 4" x 2½"; value is for complete deck in box; subtract 60% if box is missing. ★ *Repro Alert*
G $175   **VG $260**   **NM $350**

○ **315. Playing Cards;** (same as above except Beatles photographed in collarless suits with George & Ringo sitting on stools.) ★ *Repro Alert*

○ **316. Playing Cards, twin pack;** items #314 and #315 together in a deluxe twin-pack box; both designs pictured on one side of the box; "The Beatles" inscribed on reverse side; value is for complete decks in box.
G $250   **VG $375**   **NM $500**

○ **317. Pom-Pom;** 3"; black "fur ball" with two eyes attached; attachment on back.
G $35   **VG $55**   **NM $75**

311

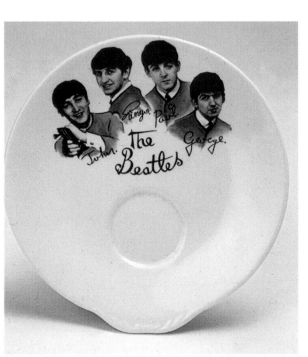

312

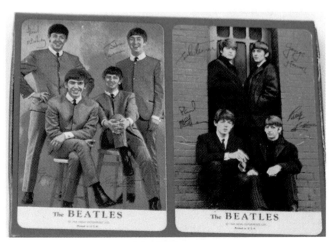

316

○ **318. Pom-Pom Display;** 28" x 16"; cardboard easel-backed display pictures the pom-pom with Beatles' faces and autographs; red with black and white print.

     G $250   **VG $375**   **NM $500**

○ **319. Pom-Pom Poster;** poster with the Beatles, their autographs and pom-poms pictured; reads "We Have Official Beatle Pom-Poms"; red with black and white print.

     G $200   **VG $300**   **NM $400**

○ **320. Portrait "Oil" Painting;** Mfd. for Beatle Buddies Fan Club; 9" x 12"; set of four prints of oil-style paintings, one of each Beatle; sold in plastic bag with header card that has a fan club card attached; painted by Leo Jansen; value is for sealed item.

     G $40   **VG $60**   **NM $80**

○ **321. Portrait "Oil" Painting;** Mfd. for Beatle Buddies' Fan Club; 16" x 20"; group painting by Leo Jansen; sold in plastic bag with header card that has a fan club card attached; value is for sealed item.

     G $40   **VG $60**   **NM $80**

○ **322. Portrait Offer;** Frito Lay; 6" x 3" (folded); paper was attached to bags of snack items, advertised 9" x 12" print included in bag and had mail-in offer on reverse for 16" x 20" print (Item #321).

     G $25   **VG $35**   **NM $50**

320

318

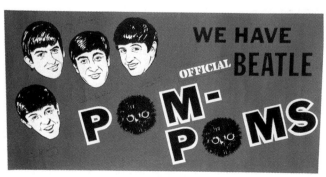

319

321

323. **Portrait "Oil" Painting;** 14" x 17"; print of group oil painting by Leo Jansen; similar to item #321 but on canvas-like material.
G $10   VG $15   NM $20

324. **Portraits, John;** Mfd. by Resco Products; B&W 12" x 12"; drawing of John; OP: clear plastic with header card; price is for item in package.
G $60   VG $90   NM $125

325. **Portraits, Paul;** (same as #324); variation #1: head on view of Paul; yellow header.

326. **Portraits, Paul;** (same as #324); variation #2: Paul's face is turned slightly; yellow header.

327. **Portraits, George;** (same as #324) green header.

328. **Portraits, Ringo;** (same as #324) orange header.

329. **Portraits, color;** 8" x 10"; one group photo and one of each Beatle; facsimile autographs on each portrait; value is for set of five.
G $20   VG $30   NM $40

330. **Portraits Store Display Poster;** 34" x 50"; color poster offering item #329; color portraits from Wagon Master Baked Beans.
G $200   VG $300   NM $400

331. **Portraits;** 14¹/₄" x 18¹/₄"; painted by Nicholas Volpe; color painting of each Beatle's face with small full-figure image of the Beatle playing instrument; OP: set of four, sealed with insert card with Capitol dome logo; insert gives a bio of the artist; add 50% to value if sealed in original package.
G $30   VG $45   NM $60

322

325

327

330

331

○ **332.** **Portraits, Punch-Out;** Mfd. by Whitman; 10" x 14"; booklet of color photos, stage, mobile, etc.; all are perforated for removal; value is for unused condition.

G $65   **VG $90**   **NM $125**

○ **333.** **Postcard (U.K.);** 3 1/2" x 5 1/2"; postcard with photo of one of the Beatles and personal message for the Variety Club of Great Britain charity fundraiser.

G $20   **VG $30**   **NM $40**

○ **334.** **Postcard (U.K.);** 1966; 5" x 8"; with photo of Beatles; reads "From us to you with best wishes" on reverse.

G $7   **VG $12**   **NM $15**

○ **335.** **Postcards;** various sizes and designs; many were produced in quantity, both in color and in B&W.

G $5   **VG $7**   **NM $10**

○ **336.** **Pouch;** Mfd. by Select-O-Pak; 10 1/2" x 15 1/4" flat zippered vinyl pouch; paper with Beatles pictured under clear plastic front.

G $100   **VG $150**   **NM $200**

○ **337.** **Purse;** Mfd. by Ramat + Co. Ltd. (U.K.); 8 1/4" x 3 3/4"; off-white zippered pouch with group photo to right; "The Beatles Purse" and autographs on left; (purse: see also Clutch Purse—item #84 & 85; handbag: see also item #208, 209, & 210).

G $100   **VG $150**   **NM $200**

○ **338.** **Puzzle (U.K.);** 11" x 17" (assembled); 340-piece jigsaw puzzle pictures the Beatles on stage at the Cavern; box measures 8" x 11"; front side of box pictures puzzle inside; all four of the puzzles in the series are pictured on the back.

G $125   **VG $190**   **NM $250**

○ **339.** **Puzzle (U.K.);** same as item #338; this puzzle pictures the Beatles in concert wearing brown suits.

○ **340.** **Puzzle (U.K.);** same as item #338; this puzzle pictures the Beatles on stage wearing blue suits.

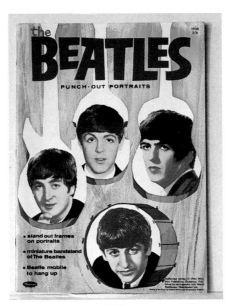

332

337

336

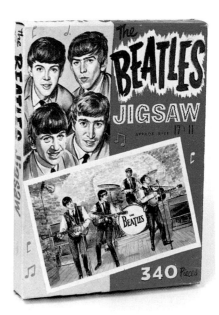

338a

○ 341. **Puzzle (U.K.);** same as item #338; this puzzle pictures the group seated with their instruments.

○ 342. **Puzzle (U.K.);** 1970; 18¹/₂" x 33" (assembled); "The Beatles Illustrated Lyrics Puzzle in a Puzzle"; puzzle contains various characterizations of Beatle songs; box measures 13" x 22"; puzzle has over 800 pieces and includes a poster of the assembled puzzle and solutions to the puzzle in an envelope; value shown is for complete puzzle with poster and solutions.
G $100   VG $150   NM $200

○ 343. **Record Box;** Mfd. by Air Flite.; 8¹/₂" x 8" x 5"; cardboard box with handle on top; designed to hold 45-rpm records (singles); group pictured on front; red or green box with a white top.
G $300   VG $450   NM $600

○ 344. **Record Box;** Mfd. by Air Flite; 12¹/₂" x 12¹/₂" x 4³/₄"; cardboard box designed to hold 33-rpm albums; group pictured on the front; red or green box with white top.
G $400   VG $600   NM $900

○ 345. **Record Cabinet (U.K.);** 37" x 24" x 15"; wood cabinet with Beatle wallpaper on outside of sliding doors; generic rock-n-roll vinyl material on top.
G $400   VG $600   NM $800

338b

343

342

344

○ **346. Record Carrier;** Mfd. by Seagull Enterprises (U.K.); 7½" x 7½" x 1½"; blue, red or white plastic carrying case for 45-rpm records; has plastic sleeves for sixteen records and retractable handles; group pictured on front (paper picture under clear plastic); several poses available.

G $175   **VG $260**   **NM $350**

○ **347. Record Carrier;** Mfd. by Creech Co.; 8¾" square; flat plastic pouch with strap handle, for 45-rpm record transport; Beatles record sleeve used for photo on front of pouch; reads "Platter Sack" on front.

G $60   **VG $90**   **NM $125**

○ **348. Record Carrier (Holland);** 7½" x 7½"; black and white carrying case has plastic sleeves for twenty 45-rpm records; group pictured on the front.

G $125   **VG $190**   **NM $250**

○ **349. Record Case;** Mfd. by Charter Industries; 1966; "Disk-Go-Case"; 8" tall, 9" diameter; round plastic case with group pictured on the front in black; available in seven colors: green, yellow, red, blue, brown, lavender, and pink; sold with a wrap-around banner and a folded hang tag; add 60% to price if banner is present and 60% to price if tag is present.

G $90   **VG $135**   **NM $180**

○ **350. Record Case Poster;** 6½" x 22"; promotional poster for the "Disk-Go-Case"; pictures the group with autographs and the "Disk-Go-Case."

G $225   **VG $340**   **NM $450**

348

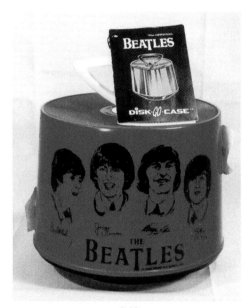

349

350

○ **351.** **Record Player;** 17¹/₂" x 10" x 6"; blue-cased four-speed record player; Beatles pictured on top and inside of lid; reads "The Beatles" on front and board next to platter; approximately 5,000 were produced; the serial number is located on a small strip of cardboard attached to the inside top of lid (please send the authors your serial number as we are trying to keep a record of these); OP: player came in a colorful box which measures 20" x 11¹/₂" x 7"; also included was an instruction booklet; instruction booklet is valued separately at $100 in NM shape; add 100% to price if the player is in the original box.

G $1,750   **VG $2,600**   **NM $3,500**

○ **352.** **Record Rack;** Mfd. by Selcol (U.K.); 10" long; orange plastic record rack held forty 45-rpm records; has autographs of group along lower front edge and pictures of group on ends.

G $400   **VG $600**   **NM $800**

○ **353.** **Ringo Roll;** Mfd. by Scotts Bakery, Liverpool (U.K.); clear cellophane package picturing group; bread product inside.

G $200   **VG $300**   **NM $400**

○ **354.** **Rug (Belgium);** 21¹/₂" x 33¹/₂"; colorful rug pictures faces, guitar, musical notes, and drum; tag on back of rug.

G $150   **VG $225**   **NM $300**

○ **355.** **Rug Sample;** Mfd. for Ohio Boys Town.; 1" square; piece of rug from the Sheraton Hotel in Cleveland, where the Beatles stayed during their 1964 tour; sold in envelope containing an affidavit.

G $40   **VG $60**   **NM $80**

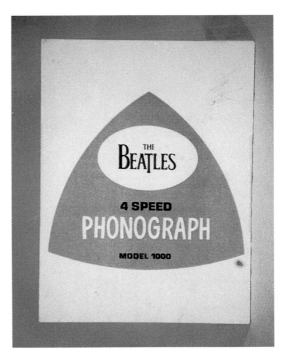

351b

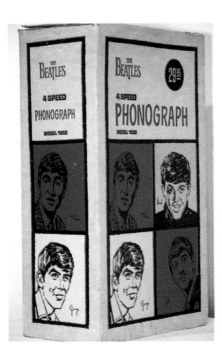

351a

353

354

○ **356.** **Saucer;** Mfd. by Washington Pottery (U.K.); 6" diameter; saucer with blue and black group picture; depression in center for cup. ★ *Repro Alert*
G $60   VG $90   NM $125

○ **357.** **Scarf;** 27" square; scarf has autographs covering entire surface; underlying design is four large records with "Beatles" in center of each; red, gold, and black print on white material.
G $50   VG $75   NM $100

○ **358.** **Scarf;** 26" square; white scarf with faces, records, and instruments in one corner; song titles printed below records; fine fringe along edge. ★ *Repro Alert*
G $25   VG $35   NM $50

○ **359.** **Scarf;** Mfd. by Blackpool Publishers (U.K.); 26" square; scarf is white with brown and pink print; several different group poses and a face shot in each corner with autographs.
G $50   VG $75   NM $100

○ **360.** **Scarf;** Mfd. by Scammonden Wollen Co. (U.K.); long scarf with beetles and first name autographs covering entire length.
G $100   VG $150   NM $200

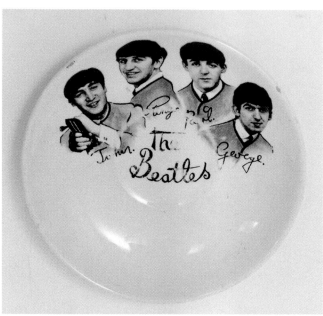

356

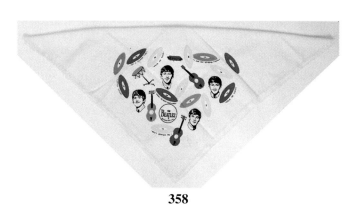

358

357

359

○ **361.** **Scarf (U.K.);** 26" x 26"; white scarf with guitar, bugs and music notes around edge; 3" Beatle faces in color in one corner with song titles; "The Beatles" above faces.
   G $45   **VG $70**   **NM $90**

○ **362.** **Scarf (Italy);** 26" x 27"; acetate twill scarf in violet or light blue, with group picture in each corner; reads "Beatlemania Sweeps Australia" in center.
   G $50   **VG $75**   **NM $100**

○ **363.** **Scarf;** triangular head scarf with ties; Beatles' faces and autographs cover entire surface; various colors; OP: plastic bag with group picture printed on top; attached to photo card; add 300% for original packaging.
   G $30   **VG $45**   **NM $60**

○ **364.** **Scarf;** (same basic design as #363, except this scarf shows group shot with "The Beatles.")
   G $40   **VG $60**   **NM $80**

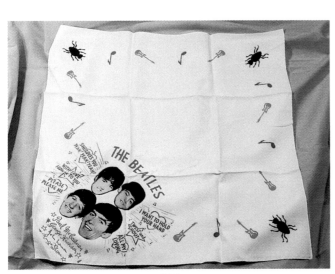

361

362

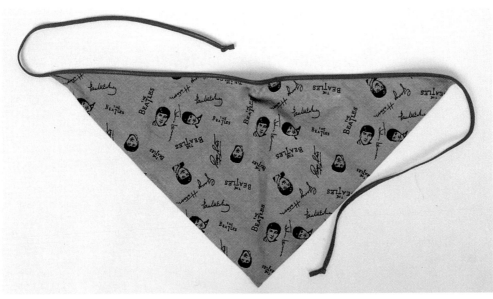

363

○ **365.   School Bag;** Mfd. by Burnel Ltd. (Canada); 12" x 9" x 3½"; tan school bag with "The Beatles" printed on flap above latch; group picture on both sides of latch; has handle on flap and shoulder strap.

G $450   VG $675   NM $900

○ **366.   School Report Cover;** Mfd. by Select-O-Pak; 9¼" x 11½"; heavy paper folder to fit 2-, 3- and 5-hole paper; Beatle faces and instruments

pictured in lower left corner; covers available include green, yellow, or blue; two different border design variations exist: straight or twisted rope-type border.

G $40   VG $60   NM $80

○ **367.   Scrapbook;** Mfd. by Whitman; 11³⁄₈" x 13½"; scrapbook with color picture of the Beatles on front and back covers; plain beige paper inside.

G $30   VG $45   NM $60

364

365

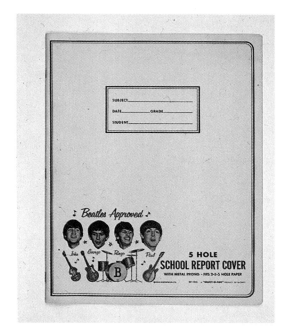

366

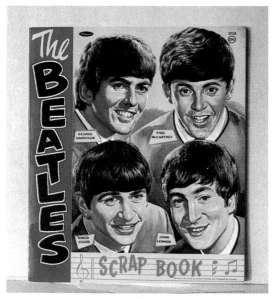

367

368. **Scrapbook (U.K.);** same as item #367 but measures 9³/₄" x 12" and has picture of Beatles on front only.
G $30   VG $45   NM $60

369. **Shampoo Box;** Mfd. by Bronson Products Co.; 3" x 7¹/₄" x 2¹/₂"; gold, black; and white box held one bottle of shampoo; faces on sides and top, with an ad for Beatles hairspray on back.
G $250   VG $375   NM $500

370. **Shampoo Shipping Carton;** Mfd. by Bronson Products Co. 8" x 13" x 8"; white cardboard box with black and blue print showing Beatle faces and autographs on all sides; held 1 dozen 8 oz. bottles of shampoo.
G $350   VG $525   NM $700

371. **Shirt;** knit white 3-button shirt with black piping; "The Beatles" and faces on upper left; tag inside neck reads "The Only Authentic Beatles shirt"; sold with hang tag that had perforated wallet photo; add 60% to price if tag is present.
G $60   VG $90   NM $120

372. **Shirt (U.K.);** red pullover cotton T-shirt with "The Beatles" and their faces on upper left.
G $50   VG $75   NM $100

373. **Shirt (U.K.);** yellow short-sleeved pullover shirt with posed group on front; pleated cuffs on sleeves and turtleneck collar.
G $100   VG $150   NM $200

374. **Shoulder Bag;** 9¹/₂" x 10"; vinyl pouch with rope or cord strap attached to top; picture of group on front, autographs below; various colors.
G $175   VG $260   NM $350

369a   369b

373

370

374

○ **375. Shoulder Bag;** 14" x 14"; white vinyl bag with black trim; Beatle faces are in color and "Beatles" is printed in red, blue, and yellow; bag has a strap and art is on both sides.

G $250   **VG $375**   **NM $500**

○ **376. Shoulder Bag (U.K.);** 14" x 9" x 6"; bag with strap reads "The Fabulous Beatles" on the front with Beatle faces, has autographs on the back side.

G $400   **VG $600**   **NM $800**

○ **377. Skateboard;** Mfd. by Surf Skater Co.; wooden board with metal wheels; group pictured on right side; "The Beatles Skateboard" on left; various models and colors; OP: box pictures group on right side, rest of box is striped design; add 50% to value for original box.

G $500   **VG $750**   **NM $1,000**

○ **378. Socks;** white crew socks with 1½" square patch picturing group on ankle; made of cotton and stretch nylon; one sock has "The Beatles" printed on sole with company name; price is per pair; OP: clear plastic bag with cardboard insert picturing the group; add 100% if in original package.

G $100   **VG $150**   **NM $200**

○ **379. Spatter Toy;** Mfd. by Spatter Toy Co.; handle attached to cord leading to two plastic knobs, with "mop-tops" attached; package measures 4" x 16" and reads "Twirl with the Beatles"; includes instructions for use.

G $50   **VG $75**   **NM $100**

○ **380. Stamps (Australia);** each stamp 1⅜"; set of four color stamps sold in block—one of each Beatle; value is for block of four.

G $20   **VG $30**   **NM $40**

○ **381. Stamps;** each stamp 1" x ½"; B&W photo stamps of each Beatle, originally sold in sheets of 48; value is for each sheet.

G $10   **VG $15**   **NM $25**

375

376

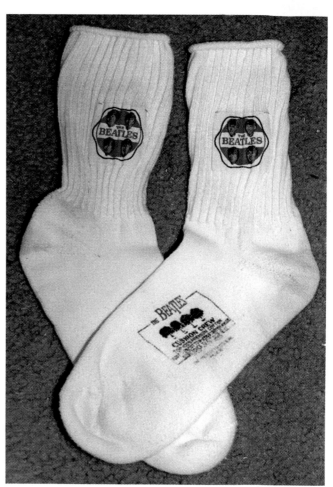

378

○ **382. Stamps Display Rack;** thin cardboard display rack which has red lettering and an easel back; held the sheets of item #381.
G $50   **VG $75**   **NM $100**

○ **383. Stamps;** Mfd. by Hallmark; $7^{1}/_{4}$" x 4", booklet with five pages of color stamps; twenty stamps per page; one page has a group picture on each stamp; the other pages each feature a different member of the group.
G $15   **VG $22**   **NM $30**

○ **384. Stamps Sales Banner;** $2^{3}/_{4}$" x 20"; promotional banner; "Yeah! Yeah! Yeah! Beatle Stamps Are Here!" on banner along with illustrations of stamps; display for item #383—Hallmark stamps.
G $20   **VG $30**   **NM $40**

○ **385. Stamps Display Box;** held item #383—Hallmark stamp packets; manila box with easel back; "100 Beatle Stamps Price 59 cents" printed in blue on front.
G $15   **VG $22**   **VG $30**

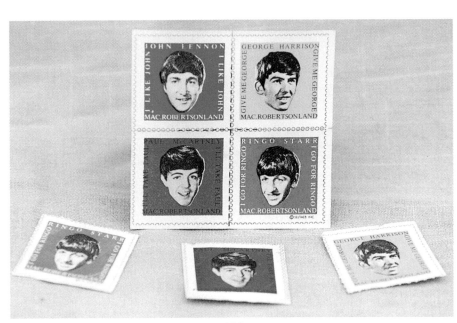

380

382

383

384

○ **386.** **Stickers;** Mfd. by Pop-Stick (U.K.); four heart-shaped vinyl stickers on paper, each with a B&W Beatle picture.; value for each.
G $10   **VG $15**   **NM $25**

○ **387.** **Suit;** cloth suit has Beatle faces and first names on jacket lining; Beatle clothes tag inside; pants did not have lining and had no Beatle markings.
G $300   **VG $450**   **NM $600**

○ **388.** **Sunglasses;** Mfd. by Solarex; black plastic wrap-around sunglasses with green lenses; small paper stickers of Beatle faces on each lens.
G $50   **VG $75**   **NM $100**

○ **389.** **Sunglasses Display Card;** Mfd. by Bachman Bros.; 22" x 14"; cardboard display with easel on back; B&W picture of group with autographs in center; across top it reads "The Beatles by Solarex"; held twelve pairs of glasses—item #388.
G $300   **VG $450**   **NM $600**

○ **390.** **Sunglasses Store Poster;** Mfd. by Solarex; 18" x 6"; paper poster which was used to promote sales of item #388; Beatle faces and signatures are shown with a blue background.
G $200   **VG $300**   **NM $400**

386

389

390

○ **391.** **Surveys;** radio hit song survey sheets were is-sued by many AM stations in the '60s; those with Beatle songs or Beatle pictures are of greatest interest.
G $2 - $5   **VG $3 - $10**   **NM $4 - $20**

○ **392.** **Sweatshirt;** white cotton long sleeve sweatshirt has posed picture of group on front; reads "The Beatles" above picture, has their autographs below.
G $40   **VG $60**   **NM $80**

392

396

○ **393.** **Sweatshirt;** same as above, but used in radio station promotion; "KYW Radio 1100 Group W" printed on shirt below autographs.
G $60   **VG $90**   **NM $120**

○ **394.** **Sweatshirt;** long sleeve sweatshirt pictures their faces with "The Beatles" below picture; above their faces reads "Yea, Yea, Yea"; color variations: black with yellow print, white with black print, or red with yellow print; short sleeve variation is light blue with black print.
G $40   **VG $60**   **NM $80**

○ **395.** **T-Shirt;** (same design as sweatshirt item #392)
G $40   **VG $60**   **NM $80**

○ **396.** **Tablecloth;** Mfd. by Ulster (Ireland); 36" square; white cotton tablecloth with group pic-ture in each corner; instruments around border; burgundy, black, and flesh colors; marked "Ulster copyright." ★ *Repro Alert*
G $175   **VG $260**   **NM $350**

○ **397.** **Tablecloth;** white paper with Beatles printed in repeating pattern; B&W print; this may have only been produced as a sample item.
G $125   **VG $185**   **NM $250**

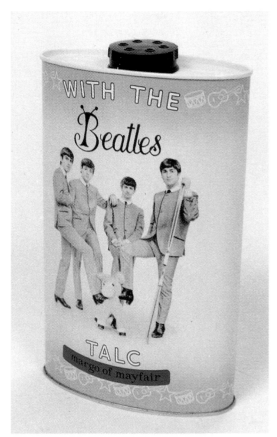
398

○ **398.** **Talcum Powder;** Mfd. by Margo of Mayfair (U.K.); 7" tall; grey and white can has pictures of group on both sides; reads "With the Beatles Talc."
G $250   **VG $375**   **NM $500**

○ **399.** **Tennis Shoes;** Mfd. by Wing Dings; low cut lace-up shoes with faces and autographs in repeating pattern over entire shoe; blue or white color; OP: box measures 11" x 4¼" x 3¼" and has pictures of each Beatle with autograph on lid; add 125% to value for original box; add 20% for blue shoes; value is per pair.
G $150   **VG $225**   **NM $300**

○ **400.** **Tennis Shoes (Canada);** same design item #399 except pink color with "made in Canada" on bottom; add 125% to price for original box.
G $175   **VG $260**   **NM $350**

○ **401.** **Tennis Shoes;** Mfd. by Wing Dings; high top, slip-on shoes; same pattern and box as item #399; available in white or blue; add 125% to value for original box; add 20% to price for blue shoes.
G $175   **VG $260**   **NM $350**

○ **402.** **Tennis Shoes Store Display;** Mfd. by Wing Dings; B&W display has Beatles pictured with voice balloons over each Beatle; Beatle tennis shoe and Wing Dings logo in right-hand corner; display has easel on back.
G $250   **VG $375**   **NM $500**

○ **403.** **Thermos;** Mfd. by Alladin; 1965; 7" tall, 3¼" diameter; blue thermos bottle pictures group on both sides; sold with lunch box (item #253) and brunch bag (item #52); came with matching light blue screw cap and light blue cup cap.
G $100   **VG $165**   **NM $225**

399

412

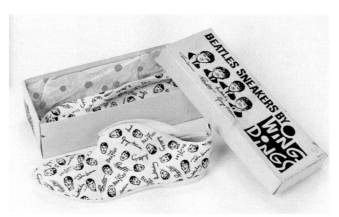

401

402

○ **404.** **Tie, Lariat;** Mfd. by Press-Initial Corp.; 1" brass disk with faces embossed on front, cord attached on back; tie is black cord with brass ends; OP: B&W photo card measures 10" x 3^1/$_2$", reads "Official Lariat Tie"; add 60% for card.
G $45 **VG $65** **NM $90**

○ **405.** **Tie, Lariat;** (same item #404, except color group picture on brass disk.)
G $60 **VG $90** **NM $120**

○ **406.** **Tiles, Group;** Mfd. by Carter Tiles (U.K.); 6" square; ceramic tile with Beatles group shot and autographs; tile is white with blue, brown, and black images; reads "The Beatles" at bottom.
G $100 **VG $150** **NM $200**

○ **407.** **Tiles, John;** same design as above; image of John with his autograph.
G $75 **VG $110** **NM $150**

○ **408.** **Tiles, Paul;** (same as above)

○ **409.** **Tiles, George;** (same as above)

○ **410.** **Tiles, Ringo;** (same as above)

○ **411.** **Tile;** Mfd. by Holman Bros. (U.K.); 4" square; white with group pictured with "The Beatles" and first name autographs below each picture in black.
G $20 **VG $30** **NM $40**

○ **412.** **Toffee Record (U.K.);** 7" square; paper envelope designed to resemble a record sleeve; held a toffee disk; Beatle song titles on front.
G $100 **VG $150** **NM $200**

○ **413.** **Towel (Holland);** 20" x 40"; white towel with black images of Beatles, song titles above, "The Beatles" below.
G $100 **VG $150** **NM $200**

○ **414.** **Towel;** Mfd. by Delsener; 2" x 2"; towel square from Riviera Hotel, used by the Beatles during their stay there in September 1964; one page with photo and info on each Beatle; value is for each.
G $25 **VG $35** **NM $75**

○ **415.** **Towel, Hollywood Bowl;** ^{1}/$_2$" towel swatch from "a towel used by the Beatles to dry their faces" on August 23, 1964 at the Hollywood Bowl concert; on a 2^1/$_2$" x 4" card.
G $40 **VG $60** **NM $80**

○ **416.** **Transfer;** 6" x 3^1/$_2$"; white iron-on transfer pictures group in classic pose; OP: white envelope with info on how to obtain additional transfers for 25 cents each.
G $20 **VG $30** **NM $40**

○ **417.** **Tray;** Mfd. by Worcester or Metal Tray Manufacturing (MTM) (U.K.); 13" x 13"; metal tray with color pictures of each Beatle on front; marked "Made in Great Britain" on lower front; issued with company sticker on back. ★ *Repro Alert*
G $30 **VG $45** **NM $60**

○ **418.** **Tumbler;** Mfd. by Burrite; 6^1/$_4$" tall; plastic glass with color picture of group on paper insert, under clear plastic sides; pink lips also printed on the top of the insert sheet; called the "Kissin' Lips Tumbler"; top and inner plastic is usually white in color; add 25% to price for pink or green colors. ★ *Repro Alert*
G $40 **VG $60** **NM $80**

○ **419.** **Tumbler;** Mfd. by Goodwill Products (Australia); 5^1/$_4$" tall; white plastic tumbler with paper color picture of group under clear plastic sides; reads "We Love You Beatles" vertically; there is also a variation which has "Spotless Cleaners" inscribed on the side of the tumbler.
G $50 **VG $75** **NM $100**

○ **420.** **Twig;** unusual toy consists of two red ^{1}/$_4$" wooden dowels, and two plastic spinners which fit on longer dowel; original plastic packaging pictures the Beatles on the enclosed instruction card, which opens up and measures 8^1/$_2$" x 3^1/$_2$".
G $175 **VG $260** **NM $350**

○ **421.** **Vase;** 14" tall; white ceramic vase with Beatle faces in color and first name autographs.
G $350 **VG $525** **NM $700**

○ **422.** **Vinyl Material (U.K.);** thin white vinyl with color Beatle group and individual poses and autographs in repeating pattern; value is for one square yard.
G $50 **VG $75** **NM $100**

○ **423.** **Vox Equipment Display (U.K.);** 16" x 20"; heavy cardboard store display for Vox musical equipment; pictures the Beatles and amplifier; easel backed.
G $250 **VG $375** **NM $500**

○ **424.** **Vox Display Photo;** 10^1/$_4$" x 13^1/$_8$"; B&W photo on heavy cardboard of the Beatles with Vox amps; Paul seated on amp, George with drumsticks.
G $40 **VG $60** **NM $80**

○ **425. Wall Hanging (Germany);** $26^1/_2$" x 19"; colorful linen-type cloth with drawing of Beatles with photos of faces
G $150   **VG $225**   **NM $300**

○ **426. Wall Plaque, John;** Mfd. by Kelsboro Ware (U.K.); 5" tall; dimensional ceramic heads; designed to be hung on a wall; they are hand-painted in color with trademark on the back.
G $200   **VG $300**   **NM $400**

○ **427. Wall Plaque, Paul;** (same as above)

○ **428. Wall Plaque, George;** (same as above)

○ **429. Wall Plaque, Ringo;** (same as above)

○ **430. Wallet;** Mfd. by Standard Plastic Products; $4^1/_4$" x $3^3/_4$"; vinyl wallet with group picture on one side, autographs on other; sold with file, comb, mirror, and two autographed photo cards inside; colors available are red, blue, yellow, tan, peach, and pink; OP: header card with Beatle faces, red and white striped; add 300% to price if in original package; price is for wallet complete with contents.
G $75   **VG $110**   **NM $150**

○ **431. Wallet Display, Mfd. by Standard Plastic Products;** held twelve wallets (item #430); two-piece cardboard display measures 17" x 23", header board pictures the Beatles; price is for card without wallets.
G $350   **VG $525**   **NM $700**

○ **432. Wallet;** $3^1/_2$" x 7"; checkbook-style wallet; vinyl with color photos of group under clear plastic on each side; has strap for closure.
G $85   **VG $130**   **NM $175**

○ **433. Wallet;** Mfd. by Ramat & Co. (Canada); $3^1/_4$" x $4^1/_2$" brown wallet has group picture on one side, autographs on reverse; has snap on side.
G $75   **VG $110**   **NM $150**

○ **434. Wallet;** Mfd. by Ramat & Co. (U.K.); $4^1/_4$" x 4"; round-top wallet with photo on front, autographs on back; has snap on top; colors include white, black, or pink.
G $75   **VG $110**   **NM $150**

○ **435. Wallet;** $3^1/_2$" x $4^1/_2$"; black vinyl with color pictures under clear plastic on both sides; no strap.
G $80   **VG $120**   **NM $160**

○ **436. Wallet;** 5" x 4"; black or white vinyl with pictures under clear plastic on both sides; brass trim around edges; snap closure.
G $70   **VG $110**   **NM $140**

417

423

434

◯ **437.** **Wallet Photo Booklet;** Mfd. by Dell; 3¹/₂" x 5"; booklet with twenty B&W fold-out photos.
G $10 **VG $15** **NM $25**

◯ **438.** **Wallet Photo Booklet Display Box;** Mfd. by Dell; 7" x 5"; red cardboard box with open front; two rows of wallet photo booklets can be displayed side by side; this countertop box has "Beatles" in white print on front of box and also on sides; value is for empty box.
G $75 **VG $110** **NM $150**

◯ **439.** **Wallpaper (Canada and U.K.);** 21" wide; rolls of wallpaper with pictures of group in re-peating pattern; 21" x 21" panel shows com-plete pattern; U.K. variety has a sizing strip along side; price is per panel.
G $15 **VG $25** **NM $35**

◯ **440.** **Watch;** Mfd. by Smiths (U.K.); Beetle-shaped brooch watch with pin attachment; OP: presen-tation box is silk lined with group picture inside lid; add 100% if original box is present.
G $100 **VG $150** **NM $200**

436

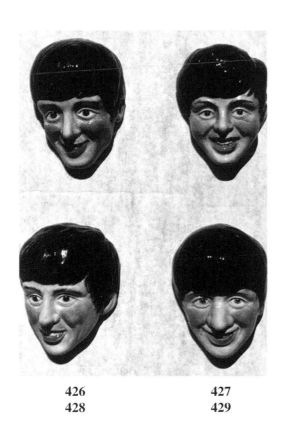

426 427
428 429

435

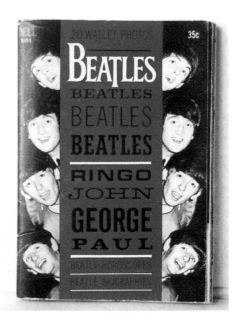

437

○ **441.** **Wig;** Mfd. by Bell Toy Co. (U.K.); formed plastic wig with "Beatle" hairstyle; OP: clear plastic bag with header card; card reads "The Beatles Wig" on front and "Be With It, Wear a Beatles Wig" on back; value is for wig in package.
G $275   **VG $400**   **NM $550**

○ **442.** **Wig;** Mfd. by Lowell Toy Manufacturing; wig of "lifelike" hair; OP: plastic bag with header card; Beatle heads are die-cut on top of header card; value is for wig in package. ★ *Repro Alert*
G $60   **VG $90**   **NM $125**

Writing Pad; see also Notebook (item #277)

439

441

440

442

2

Yellow Submarine

The 1968 release of the movie *Yellow Submarine* was coupled with the licensing of scores of related products. One page from the *Yellow Submarine* pressbook (which was sent to theater owners prior to the booking of the movie) was headed with " 'Yellow Submarine' Offers Tremendous Merchandise Promotion Opportunity!" That page listed over twenty-five companies which were licensed to produce *Yellow Submarine*-related products. The only *Yellow Submarine* items not listed in this chapter are: movie posters (see chapter 9), record promotional items (see chapter 10), and trading cards (see chapter 13). These items are excluded from this chapter because we thought the listings would be more appropriate in the specific categories. All the items in this chapter are alphabetically arranged by item name. All items in this chapter were manufactured in 1968.

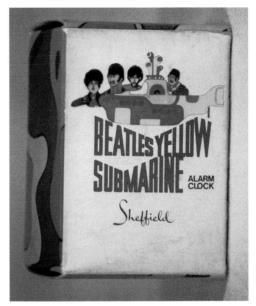

443a

○ **443.** **Alarm Clock;** Mfd. by Sheffield Watch, Inc.; metal clock with Beatles and Yellow Submarine pictured under glass face; clock is yellow with psychedelic designs on sides; OP: box with design similar to clock; add 60% to value if box is present. ★ *Repro Alert*
　　G $400　　　**VG $600**　　　**NM $800**

○ **444.** **Bank, John;** Mfd. by Pride Creatios; 8" tall; brightly colored papier-mâché bank of John from waist up; coin slot in back of head, rubber plug and two stickers on the bottom; one is a King Features sticker and the other is a Pride Creations sticker; OP: plain green cardboard box with name stamped on end; add 25% to price if box is present. ★ *Repro Alert*
　　G $225　　　**VG $335**　　　**NM $450**

443b

○ **445.   Bank, Paul;** (same as above)

○ **446.   Bank, George;** (same as above)

○ **447.   Bank, Ringo;** (same as above)

○ **448.   Bicycle Seat;** Mfd. by Huffy; Sunline model; yellow bicycle seat with a yellow submarine across top.
G $125   VG $190   NM $250

○ **449.   Binder;** Mfd. by Vernon Royal; $11^1/_2$" x $10^1/_4$"; 3-ring binder pictures assorted *Yellow Submarine* characters on both front and back; color illustrations on white background.
G $125   VG $190   NM $250

○ **450.   Book, *Yellow Submarine;*** 4" x 7"; hardcover published by World Press, written by Max Wilk.
G $30   VG $45   NM $60

○ **451.   Book, *Yellow Submarine;*** $4^1/_4$" x 7"; paperback published by Signet, written by Max Wilk.
G $7   VG $14   NM $20

○ **452.   Bookmarks;** Mfd. by Unicorn Creations, Inc.; 3" x 9"; with a plain back; set of six includes: Apple Bonker, one of each Beatle, and Old Fred; value is for each.
G $7   VG $12   NM $15

450

444   445   446   447

449

452

○ **453.** **Bulletin Board, Beatles;** Mfd. by Unicorn Creations, Inc.; $7^1/_2$" x 23"; corrugated cardboard bulletin board with four pressure-sensitive tape strips on back for mounting; OP: shrink wrapped with round paper tag insert; value is for sealed item; deduct 50% if not sealed.
   G $60   **VG $90**   **NM $125**

○ **454.** **Bulletin Board, Head Meanie;** (same description as above.)
   G $35   **VG $55**   **NM $75**

○ **455.** **Bulletin Board, Snapping Turk;** (same description and price as #454.)

○ **456.** **Bulletin Board, Stamp Out Fun!;** (same description and price as #454.)

○ **457.** **Bulletin Board, The Beatles;** Mfd. by Unicorn Creations, Inc.; 24" x 24"; corrugated cardboard bulletin board; OP: plastic bag with header card and tacks; value is for sealed item.
   G $150   **VG $225**   **NM $300**

○ **458.** **Bulletin Board, John;** (same description and price as item #457.)

○ **459.** **Bulletin Board, Paul;** (same as item #457.)

○ **460.** **Bulletin Board, George;** (same as item #457.)

○ **461.** **Bulletin Board, Ringo;** (same as item #457.)

458

453   454   456   455

457

459

462

462. Bulletin Board, Yellow Submarine; (same as item #457.)

463. Buttons; Mfd. by Yellow Submarine Enterprises; 1³/₄" diameter; set of six pinback buttons; one of each Beatle, a blue meanie, and the submarine; value is for each.
G $7   **VG $10**   **NM $15**

464. Buttons; 3" diameter; set of four pinback buttons; one of each Beatle against a different color solid background; value is for each. ★ *Repro Alert*
G $5   **VG $7**   **NM $10**

465. Buttons; Mfd. by A & M Leatherline; 2" diameter; buttons with *Yellow Submarine* characters and slogans; slogans are: "All you need is love," "Stomp out Blue Meanies," "We all live in a yellow submarine," "All together now," and "Sgt. Pepper's Lonely Hearts Club Band."
G $6   **VG $9**   **NM $12**

466. Button Box; 10" x 6" x 3"; white cardboard box; "Buttons Yellow Submarine" printed on box top; box has hole to mount one button for display.
G $70   **VG $100**   **NM $140**

465

467. **Calendar;** Mfd. by Golden Press; 12" x 12"; colorful spiral-bound calendar with scenes from the movie for each month; OP: brown paper envelope marked "The Beatles 1969 Calendar"; add 30% with original envelope.

G $75   VG $110   NM $150

468. **Candle;** Mfd. by Concept/Development; glass or tin container with 8$\frac{1}{2}$" x 4$\frac{1}{2}$" color sticker wrapped around side; sticker pictures characters from movie.

G $250   VG $375   NM $500

Cards; see Trading Cards #1239 through #1244

469. **Cels:** Original artwork from the film, painted on celluloid. These were sold at art galleries and bookstores in the early 1970s with a "Certificate of Authenticity." Some were given away as prizes by radio stations. The certificate measures 8" x 10", it is on a parchment-type paper and has a gold foil seal. The celluloid measures 12$\frac{1}{2}$" x 16". At the bottom of the cel are peg holes for lining up the animation drawing to the cel and eventually the cel with the background and camera. At the bottom of the cel are hand-written numbers and letters. These would denote the scene and sequence in which the cels would appear. Most cels were sold in groups of three or four cels. Each cel contains a character or image.

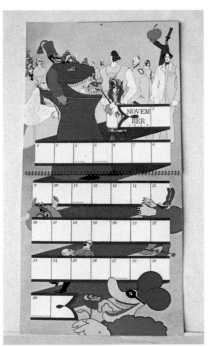

467

469a

468

469b

The value depends on the content and visual appeal of the cels. Characters can be found in sizes from 1" to 12$\frac{1}{2}$". Generally, the larger the character image the higher the value. Full-figure characters, not missing body parts, are most desirable. Occasionally a cel would include one of the Beatles only shown from the waist up. Characters with their "backs to the camera," so to speak, are not as desirable. Characters over 6" are not often found and bring a higher price. Many times these sets of three to four cels may not have appeared in the same configuration in the movie and have been placed together for the sale of the artwork. We can only list general price guidelines due to the unique nature of this one-of-a-kind artwork. Cel sets that contain all four Beatles would be the most sought after.

Price for cels that contain the Beatles: $300 to $800 per Beatle (less if the Beatle is very small.)

Price for cels that contain other *Yellow Submarine* characters: $150 to $400 depending on the size or importance of the character. (Less if the character is not full figure or is very small.)

Add $50 if "Certificate of Authenticity" is present.

Paint separation, line wear (black ink outlines of characters worn off), or cel trimming will reduce the value of the cel.

○ **470.** **Coasters;** Mfd. by K. Cennar Ent.; 3$\frac{3}{4}$" square; cardboard drink coasters with color pictures of the Beatles and movie characters; sold in a package of twelve with header card; value is for sealed package.

| G $75 | VG $110 | NM $150 |

○ **471.** **Coloring Book;** Pub. by World Distributors (U.K.); 64 pages of drawings to color; Beatles and movie characters pictured in color on the cover.

| G $100 | VG $150 | NM $200 |

○ **472.** **Comic Book;** Pub. by Gold Key Comics; comic book is based on the movie; includes 15$\frac{1}{2}$" x 20" pullout poster; deduct 50% if poster is missing.

| G $60 | VG $90 | NM $125 |

○ **473.** **Dimensional, The Beatles, D-1;** Mfd. by Craftmaster Paper; kit that is assembled to make a wall hanging; envelope measures 15" x 18", and shows the assembled kit on the front, with the assembly instructions on the reverse; price is for unassembled kit with envelope.

| G $250 | VG $375 | NM $500 |

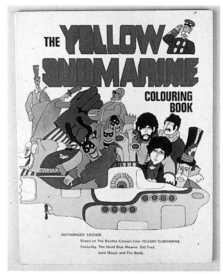

471

470

472

○ **474. Dimensional, Lord Mayor, D-2;** (same description as above.)
　　G $200　　　**VG $300**　　　**NM $400**

○ **475. Dimensional, Yellow Submarine, D-3;** (same description and price as #474.)

○ **476. Dimensional, The Boob, D-4;** (same description and price as #474.)

○ **477. Dimensional, Blue Meanie, D-5;** (same description and price as #474.)

○ **478. Dimensional, The Flying Glove, D-6;** (same description and price as #474.)

○ **479. Giftbook;** Pub. by World Distributors (U.K.); 8$^1/_4$" x 12"; hardcover; a 60-page book following the storyline of the movie.

　　G $35　　　**VG $50**　　　**NM $75**

473

474

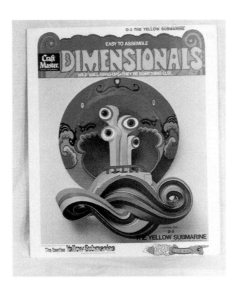

475

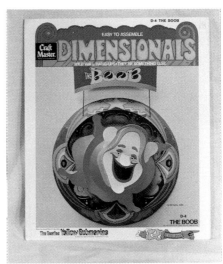

476

477

478

479

○ **480.   Glove Puppets Candy Display Box;** Mfd. by J. Bellamy Ltd. (U.K.); 10³/₄" x 9" x 3¹/₂"; colorful display box pictures the Yellow Sub Beatles and held twelve "Glove"-shaped packages of four different flavors of candy; top of the box lifts off from bottom of box; both top and bottom have graphics.
G $800   VG $1,200   NM $1,600

○ **481.   Goebel Figurine, John;** Mfd. by Goebel (W. Germany); 8¹/₂" tall; colorfully-painted porcelain figure; marked on the bottom with Goebel Hummel trademark.
G $600   VG $900   NM $1,200

○ **482.   Goebel Figurine, Paul;** (same as above).

○ **483.   Goebel Figurine, George;** (same as above).

○ **484.   Goebel Figurine, Ringo;** (same as above).

480

481   482   483   484

○ **485.** **Greeting Cards;** Mfd. by Sunshine Card Co.; box of fourteen 4^1/$_2$" x 9" color cards with envelopes; box has the Beatles and the Yellow Sub conning tower on lid.
G $65   **VG $95**   **NM $125**

○ **486.** **Greeting Cards;** Mfd. by Sunshine Card Co.; box of eighteen 4^1/$_2$" x 9" color cards with envelopes; box lid has John and Ringo with periscopes and side view of the Yellow Submarine.
G $65   **VG $95**   **NM $125**

○ **487.** **Greeting Cards;** Mfd. by Sunshine Card Co.; box of fifteen 5" x 7" color cards with envelopes; box has psychedelic theme on lid.
G $65   **VG $95**   **NM $125**

○ **488.** **Greeting Cards;** Mfd. by Sunshine Card Co.; box of twenty 5" x 7" color cards with envelopes; box pictures the Sgt. Pepper Band Lonely Hearts Club on lid.
G $50   **VG $75**   **NM $100**

○ **489.** **Halloween Costume;** Mfd. by Collegeville Costumes; pink, blue, and yellow Blue Meanie costume and mask; the Beatles, Yellow Submarine, and various characters are on the chest of the costume; OP: box measures 11" x 8^1/$_2$" and has "Yellow Submarine" stamped on end; add 200% to value if box is present.
G $125   **VG $185**   **NM $250**

485

488

487

489

○ **490.   Halloween Costume;** Mfd. by Collegeville Costumes; deluxe style costume of Blue Meanie with flasher light in forehead of mask (battery powered); Blue Meanies on chest of costume; OP: box is similar in size as above, and has "Blue Meanie" stamped on end; add 200% to value if box is present.

G $150   VG $275   NM $300

○ **491.   Hangers;** Mfd. by Henderson-Haggard, Inc.; 16" tall; color two-sided clothes hanger with translucent plastic hook; John, Paul, George, and Ringo were sold as a set; OP: clear vinyl with colorful psychedelic border; "Closet Carnival" and "Picture Hangers" on either side of front; value is for each hanger; add 35% to set if in the original packaging.

G $60   VG $90   NM $120

Jigsaw Puzzle; see item #528-#541 (Puzzles)

○ **492.   Keychain, John;** Mfd. by Pride Creations; 2½" x 6"; color plastic rectangle with metal keyring attached.

G $10   VG $17   NM $25

○ **493.   Keychain, Paul;** (same as above).

○ **494.   Keychain, George;** (same as above).

○ **495.   Keychain, Ringo;** (same as above).

○ **496.   Keychain, Yellow Submarine;** (same description as above).

G $25   VG $35   NM $50

○ **497.   Keychain, Apple Bonkers;** Mfd. by Pride Creations; 4" diameter; color round plastic disk with metal keyring attached.

G $25   VG $35   NM $50

490

491

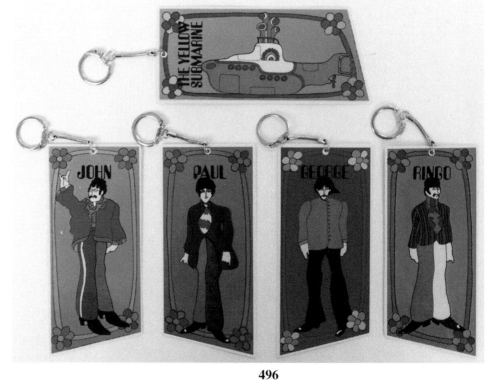

496

492   493   494   495

○ **498.** **Keychain, Blue Meanie;** (same as item #497).

○ **499.** **Keychain, The Boob;** (same as item #497).

○ **500.** **Keychain, Jack the Nipper;** (same as item #497).

○ **501.** **Keychain, Mini Meanie;** (same as item #497).

○ **502.** **Keychain, Robin the Butterfly Stomper;** (same as item #497).

○ **503.** **Letter Holder;** Mfd. by A + M Leatherline; U-shaped holder pictures Beatles, Submarine, and The Boob.
G $350   **VG $525**   **NM $700**

Lobby Cards; also see Movie Items #1027

○ **504.** **Lunchbox;** Mfd. by Thermos; 6³/₄" x 8³/₄" x 4"; metal lunchbox pictures Beatles Sgt. Pepper Band and others; value is for lunchbox only; see #561 for thermos.
G $250   **VG $400**   **NM $700**

○ **505.** **Magazine;** Pub. by Pyramid Publications; *The Official Yellow Submarine Magazine* contains the storyline of the movie with color pages; 48 pages (no cover price); newsstand edition exists with 60-cent cover price and has twelve added pages of Beatle features; valued the same as the 48-page edition.
G $15   **VG $25**   **NM $30**

○ **506.** **Magnetic Poster (Italy);** one metal sheet with scenery from the movie; one magnetic sheet with over 40 punch-out characters and the Beatles; these can be detached and placed on the metal sheet; OP: sealed in plastic with header card; add 50% to value if in original packaging.
G $400   **VG $600**   **NM $800**

504

502   499   497
500   501   498

505

○ **507.** **Mobile;** Mfd. by Sunshine Art Studios; color cardboard characters mounted on 9³/₄" x 14¹/₄" backing; sold with black string to hang figures; value is for unassembled item.

| G $65 | VG $95 | NM $125 |

○ **508.** **Model;** Mfd. by Model Products Corp. (MPC); plastic model kit of submarine with four 3-D plastic Beatles, decal sheet, and instructions; box measures 9" x 6" x 3"; value is for unassembled model in box; add 25% to value if the model is sealed in original shrink wrap; value for built-up model without box is $75 in NM shape. ★ *Repro Alert*

| G $175 | VG $260 | NM $350 |

Movie Posters; see Movie Item #1028-1030.

○ **509.** **Notebook;** Mfg. by Vernon Royal.; 5" x 7¹/₂"; side spiral-bound ruled notebook pictures Beatles, Yellow Submarine, and other characters on the cover.

| G $40 | VG $60 | NM $80 |

○ **510.** **Notebook;** Mfg. by Vernon Royal; same description as above, except this is a full-size notebook measuring 8" x 10¹/₂".

| G $75 | VG $110 | NM $150 |

○ **511.** **Pen Holder;** Mfd. by A & M Leatherline; 3" x 5" x 1"; white block with the Sgt. Pepper band, The Boob and sub pictured on it; brass pen holder attached.

| G $350 | VG $525 | NM $700 |

506

508

507

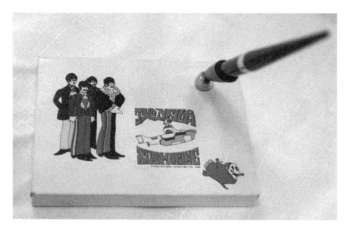

511

○ **512. Pencil Holder;** Mfd. by A & M Leatherline; 4" tall x 3" in diameter; cork-lined circular container; each Beatle is pictured on the outside.
G $300   **VG $450**   **NM $600**

○ **513. Pennant;** 5" x 7"; colorful cloth pennant which reads "Beatles Yellow Submarine"; the Beatles and various characters from the movie are shown.
G $60   **VG $90**   **NM $120**

○ **514. Photo Album;** Mfd. by A & M Leatherline; 4½" x 3¾"; cover of this photo album reads "Beatle Photos" and pictures the Sgt. Pepper Band; designed to display twelve photos—one per page.
G $150   **VG $225**   **NM $300**

○ **515. Photo Album;** Mfd. by A & M Leatherline; 7½" x 10"; 3-ring binder pictures the Sgt. Pepper Band; "The Beatles Photo Album" written on cover.
G $225   **VG $340**   **NM $450**

○ **516. Planter;** Mfd. by MY-LO Inc.; 9" long x 6" tall; plaster plant holder which is yellow with red and blue highlights.
G $150   **VG $225**   **NM $300**

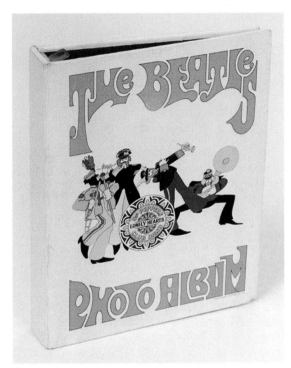
515

512

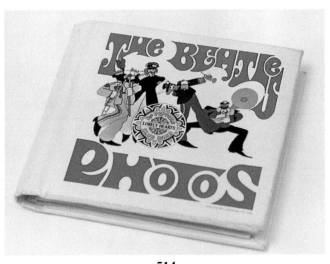
514

516

○ **517. Pop-Out Art Decorations;** Mfd. by Western Publishing Co.; book of perforated figures to remove; booklet measures $9^1/_2$" x 15"; Beatles and other characters are printed on thin cardboard and can be used to make a mobile, display, etc.

G $15   **VG $25**   **NM $30**

○ **518. Postcards;** Mfd. by Personality Posters; 10" x $5^1/_2$"; five different color postcards in series; four individual Beatles and the Yellow Submarine; value is per postcard.

G $5   **VG $7**   **NM $10**

○ **519. Postcards;** Mfd. by Unicorn Creations; 10 $^1/_4$" x 14$^1/_2$"; six different postcards in this set; the individual Beatles, the Sgt. Pepper Band, and the Yellow Submarine; price is per postcard.

G $6   **VG $10**   **NM $15**

○ **520. Poster, All You Need Is Love;** Mfd. by Poster Prints; 24" x 36"; day-glo poster which pictures the group.

G $25   **VG $35**   **NM $50**

○ **521. Poster, Beatles;** 21" x 29"; poster of the Beatles from the movie; sold through mail order.

G $25   **VG $35**   **NM $50**

517

519

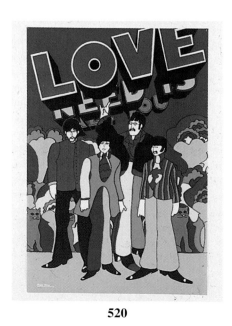

520

521

○ **522. Poster, All You Need is Love;** features the Lord Mayor; (same as item #521).

○ **523. Poster, Blue Meanies;** (same as item #521).

○ **524. Poster, Sgt. Pepper Band;** (same as item #521).

○ **525. Poster Put-Ons, The Beatles;** Mfd. by Craftmaster; 21" x 15"; poster to which you apply over 60 stickers; poster comes rolled in a 15" long x 2" x 2" box.
G $100   **VG $150**   **NM $200**

○ **526. Poster Put-Ons, Sgt. Pepper Band;** (same as above).

Press Information Kit; see Movie Item #1032.

○ **527. Press-Out Book;** Mfd. by World Distributors (U.K.); 8½" x 11½"; six pages of punch-outs and eight pages to color.
G $125   **VG $190**   **NM $250**

Pressbook; see Movie Item #1033.

Program; see Movie Item #1034

Puzzles; Mfd. by Jaymar Specialty Company. There are six different titles of the large and medium size *Yellow Submarine* puzzles. There are eight titles of the small puzzles making a total of twenty different *Yellow Submarine* puzzles. The medium and small puzzles show progressively smaller portions of the scenes shown in the large puzzle. (There may have been four more small puzzles, but we have been unable to verify the titles.)

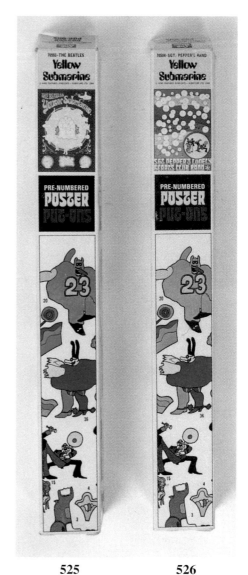

525   526

524

527

Puzzle Size	Number of pieces	Completed Size	G	VG	NM
Pockct (small)	over 100	5" x 7"	$45	$65	$90
Medium	over 100	13" x 18"	$40	$60	$80
Large	over 650	19" x 19"	$60	$90	$120

Box size: small $3^3/_4$" x $5^3/_4$" x $1^1/_2$"
           medium   8" x $9^1/_2$" x 2"
           large $12^1/_4$" x $12^1/_4$" x $1^1/_2$"

Large and Medium Puzzles

○ **528.   Puzzle, Beatles in Pepperland.**

○ **529.   Puzzle, Blue Meanies Attack.**

○ **530.   Puzzle, In The Yellow Sub.**

○ **531.   Puzzle, Meanies Invade Pepperland.**

○ **532.   Puzzle, Sea of Monsters.**

○ **533.   Puzzle, Sgt. Peppers Band.**

529

528

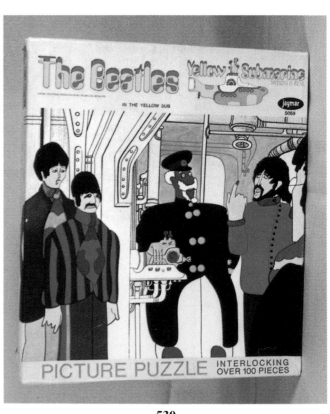

530

Small (Pocket) Puzzles

○ **534.**   **Puzzle, Beatles in Pepperland.**

○ **535.**   **Puzzle, The Bugler;** a scene from the larger "Sgt. Peppers Band" puzzle.

○ **536.**   **Puzzle, Flying High;** a scene from the larger "Beatles in Pepperland" puzzle.

○ **537.**   **Puzzle, Fyfe & Drum;** a scene from the larger "Sgt. Peppers Band" puzzle.

○ **538.**   **Puzzle, In The Yellow Sub.**

○ **539.**   **Puzzle, Meanies Invade Pepperland.**

○ **540.**   **Puzzle, Nothing is Real.**

○ **541.**   **Puzzle, Sgt. Peppers Band.**

○ **542.**   **Rub-Ons;** $2^1/_2$" x $3^1/_2$"; eight individually numbered sheets of six to eight rub-ons; each pictures various characters from the movie; packaged in plain white sealed wrapper with instruction sheet; distributed in boxes of Wheat Honeys or Rice Honeys cereal; value is per sheet with instructions.
G $25   **VG $35**   **NM $50**

○ **543.**   **Rub-Ons Offer on Cereal Box;** Mfd. by Nabisco; boxes of Wheat Honeys or Rice Honeys which contained rub-ons (item #542); box is heavily illustrated with *Yellow Submarine* characters; there is a coupon on the side to order a complete set of the eight rub-ons sheets. ★ *Repro Alert*
G $400   **VG $600**   **NM $800**

536   **535**

543a

543b

544. **Scrapbook;** Mfd. by A & M Leatherline; 12 ¹/₄" x 14¹/₂"; a blank-paged scrapbook with the Sgt. Pepper Band on the cover.
G $250   **VG $375**   **NM $500**

545. **Snow Dome (Hong Kong);** 2" tall x 3" long; clear domed plastic container with a yellow submarine and "snow" inside water.
G $150   **VG $225**   **NM $300**

546. **Stationery;** Mfd. by Unicorn Creations; 8¹/₂" x 10¹/₂"; sheets of paper with Yellow Submarine characters on them; sold in boxes of twenty sheets with twenty matching envelopes; eighteen different designs were issued; value is per complete box; add 50% to value for designs featuring a Beatle. Available designs are:

1. John	10. Beatles on rainbow
2. Paul	11. Chief Blue Meanie
3. George	12. Jeremy the Boob
4. Ringo	13. Snapping Turtle Turk
5. Max	14. Lonely People
6. Max (front view)	15. All You Need Is Love
7. Hidden Persuader	16. Flying Glove
8. Flying Horsemen	17. Apple Bonkers
9. The Yellow Sub	18. John under tree

G $30   **VG $45**   **NM $60**

544

545

546a

546b

546c

547. **Stickers, The Beatles;** Mfd. by DAL Manufacturing Corp.; sheet measures 9" x 12"; sheet of color plastic stickers; sold sealed in plastic with insert page on reverse; marketed as "Pop-Stickles"; value is for sealed item.
G $30   **VG $45**   **NM $60**

548. **Stickers, The Glove;** (same description as above).
G $15   **VG $25**   **NM $30**

549. **Stickers, Yellow Submarine;** (same description as #547, same price as #548).

550. **Stick-Ons;** Mfd. by Beemans; set of four stickers each on a 7" x 7" backing paper; includes: The Beatles, the sub, Blue Meanie, and Old Fred; value is for set of four.
G $50   **VG $75**   **NM $100**

551. **Stick-Ons Store Display;** Mfd. by Beemans (Gum Company); 19" x 20"; two-sided colorful cardboard display for the Yellow Submarine stick-ons (see item #550); pictures various characters including Sgt. Peppers Band; mail-in coupons were attached in the lower corner.
G $400   **VG $600**   **NM $800**

552. **Stickers;** comes in 2" x 2" sizes and 1$^1/_2$" x 1$^1/_2$" sizes; peel and stick stickers given away as premiums in various products; various characters were illustrated on these stickers.
G $10   **VG $15**   **NM $20**

547

551

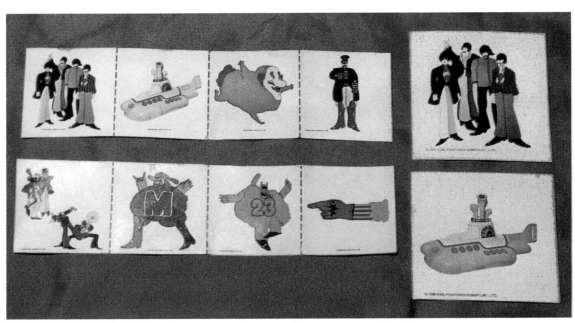

552

○ **553.** **Stickers Display;** Mfd. by Laura Scudder's Potato Chips; cardboard display reads "We've got Beatles in our potato chips"; the Beatles and the Yellow Sub are pictured; the stickers (item #552) were given away in twin packs and variety packs of their potato chips.
G $350   **VG $525**   **NM $700**

○ **554.** **Sticker Fun Book (U.K.);** $10^1/_4$" x 12"; twelve-page book has four pages of color stickers to mount on eight pages of scenes from the movie; the color cover pictures many characters.
G $125   **VG $190**   **NM $250**

Stills; see Movie Item #1035 and 1036.

○ **555.** **Submarine;** Mfd. by Corgi; $5^1/_4$" long; a die-cast metal yellow submarine with rotating periscope and pop-up hatches from which the Beatles spring; OP: box with cellophane window and a blue/green plastic "sea" insert which the sub rests on; add 150% to value if complete with box and insert; add 25% to value for sub with one white and one yellow hatch. ★ *Repro Alert*
G $125   **VG $190**   **NM $250**

○ **556.** **Switchplate Cover, The Beatles;** Mfd. by DAL Manufacturing Corp.; cardboard light switch cover pictures the four Beatles; measures $6^1/_4$" x $11^3/_4$"; OP: sealed in plastic with header card; price is for sealed item.
G $25   **VG $35**   **NM $50**

553

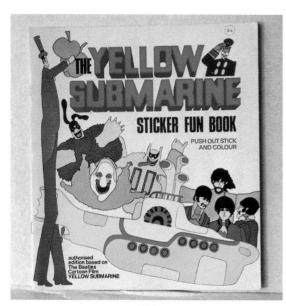

554

555

556

560

558

○ **557.** **Switchplate Cover, Glove;** (same description as above).
G $20   **VG $30**   **NM $40**

○ **558.** **Switchplate Cover, Blue Meanie;** Meanie pictured holding flowers; (same description and price as #557).

○ **559.** **Switchplate Cover, Snapping Turtle Turk;** (same as above).

○ **560.** **Switchplate Cover, Stamp Out Fun!;** Meanie pictured; (same as above).

○ **561.** **Thermos;** Mfd. by Thermos; $6\frac{1}{2}$" tall; pink thermos pictures Sgt. Pepper's Band and Old Fred; issued with a tan colored inner vacuum cap and a yellow colored outer "cup" cap both of which screwed on; sold with the *Yellow Submarine* lunchbox (item #504); deduct $25 for each missing original cap.
G $100   **VG $150**   **NM $200**

○ **562.** **Wall Plaque, John;** Mfd. by K. Cennar Ent.; 9" x 21"; cardboard wall hanging which pictures John; has hole at top for hanging.
G $30   **VG $45**   **NM $60**

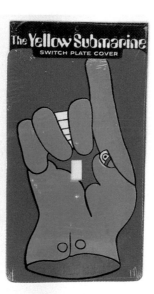

559   **557**

561

563a   **562**

563b

○ **563.** **Wall Plaque, Paul;** (same description as above); available with two different backgrounds: wave pattern or flower pattern; add 50% to value for flower background pattern.
G $30   **VG $45**   **NM $60**

○ **564.** **Wall Plaque, George;** (same description and value as item #562).

○ **565.** **Wall Plaque, Ringo;** (same description as item #562); available with two different backgrounds: black squares or yellow squares; add 50% to value for yellow squares background.
G $30   **VG $45**   **NM $60**

○ **566.** **Wall Plaque, Glove;** (same description as item #562).
G $25   **VG $35**   **NM $50**

○ **567.** **Wall Plaque, Yellow Submarine;** (similar to above, but measures 12" x 21").
G $ 65   **VG $ 90**   **NM $125**

○ **568.** **Water Color Set;** Mfd. by Craftmaster; 6" x 8"; four ready-to-paint pictures, sold in a box with a paint tray and brush; Beatles pictured on box; value is for an unused set.
G $50   **VG $75**   **NM $100**

○ **569.** **Water Color Set;** Mfd. by Craftmaster; 8" x 10"; six ready-to-paint pictures, sold in a box with a paint tray and brush; value is for an unused set.
G $75   **VG $110**   **NM $150**

○ **570.** **Wrist Watch;** Mfd. by Sheffield; yellow brass watch with 8" band; both band and watch picture the Beatles; watch face reads "Beatles Yellow Submarine Love." ★ *Repro Alert*
G $600   **VG $900**   **NM $1,200**

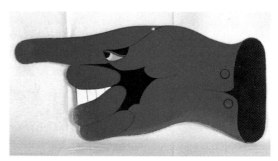

566

565   564

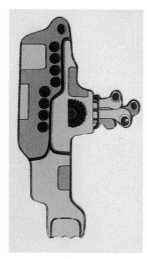

567   568

570

3

Jewelry

Some jewelry pieces came with their own specific backing card, while others used one of a limited number of "generic" cards, which were holed to fit a particular piece. Original display cards increase the value of most items substantially, with cards designed for a particular piece being more valuable than those which were used for various pieces. Listed below are the jewelry cards which were used for more than one style.

Jewelry Display Cards

Type A: Press-Initial Corp.; 6" x 5"; card has guitar-shaped outline along left side; in the right upper quarter is a photo of the group; right lower quarter reads "The Beatles" with autographs.

Type B: Press-Initial Corp.; 6" x 3½"; card has color wallet-sized photo on top; reads "Official Beatles" in center.

Type C: Invicta Plastics; 5¾" x 5¾"; card with color picture of group on right side; reads "Official Beatles" across top, with autographs.

Type D: Randall; 8½" x 3¾"; card pictures group on yellow background on top, with "The Beatles Official" in center and song titles at bottom.

Type E: Randall; 6" x 2⅜"; card pictures faces at top, reads "The Beatles" on bottom.

○ **571.** **Barrette;** 1¼" oval brass hair clip with ⅞" group B&W photo disk attached.
G $40   VG $60   NM $80

○ **572.** **Bracelet;** Mfd. by Randall; 1"-diameter brass mounting with ⅞" group B&W photo disk attached; "Yeh Yeh Yeh" on back of mounting; on 6" chain.
G $30   VG $45   NM $60

○ **573.** **Bracelet;** chain with one or more of the 1" pinback buttons (by Green Duck Co.—see item #650) as charms; the pinback has been replaced with a flat brass disk; add $10 for each button over one on chain.
G $10   VG $15   NM $20

572

93

○ **574. Bracelet;** two charms attached to either end of a 7" chain; one is a 2" leather disk with "The Beatles" printed on one side and a group picture printed on the reverse; the other charm is a 1¼" brass disk with "The Beatles" on one side and their first names on the reverse.
G $50   **VG $75**   **NM $100**

○ **575. Bracelet;** three charms on 7" heavy brass chain; two charms are 1⅞" leather disks with "The Beatles" engraved on one side.
G $45   **VG $70**   **NM $90**

○ **576. Bracelet;** 2"-wide oval piece of worked leather with 1¾" oval brass piece affixed to front; reads "The Beatles"; brass chain attached at both ends; OP: color card with clear plastic package stapled to front; reads "The Beatles Official Leather ID Bracelet"; add 100% if sealed with card.
G $50   **VG $75**   **NM $100**

○ **577. Bracelet;** four 1" brass mountings with ⅞" B&W photo disks attached to each; one Beatle pictured on each, with their first names on back; charms are strung on a 7" chain.
G $40   **VG $60**   **NM $80**

○ **578. Bracelet;** Mfd. by U.S. Ceramic Company; color drawings of each Beatle on ⅞" disks; each is mounted on a smooth-back 1" brass disk; on chain.
G $60   **VG $85**   **NM $110**

○ **579. Bracelet;** brass charm bracelet with the following charms attached: drum, wig, guitar, and first name autographs.
G $45   **VG $70**   **NM $90**

○ **580. Bracelet;** 2" oval leather piece with 1¾" oval brass piece affixed to front; reads "The Beatles" on the brass piece.
G $50   **VG $75**   **NM $100**

○ **581. Bracelet;** 7"-long brass chain with 1½" round open brass ring with first name autographs inset.
G $50   **VG $75**   **NM $100**

○ **582. Bracelet;** 6"-long gold-colored chain with letters suspended below spelling "Beatles"; guitar and beetle charms at each end.
G $45   **VG $70**   **NM $90**

581
583

574   579   582   578
        576   575

577

585

586

590

587

589

○ **583. Bracelet (Australia);** 7" chain with nine charms attached, four picture individual Beatles; original display card 7¹/₂" x 1¹/₂" and reads "The Beatles Bracelet"; add 50% for original card.
G $50   VG $75   NM $100

○ **584. Bracelet;** Mfd. by Sheffield (U.K.); stainless steel bracelet measures 3" in diameter and 1" wide; engraved around the circumference are the Beatles' faces, and "Sheffield" is engraved inside.
G $65   VG $90   NM $125

○ **585. Bracelet;** Mfd. by Celebrity Novelty Ltd. (U.K.); five gold colored charms; four are faces of the Beatles and middle one is guitar-playing figure; OP: white card with "Beatles" at top and first names below each charm; add 50% for original card.
G $55   VG $80   NM $110

○ **586. Bracelet;** unusual piece has four wooden balls decorated to resemble Beatle heads; display card is white with black print including autographs; card measures 5" x 2"; add 100% to value if on original card.
G $30   VG $45   NM $60

○ **587. Brooch;** Mfd. by Randall; brass disk with pin and autographs on back measures 2" diameter; attached to front is a 1³/₄" B&W photo disk of the group.
G $35   VG $55   NM $75

○ **588. Brooch;** brass disk with pin and autographs on back; attached to front is a 1³/₄" photo disk with each Beatle pictured with his autograph below.
G $60   VG $90   NM $120

○ **589. Brooch;** plastic beetle in various colors, including white, pink, and blue; measures 2¹/₄" long and has a pin attachment on its underside; a 1" round color photo of a Beatle is inset under clear plastic on its back; add 100% to value for card (individual or group card).
G $40   VG $60   NM $80

○ **590. Brooch (U.K.);** similar to above, but a 2" black beetle with gold trim; OP: 5¹/₂" x 2" card with "Beatle Brooch" at top and autographs below; add 50% if on original card.
G $40   VG $60   NM $80

○ **591. Brooch;** blue plastic square with pin attachment on back; suspended below it is a 1¹/₄" x 1¹/₄" flasher that changes from a picture of George to Ringo on one side and from Paul to John on the reverse.
G $20   VG $30   NM $40

○ **592. Brooch;** plastic guitar measures 4" long; has pin attachment on back; group or individual members of the group are featured in 1" round paper photos which are inset on body of guitar with a clear plastic lens over it; there are two different photos of Ringo available; guitar most commonly seen in black, but other colors are known; add 150% for guitars which are other than black; OP: 5" x 2" display card with scalloped edge; card reads "The Fabulous Beatles Jewelry Brooch"; add 50% if on card. ★ *Repro Alert*
G $10   VG $15   NM $20

○ **593. Brooch Box;** original store display box for item #592; measures 11" x 5³/₄" x 2"; reads "The Fabulous Beatles Jewelry Brooch" on all sides and top; box is red, white, and black.
G $250   VG $375   NM $500

○ **594. Brooch (U.K.);** 3¹/₂"-long plastic guitar in black, white or cream with Beatles group picture under clear plastic dome.
G $20   VG $30   NM $40

○ **595. Brooch;** brass guitar measures 4" long; has a ⁷/₈" B&W group photo disk inset on front; pin attachment is on back.
G $55   VG $80   NM $110

592c

593

592a

592b

594

595

600

596

602

598

603

○ **596.** **Brooch;** heart-shaped brass brooch with $7/8$" group photo disk inset in middle; cast-brass drum, guitar and "The Beatles" is above photo disk.
G $45   **VG $70**   **NM $90**

○ **597.** **Brooch;** Mfd. by Novelty Brooch Co. (U.K.); silver- or gold-finished letter $1^1/2$"-tall "B" with pin on back; four small black pointed figures attached at various points.
G $50   **VG $75**   **NM $100**

○ **598.** **Brooch;** brass mop-topped figure with painted pearl "face," playing guitar; pin attachment on back of arms.
G $50   **VG $75**   **NM $100**

○ **599.** **Brooch (Hong Kong);** $4^7/8$" plastic guitar with white front and black back with rubber bands for "strings"; lapel clip on back; guitar has "Beatles" and their first names printed on front.
G $40   **VG $60**   **NM $80**

○ **600.** **Brooch;** Mfd. by Mastro; $5^1/2$"-tall pink plastic guitar with two rubber bands as "strings" and lapel clip on back; Beatle faces and first name autographs on front.
G $65   **VG $95**   **NM $130**

○ **601.** **Brooch Display Card;** 10" x 10" store card which held one dozen of the pink guitar brooches (item #600); Beatles pictured on card; price is for empty card.
G $150   **VG $225**   **NM $300**

○ **602.** **Brooch, Record (U.K.);** $1^3/4$" diameter; black plastic disk designed to resemble a record; individual or group color picture under plastic dome in center; original card measures $5^1/2$" x 2" with scalloped edges; add 50% to value if on original card.
G $20   **VG $30**   **NM $40**

○ **603.** **Brooch Box (U.K.);** $11^1/4$" x $5^3/4$" x $2^3/4$"; red and black display box with die-cut lid that folds to provide backdrop for contents; contained either the guitar brooches (item #592) or round "record" brooches (item #602); value is for empty box.
G $225   **VG $335**   **NM $450**

○ **604.** **Charm;** metal disk measures $1^1/4$" diameter; on one side the Beatles' faces are embossed, with their first names below each face; on the reverse it reads "The Beatles MCMLXIV"; chain attachment on top.
G $12   **VG $18**   **NM $25**

○ **605.** **Charm;** rectangular worked leather piece measuring 2" x $1^1/4$" with chain attachment on top; attached to the front is a $7/8$" group color photo disk.
G $30   **VG $45**   **NM $60**

○ **606.** **Cuff Links;** Mfd. by Press-Initial Corp.; brass 1" disk with cuff link attachment on back; mounted on front is a $^7/_8$" color group photo disk; value is for pair.
G $60   **VG $90**   **NM $120**

○ **607.** **Cuff Links;** Mfd. by Press-Initial Corp.; brass 1"-diameter disks with the Beatles faces embossed on the front and cuff link attachment on back; OP: card measures $6^1/_2$" x $3^1/_2$" and has a B&W wallet photo of the Beatles at top; reads "Official Cuff Links" on bottom; value is for pair of cuff links; add 50% for card.
G $50   **VG $75**   **NM $100**

○ **608.** **Hair Clip;** 2"-long brass spring-loaded clip with mop-topped figure at right; reads "Yeh Yeh Yeh" from end.
G $40   **VG $60**   **NM $80**

○ **609.** **Locket;** leather-covered 1"-square booklet with eleven fold-out B&W photos inside; reads "The Beatles" on cover; booklet snaps shut on back; various colors including: gray, brown, black, white, and red; had pin or chain attachment.
G $25   **VG $35**   **NM $50**

○ **610.** **Locket;** brass $1^1/_4$" x 1" locket reads "The Beatles" in raised lettering on the front; it opens up to reveal four B&W photos, one of each Beatle.
G $60   **VG $90**   **NM $120**

○ **611.** **Locket;** brass letters read "Yeh Yeh Yeh" with pin attachment on back; suspended below them is a $1^1/_4$"-diameter round brass locket with "The Beatles" in raised letters on the lid; inside is a $^7/_8$" B&W photo disk.
G $60   **VG $90**   **NM $120**

○ **612.** **Locket (U.K.);** square 1" brass locket with B&W photos under clear plastic for cover; inside are ten fold-out B&W photos; came with pin attachment.
G $60   **VG $90**   **NM $120**

○ **613.** **Necklace;** Mfd. by Randall; gold-colored music treble clef with $^7/_8$" B&W photo disk mounted in center; attached is a gold-colored chain.
G $50   **VG $75**   **NM $100**

○ **614.** **Necklace;** brass chain with $1^1/_4$" round locket worn as a pendant; "The Beatles" in raised letters; inside is a $^7/_8$" photo disk.
G $60   **VG $90**   **NM $120**

○ **615.** **Necklace;** Mfd. by U.S. Ceramic Co.; flat 1" brass disk with $^7/_8$" color drawing disk of one Beatle on front; each is attached to a 17" fine chain; value is for each.
G $30   **VG $45**   **NM $60**

606   **607**

608   **611**

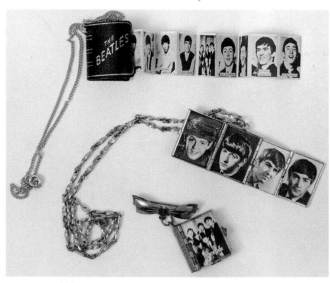

609   **610**

612

613   **614**

○ **616.** **Necklace;** Mfd. by U.S. Ceramic Co.; brass 2" disk with group color drawing disk attached to front; chain attachment at top.

G $60   VG $90   NM $120

○ **617.** **Necklace (U.K.);** brass beetle measures $1\frac{1}{2}$" long; with B&W photo of group under clear plastic on its back; chain attachment at mouth.

G $40   VG $60   NM $80

○ **618.** **Necklace;** gold-colored grooved plastic $1\frac{1}{4}$" disk with B&W photo mounted in center, on fine gold colored chain.

G $30   VG $45   NM $60

○ **619.** **Necklace;** Mfd. by Randall; $1\frac{3}{8}$"-tall heart-shaped backing with $\frac{7}{8}$" photo disk inset on front; "Yeh Yeh Yeh" on back; 17" chain.
★ *Repro Alert*

G $50   VG $75   NM $100

○ **620.** **Necklace;** $1\frac{7}{8}$"-diameter brown leather disk with group picture on front; "The Beatles" printed on back; 19" heavy chain.

G $50   VG $75   NM $100

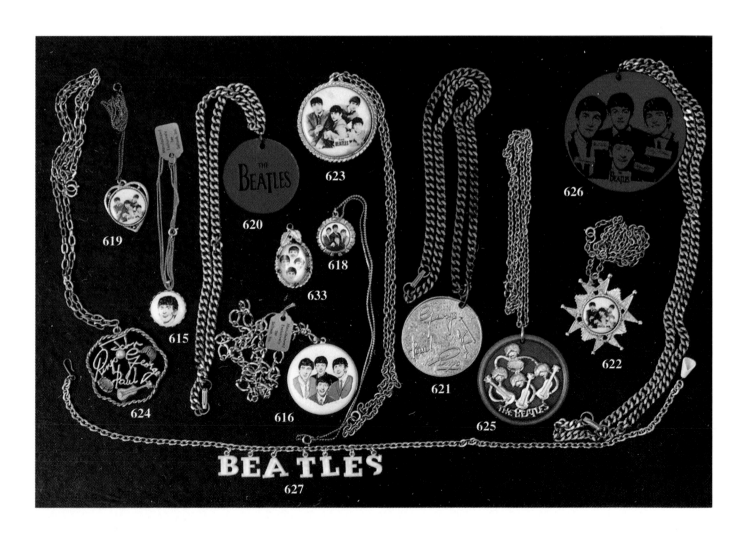

○ **621.** **Necklace;** 2"-diameter heavy brass disk on heavy 24" chain; "The Beatles" on one side of the disk; first name autographs on reverse.
G $65   **VG $95**   **NM $130**

○ **622.** **Necklace;** 2"-diameter eight-pointed star with ⅞" photo disk insert on front; "Yeh Yeh Yeh" on back; 22" chain.
G $60   **VG $90**   **NM $120**

○ **623.** **Necklace;** brass 2" round pendant with first names on back; group B&W photo disk on front; suspended from 22" chain.
G $40   **VG $60**   **NM $80**

○ **624.** **Necklace;** brass 2" round open-weave piece with first name autographs, wig, drum, guitar and pearl in design; on a brass chain.
G $60   **VG $85**   **NM $110**

○ **625.** **Necklace;** 2¼" wooden disk with raised edge; four moptop figures with guitars, drum and "The Beatles" are inset; hole at top with chain attached.
G $50   **VG $75**   **NM $100**

○ **626.** **Necklace;** 3"-diameter red leather disk with group picture in black print on front; "The Beatles" on back; 24" heavy chain.
G $60   **VG $90**   **NM $120**

○ **627.** **Necklace (U.K.);** black or white plastic letters on a 14"-long chain spell out "Beatles."
G $40   **VG $60**   **NM $80**

○ **628.** **Necklace;** Mfd. by A + R.C. Ltd. (U.K.); silver-colored 1½" x 1¼" pendant with B&W group picture under domed plastic; 16" silver colored chain; OP: 5½" x 2½" white cardboard with "The Beatles" at top; add 50% if on original card.
G $50   **VG $75**   **NM $100**

○ **629.** **Necklace (U.K.);** gold-colored 1" setting with round ¾" B&W photo inset; attached is a 22" fine chain.
G $40   **VG $60**   **NM $80**

○ **630.** **Necklace;** brass 1" round pendant reads "Yeh Yeh Yeh" on back; on front is mounted a ⅞" group B&W photo disk; on brass chain.
G $30   **VG $45**   **NM $60**

○ **631.** **Necklace;** Mfd. by Randall; 2⅜"-long gold-colored metal guitar and drum joined by lettering of "The Beatles"; chain is attached at top of guitar.
G $40   **VG $60**   **NM $80**

○ **632.** **Necklace** (U.K.); 1" x ¾"; rectangular metal-backed B&W photo of group; attached at top to 26" fine chain.
G $20   **VG $30**   **NM $40**

627

○ **633.** **Necklace (U.K.);** silver-colored 2" x 1" oval pendant with Beatle faces in B&W under domed piece of thick plastic, leaf design around edge; attached to silver-colored chain.
G $50   **VG $75**   **NM $100**

○ **634.** **Necklace;** Mfd. by Novelty Brooch Co. (U.K.); silver-colored 1½"-tall letter "B" with four small black painted figures attached at various points; on 30" chain.
G $60   **VG $80**   **NM $100**

○ **635.** **Necklace (U.K.);** 2¼" oval pendant with "flasher" B&W photo that changes from John and Ringo to Paul and George; attached to a 27" brass chain.
G $50   **VG $75**   **NM $100**

○ **636.** **Pin;** Mfd. by Randall; 2⅜"-long cast gold-colored metal guitar and drum joined by lettering of "The Beatles"; pin on back.
G $40   **VG $60**   **NM $80**

○ **637.** **Pin;** Mfd. by Randall; cast-metal guitar, drum and "The Beatles" with pin on back; suspended below is a 1" metal disk with ⅞" group B&W photo disk attached to front.
G $50   **VG $75**   **NM $100**

○ **638.** **Pin (Holland);** brass piece measures 1" x ½", with a 1½" pin attached on back; reads "The Beatles" in horseshoe design with faces.
G $15   **VG $22**   **NM $30**

○ **639.** **Pin;** Mfd. by Astor; small circular photo with "The Beatles" written in white at bottom; ¾" brass casing has 2"-long pin attached.
G $40   **VG $60**   **NM $80**

○ **640.** **Pin (U.K.);** brass beetle measures 1½" long, with pin on underside; B&W photo of group under clear plastic on insect's back; various photos were used.
G $40   **VG $60**   **NM $80**

○ **641.** **Pin;** "The Beatles" inset on 1½" x ¼" brass name tag, with pin on back; suspended below is a 1¼"-long metal beetle with music notes etched on its shell.
G $30   **VG $45**   **NM $60**

636   **642**

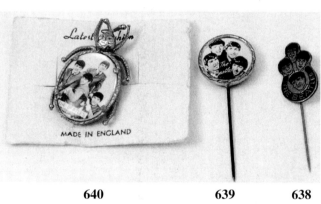

640   **639**   **638**

647   **643**
588   **597**

○ **642.** **Pin;** 2" oval leather piece with Beatle faces on lower section; attached to upper section is 1" oval brass piece with "The Beatles" in raised lettering; clasp on back.
G $50   **VG $75**   **NM $100**

○ **643.** **Pin;** open-weave 2½"-diameter metal pin, with autographs, drum, guitar, and small pearl-type inset.
G $50   **VG $75**   **NM $100**

○ **644.** **Pin;** Mfd. by Randall; B&W ⅞" photo disk inset on a 2"-wide eight-point brass star.
G $60   **VG $90**   **NM $120**

○ **645.** **Pin;** detailed plastic 2½"-tall figures with instruments; attached to back is circular grooved white or red plastic disk with lapel hook on back; one of each Beatle; (same figures as #143).
G $25   **VG $35**   **NM $50**

○ **646.** **Pin Display Card;** easel-backed 20" x 11" card held twenty-four of item #645; reads "The Beatles Official Pins" at top, with each Beatle pictured.
G $225   **VG $350**   **NM $450**

○ **647.** **Pin (U.K.);** brass beetle measures 2" long, with B&W photo of group under plastic on its back; pin attachment on underside.
G $60   **VG $90**   **NM $120**

○ **648.** **Pin (U.K.);** same beetle as #647, except this one has music notes on its back instead of a photo.
G $30   **VG $45**   **NM $60**

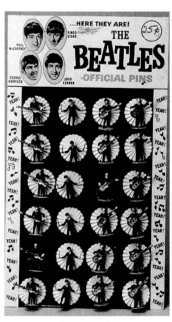

644   **645 & 646**

649. **Ring;** brass with ⁷/₈" B&W group photo disk inset in mounting.
G $35   VG $50   NM $70

650. **Ring (Hong Kong);** silver-colored cheap metal flasher ring changes from B&W group picture to "The Beatles"; ring is adjustable.
G $25   VG $35   NM $50

651. **Rings;** ³/₄" round paper pictures of each Beatle inset in color plastic rings; each Beatle is pictured on a different color ring: red, green, blue or yellow; value is for each.
G $10   VG $15   NM $20

652. **Ring Display Card;** Mfd. by Saymore Co.; 8" x 4"; has two 4" flaps which fold back to hold up display; reads "Official Beatle Rings 15 cents" with photo of each Beatle with their name below; held six rings (item #651)
G $100   VG $150   NM $200

653. **Rings;** gold- or silver-finish plastic flasher rings that change from photo of each Beatles' face to their name; one of each Beatle; value is per ring.★ *Repro Alert*
G $7   VG $12   NM $15

654. **Rings Display Card;** Mfd. Saymore Co.; easel-backed 12" x 8" card which held twenty-four of the flasher rings (item #641), which originally sold for 29 cents each; each Beatle is pictured at the top of the pink, red and black card; value is for empty card.★ *Repro Alert*
G $200   VG $300   NM $400

655. **Rings;** Mfd. by A + R.C. Ltd. (U.K.); silver-finished plastic ring with B&W photo inset.
G $15   VG $22   NM $30

656. **Rings Display Card;** Mfd. by A + R.C. Ltd. (U.K.); 15" x 8" easel-backed harp-shaped cardboard display which held thirty-six of item #643; marked "Beatle Rings" at top; value is for empty card.
G $200   VG $300   NM $400

657. **Tac;** Mfd. by Press-Initial Corp.; color group picture on ⁷/₈" disk, brass mounting has tac on back; OP: card measures 6" x 3¹/₂"; reads "Official Beatle Tac" on bottom, has color wallet photo at top; add 50% for original card.
G $35   VG $55   NM $70

658. **Tac;** Mfd. by Press-Initial Corp.; cast ¹/₂"-tall heads of each Beatle with tac on back; gold or pewter finish; OP: sealed individually on 3¹/₂" x 5¹/₂" B&W photo cards, or in sets on color photo cards; add 200% for individual B&W cards, 25% for color group card.★ *Repro Alert*
G $3   VG $4   NM $6

659. **Tac;** Mfd. by Press-Initial Corp.; 1¹/₂"-long cast-metal guitar with four small heads and "Beatles" on it.
G $20   VG $30   NM $40

660. **Tie Clip;** Mfd. by Press-Initial Corp.; brass 1"-diameter mounting with tie clip on back; ¹/₂" color photo disk on front.
G $40   VG $60   NM $80

661. **Tie Clip;** Mfd. by Press-Initial Corp.; brass 1" disk with Beatle faces embossed on front, tie clip on back; OP: card reads "Official Tie Clip," has B&W wallet size photo on top; add 100% for original card.
G $30   VG $45   NM $60

651 & 652   653 & 654

657   661

4

Pinback Buttons

American-made pinback buttons fall into three general sizes: 1" gumball machine buttons; $2^1/_2$" 'flasher' buttons; and 3" slogan or picture buttons. Little is known about the companies which produced $3^1/_2$" buttons, but similarities in style fit most of them into a couple groups obviously made by the same manufacturer.

Some of the buttons listed herein were made with different color printing or background coloration. Such differences from the ones we describe do not necessarily translate into a higher value. Buttons were usually sold loose out of boxes, with no individual packaging. ★ *Repro Alert*

○ **662. 1", Gumball;** Mfd. by Green Duck Co.; nine different button designs, originally sold in gumball machines; four of the buttons picture a Beatle with his name; the other five have these slogans: "I love the Beatles," "I'm a Beatle bug," "I'm 4 Beatles," "I'm a Beatle booster," and "Member Beatles fan club"; add 100% to value for pins which have blue printing or blue background; the blue printing/blue background pins have been found sealed in wax paper and may have been given away as premiums. ★ *Repro Alert*
   G $3   **VG $5**   **NM $7**

○ **663. 1"-Button Offer;** Mfd. by Rold Gold; 6" long, 4" wide; triangular paper was attached to snack products; advertised 1" button (items #662) included in the snack product.
   G $20   **VG $30**   **NM $45**

○ **664. 1";** slogan reads "Ringo for President"; blue or red print on white.
   G $15   **VG $22**   **NM $30**

○ **665. 1";** Mfd. by Creative House; slogan reads "Beattles Are Bugs"; shows mop-topped character, yellow background.
   G $7   **VG $10**   **NM $15**

○ **666. $1^1/_4$", Photo;** Mfd. by Norman Drees Associates (U.K.); face shot of each Beatle with "The Beatles" above, their first names below; photos are B&W, printing is orange; price is for each.
   G $15   **VG $22**   **NM $30**

○ **667. $1^1/_2$";** 1965; "KCBQ—Beatle Day Aug. 28"; blue print on white; San Diego concert souvenir.
   G $25   **VG $35**   **NM $50**

○ **668. $1^1/_2$"** (Japan); set of four color tinplate buttons; each pictures a Beatle with their first name; value is for each button.
   G $10   **VG $15**   **NM $20**

○ **669. $1^3/_4$";** slogan reads "I Dig the Beatles on KRLA"; white with red print.
   G $20   **VG $30**   **NM $40**

○ **670. $2^1/_8$"** (U.K.); "Sgt. Pepper's Lonely Hearts Club Band"; yellow button with drum logo in red and blue.
   G $10   **VG $15**   **NM $2**

○ **671. $2^1/_4$";** slogan reads "The Beatles Sound Best on KRLA"; blue print on a white background, with red circle around the outside.
   G $20   **VG $30**   **NM $40**

○ **672. $2^1/_2$", Flip;** Mfd. by Vari-Vue; B&W flicker button changes from "Beatle Booster" with faces to first name with mop tops.
   G $7   **VG $10**   **NM $15**

○ **673. $2^1/_2$", Flip;** Mfd. by Vari-Vue; color flicker button changes from "I Like Beatles" with guitars to faces.
   G $7   **VG $10**   **NM $15**

○ **674. $2^1/_2$", Flip;** Mfd. by Vari-Vue; color flicker changes from "I Like Beatles" with first names to faces.
   G $7   **VG $10**   **NM $15**

From top to bottom, left to right: First row—items #662; *Second row*—items #662, #664 and #667; *Third row*— items #668, #669 and #671; *Fourth row*—items #679, #680, #681 and #686.

663

666

675 & 676

677

○ **675.** **2¹/₂", Flip;** Mfd. by Vari-Vue; flicker button changes from "I Like (John, Paul, George, or Ringo)" to B&W photo of that Beatle; price is for each.
G $7   VG $10   NM $15

○ **676.** **2¹/₂"-Flip Button Display Card;** Mfd. by Saymore Co.; yellow cardboard display measures 14" x 11" and held twelve of the flicker buttons (#675); B&W photo of each Beatle on top, easel on back; price is for empty card.
★ *Repro Alert*
G $225   VG $350   NM $450

○ **677.** **2¹/₂"-Flip Button Banner;** 17¹/₂" x 5¹/₄"; store poster for 2¹/₂"-flicker buttons (item #675); black with red and white print; reads "Official Beatle Flips."
G $75   VG $110   NM $150

○ **678.** **2¹/₂" (U.K.);** color photo of the Beatles in disguises; reads "Guess Who?" at bottom.
G $10   VG $15   NM $20

○ **679.** **3";** slogan reads "Be a BEATLE Booster!"; button is colored plastic backing with clear plastic covering B&W photos of the their faces; advertised as "Snap-Pix."
G $10   VG $15   NM $20

○ **680.** **3",** same as above, with slogan reading "The Beatles" and a posed photo of the group.
G $10   VG $15   NM $20

○ **681.** **3";** slogan reads "Paul Lives WMCA Swings"; yellow background with black print.
G $20   VG $30   NM $40

○ **682.** **3¹/₂", Photo;** group photo in B&W, with "The Beatles" below.
G $15   VG $22   NM $30

○ **683.** **3¹/₂", Photo;** group photo in B&W; reads "The Beatles" above the photo, full names underneath.
G $15   VG $22   NM $30

○ **684.** **3¹/₂", Photo;** group photo in B&W; reads "The Beatles" above the photo, first names underneath; "Made in U.S.A." on edge.
G $15   VG $22   NM $30

○ **685.** **3¹/₂", Photo;** group photo in B&W; reads "The Beatles" below the photo; Paul and John are standing while George and Ringo crouch.
G $15   VG $22   NM $30

○ **686.** **3¹/₂";** slogan reads "Beatlemania"; blue print on white.
G $10   VG $15   NM $20

○ **687.** **3¹/₂";** slogan reads "Help stamp out Beetles"; blue print on white background.
G $12   VG $18   NM $25

○ **688.** **3¹/₂";** slogan reads "I Hate the Beatles"; blue and red print on white background.
G $20   VG $30   NM $40

○ **689.** **3¹/₂";** slogan reads "I Hate the Beatles"; blue and red print on white background with music notes below slogan.
G $25   VG $35   NM $50

○ **690.** **3¹/₂";** slogan reads "I Love Beetles"; blue print on pink background.
G $10   VG $15   NM $20

○ **691.** **3¹/₂";** slogan reads "I Love the Beatles"; blue print on white background.
G $8   VG $12   NM $15

○ **692.** **3¹/₂";** slogan reads "I Love the Beatles"; blue and red print with music notes below slogan; "Made in U.S.A." on edge.
G $12   VG $18   NM $25

○ **693.** **3¹/₂";** slogan reads "I Still Love the Beatles"; white and blue lettering on red and white background.
G $15   VG $22   NM $30

From top to bottom, left to right: First row—items #697; Second row—items #694; Third row—items #695.

○ **694.** 3¹/₂"; slogan reads "I Love (John, Paul, George or Ringo)"; blue print on white background; price is each.
   G $7   **VG $12**   **NM $15**

○ **695.** 3¹/₂"; slogan reads "I Love (John, Paul, George or Ringo)"; red and blue print with music notes below slogan; price is for each; beware of re-pros dated 1965.
   G $10   **VG $15**   **NM $20**

○ **696.** 3¹/₂"; slogan reads "I Want to Hold Your Hand"; red and blue print on white background.
   G $12   **VG $18**   **NM $25**

○ **697.** 3¹/₂"; slogan reads "I'm a Beatle Fan, In Case of Emergency Call (John, Paul, George or Ringo)"; red and blue print on white background; price is for each.
   G $12   **VG $18**   **NM $25**

○ **698.** 3¹/₂"; slogan reads "I'm A Beatle Fan, In Case of Emergency Call Paul or Ringo"; red and blue print on white background.
   G $12   **VG $18**   **NM $25**

○ **699.** 3¹/₂"; slogan reads "I'm a Beatle Fan, in Case of Emergency place my vote for LBJ"; red and blue print on white background.
   G $15   **VG $22**   **NM $30**

○ **700.** 3¹/₂"; slogan reads "Ringo for President"; white print on red background.
   G $15   **VG $22**   **NM $30**

○ **701.** 3¹/₂"; slogan reads "If I were 21, I'd Vote for (Paul or Ringo)"; blue and red print on white background; price is for each.
   G $12   **VG $18**   **NM $25**

From top to bottom, left to right: First row—items #705; Second row—items #707, #691, #692 and #693; Third row—items #690, #702, #687 and #688.

○ **702.** 3¹/₂"; slogan reads "I'm Bugs About the Beatles"; red or blue print on white background.
G $10   **VG $15**   **NM $20**

○ **703.** 3¹/₂"; slogan reads "Oh Bring Back my 'Beatles' To Me"; blue print on white background.
G $12   **VG $18**   **NM $25**

○ **704.** 3¹/₂", **Photo (U.K.);** slogan reads "With Love From Us to You" around top edge; faces in color in center, red and blue print.
G $20   **VG $30**   **NM $40**

○ **705.** 3¹/₂", **Photo (U.K.);** same as above, but individual Beatle pictured with autograph below; value is for each.
G $20   **VG $30**   **NM $40**

○ **706.** 3¹/₂", slogan reads "I Love You" at top, "Yeah Yeah Yeah" at bottom; blank faced "Beatle" in center, with place to glue your own photo.
G $10   **VG $15**   **NM $20**

○ **707.** 3¹/₂"; slogan reads "I Like The Beatles"; blue and red print on white background.
G $10   **VG $15**   **NM $20**

○ **708.** 3¹/₂"; slogan reads "Yeah, Yeah, Yeah!"; blue print on white background.
G $12   **VG $18**   **NM $25**

○ **709.** 3¹/₂" or 4", **Photo;** Mfd. by the Green Duck Co.; slogan reads "I'm a Official Beatles Fan"; B&W faces on red and white background.
G $10   **VG $15**   **NM $20**

From top to bottom, left to right: First row—items #703, #708, #696 and #698; Second row—items #682, #684, #685 and #683; Third row—items #704, #701, and #709.

○ **710.** **3"- or 4"-Button Display Card;** cardboard display card for the Green Duck photo pins (item #709); display was intended to stand up in back of "Official Beatles Fan" button box; card measures 9" x 10"; shows faces in blue-print with area to mount one button for display.
G $50   **VG $75**   **NM $100**

○ **711.** **Button Display Poster;** for Green Duck Buttons; 9" x 10" color paper poster reads "Get Your Beatles Fan Club Buttons Here" and shows the Beatles' faces; ★ *Repro Alert*
G $40   **VG $60**   **NM $80**

○ **712.** **7";** slogan reads "I Love the Beatles"; blue print on white background with music notes at sides.
G $30   **VG $45**   **NM $60**

709 & 710

Pennants and Posters

There were plenty of options to help Beatles fans decorate their walls. Felt or cloth pennants were available in many sizes and colors, and posters, from the very stylistic to the photographic fan shot, were also popular wall coverings. Because so many commercially produced posters were sold in the 1960s, only a selection can be listed in this chapter. **General price guidelines for posters not individually listed here are as follows: $6-$10 in good (G) condition; $10-$20 in very good (VG) condition; and $20-$35 in near mint (NM) condition.**

Promotional posters, fan club posters, and movie posters are not included in this chapter. Prices for those posters can be found in Chapter 10, Record Promotion Items; Chapter 12, Fan Club Items; and Chapter 9, Movie Items. The pennants and posters listed in this chapter are arranged by size. All were made in 1964 in the United States unless otherwise noted.

713
714

○ **713. Pennant, John;** Mfd. by Irwin Specialties (Canada); 5$^1/_4$" miniature pennant reads "The Beatles" and "John Lennon"; black print on white.
G $25   VG $35   NM $50

○ **714. Pennant, Paul;** (same as item #713.)

○ **715. Pennant, George;** (same as item #713.)

○ **716. Pennant, Ringo;** (same as item #713.)

○ **717. Pennant, Bike Flags;** 6" x 4"; set of five plastic flags designed to be attached to bike handlebars; one flag has "The Beatles" printed on it; each of the other four has a drawing of one of the Beatles playing an instrument with a first name autograph; value is for set of five with metal holder (which was designed to attach to handlebars of bike and hold flags); OP: all five pennants with sticks and metal holder in a plastic bag; bag has "Official The Beatles 5 Flags Bicycle Set" printed at top; drawings of the Beatles and assembly instructions below; add 50% to value if in original package.
G $100   VG $150   NM $200

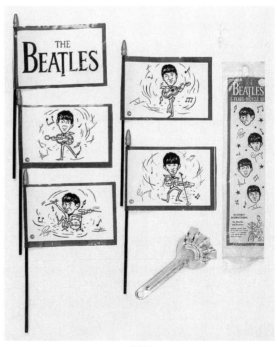

717

○ **718.   Pennant, Group (Germany);** 9¹/₂" x 6"; carnival prize pennant is red with faces and first names; "Die Beatles" printed on left.
G $25   VG $35   NM $50

○ **719.   Pennant, John (Germany);** 5" x 3"; carnival prize pennant is red with picture and drawing of guitar; "Die Beatles" printed on left, "John" printed on right.
G $30   VG $45   NM $60

○ **720.   Pennant, Paul (Germany);** 5" x 3"; carnival prize pennant is green with picture and drawing of saxophone; "Die Beatles" printed on left, "Paul" printed on right.
G $30   VG $45   NM $60

○ **721.   Pennant, George;** (similar to item #719.)

○ **722.   Pennant, Ringo;** (similar to item #719.)

○ **723.   Pennant;** 8¹/₂" x 10"; rectangular pennant was sold at 1966 Cleveland concert; pictures group with "The Beatles" below; found in black or blue with white background.
G $30   VG $45   NM $60

○ **724.   Pennant (Germany);** 1966; 11" long; vertical pennant sold by the Fan Club; pictures group at top with "The Official Beatles Fans" below; red with black, green, and white print.
G $80   VG $120   NM $160

○ **725.   Pennant;** 12"; black pennant with white print reads "International Beatles Fan Club."
G $50   VG $75   NM $100

○ **726.   Pennant;** 12"; yellow pennant with blue lettering; reads "Welcome KEW—Beatles."
G $50   VG $75   NM $100

○ **727.   Pennant (U.K.);** 12¹/₂"; pennant is designed to be hung vertically; pictures faces with song titles and autographs.
G $60   VG $90   NM $120

○ **728.   Pennant (Australia);** 17¹/₂"; red pennant with faces and autographs; this was a mail order item in 1964.
G $45   VG $70   NM $90

○ **729.   Pennant (Japan);** 1966; 17¹/₂"; red pennant with white print; faces and names to the left of "The Beatles."
G $100   VG $150   NM $200

○ **730.   Pennant (Canada);** 19¹/₂"; white pennant reads "The Beatles" on left, with face in music notes below; "Yeah Yeah Yeah" on right.
G $60   VG $90   NM $120

718

720

723

725   726   724

727

729

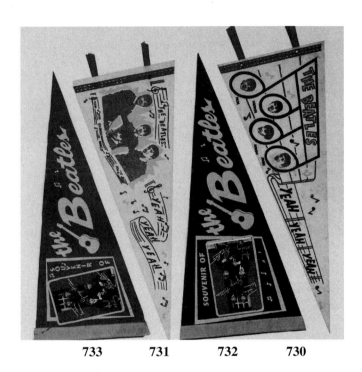

733   731   732   730

○ **731.** **Pennant (Canada);** 19$^1/_2$"; group picture with first names below on left; "Yeah" printed on right.
G $100   **VG $150**   **NM $200**

○ **732.** **Pennant;** 19$^3/_4$"; black pennant reads "Souvenir of the Beatles" in gold; has cut-out with color postcard inserted horizontally.
G $75   **VG $110**   **NM $150**

○ **733.** **Pennant;** 19$^3/_4$"; red pennant reads "Souvenir of the Beatles" in gold; has cut-out with color postcard inserted vertically; back marked "Full color post card pennant—Fund Ways Inc."
G $75   **VG $110**   **NM $150**

○ **734.** **Pennant;** Mfd. by Irwin Specialties (Canada); 22$^1/_2$"; white pennant with red print; designed to be hung vertically; posed group picture at top with "The Beatles" below, and first name autographs.
G $75   **VG $110**   **NM $150**

○ **735.** **Pennant;** Mfd. by Irwin Specialties (Canada); 22$^1/_2$"; white pennant pictures Beatles on stage to left, autographs in center, "The Beatles" on right.
G $60   **VG $90**   **NM $120**

○ **736.** **Pennant;** Mfd. by Irwin Specialties (Canada); 22$^1/_2$" white pennant with black and red print; group picture on left with first name autographs, "The Beatles" in center, instruments pictured at right.
G $60   **VG $90**   **NM $120**

○ **737.** **Pennant;** Mfd. by Irwin Specialties (Canada); 22$^1/_2$" white pennant reads "Beatles" in large letters, with faces of each inside letters; also reads "Yeah Yeah Yeah" and pictures musical notes.
G $60   **VG $90**   **NM $120**

740   739   734   735

737   741   738   736

742   744   728

○ **738. Pennant, John;** Mfd. by Irwin Specialties (Canada); 25¹/₂"; white pennant pictures John's face with autograph and "The Beatles" on far right; black and red print.
G $50   **VG $75**   **NM $100**

○ **739. Pennant, Paul;** (same as item #738.)

○ **740. Pennant, George;** (same as item #738.)

○ **741. Pennant, Ringo;** (same as item #738.)

○ **742. Pennant;** 27"; white pennant reads "The Beatles"; features drawing of the group playing instruments; blue print.
G $45   **VG $70**   **NM $90**

○ **743. Pennant;** 29"; pennant reads "i love the Beatles"; pictures five hearts; available in several color combinations including: red with white letters and green with white letters.
G $45   **VG $70**   **NM $90**

743

○ **744. Pennant;** 29"; pennant reads "i luv the Beatles"; pictures five hearts; available in various colors.
G $50   **VG $75**   **NM $100**

○ **745. Pennant;** 29"; yellow pennant reads "The Beatles" on right, to left is group picture with first names printed below; red print.
G $75   **VG $115**   **NM $150**

○ **746. Pennant;** 29"; pennant reads "BEATLES'; shows four mop-tops with first names printed alongside; various color combinations including: blue with white print. ★ *Repro Alert*
G $50   **VG $75**   **NM $100**

745   750   746

○ **747. Pennant;** 29"; pennant reads "We Love You Beatles"; white with red print or white with blue letters and red notes.
G $75   **VG $110**   **NM $150**

○ **748. Pennant;** 29"; pennant shows faces in circle; reads "Beatles" with their first names; various color combinations; no other markings. ★ *Repro Alert*
G $15   **VG $22**   **NM $30**

747

○ **749. Pennant;** 29¹/₂"; pennant reads "I LOVE the BEATLES"; has side view of faces and full names printed on left side; various color combinations including: blue with white print.
G $60   **VG $90**   **NM $120**

○ **750. Pennant;** 29¹/₂"; pennant reads "WE LUV YOU BEATLES"; pictures hearts with "George" and "Ringo" inside; red print on white.
G $40   **VG $60**   **NM $80**

749

POSTERS

○ **751.** **Poster;** "Litho by Louis F. Dow Co. USA"; London Palladium poster shows the Beatles posed in a doorway; sold in various sizes on glossy paper stock; also sold on thin cardboard; add 50% to price for cardboard variation; also available via mail order in 1964 with personalized feature—"With (your name) at the" would be printed on line above London Palladium; add 50% with this feature. ★ *Repro Alert*
G $25   **VG $35**   **NM $50**

○ **752.** **Poster;** Mfd. by *Sixteen* magazine; set of four 11" x 17" B&W photos, one of each Beatle; mail order item; value is for set.
G $30   **VG $45**   **NM $60**

○ **753.** **Poster;** Mfd. by JER Products; 20" x 22"; "Ringo For President"; black drawing of Ringo.
G $25   **VG $35**   **NM $50**

○ **754.** **Poster;** Mfd. by Celestial Arts; 1969; $23\frac{1}{4}$" x 24" depiction of the Beatles seated around table, dressed in medieval costumes; titled "Renaissance Minstrels."
G $20   **VG $30**   **NM $40**

○ **755.** **Poster, Group;** Mfd. by *Look* magazine; 1968; 16" x 42"; B&W banner poster of the Beatles by Richard Avedon.
G $25   **VG $35**   **NM $50**

○ **756.** **Poster, John;** Mfd. by *Look* magazine; 1968; $22\frac{1}{2}$" x $31\frac{1}{2}$"; color poster of John by Avedon.
G $40   **VG $60**   **NM $80**

○ **757.** **Poster, Paul;** (same description as item #756.)
G $30   **VG $45**   **NM $60**

○ **758.** **Poster, George;** (same as item #756.)

754

757

753

758

○ **759.** **Poster, Ringo;** (same as item #756.)

○ **760.** **Poster Display Box;** Avedon; 10" x 18¹/₂" x 24"; box held thirteen sets of color Avedon posters (items #756–#759) and eight of the Avedon banner posters (item #755); has header card that attaches for display; value is for empty box.
G $250   **VG $375**   **NM $500**

○ **761.** **Poster;** Mfd. by The Food; 1967; 23¹/₂" x 36"; photo by Jacobs; sepia photo of George at Golden Gate Park wearing heart-shaped glasses which are tinted pink on the poster.
G $30   **VG $45**   **NM $60**

○ **762.** **Poster;** Mfd. by *Sixteen* magazine; this 1966 magazine offer measures 24¹/₄" x 36¹/₂"; color poster features the Beatles casually dressed.
G $20   **VG $30**   **NM $40**

○ **763.** **Poster;** Mfd. by *Life*; 1967; 26" x 34"; color enlargement of Beatles on the cover of *Life* magazine Asia Edition from July 24, 1967; "The New Far-Out Beatles" (same photo which was used on the interior article from the U.S. edition of *Life* magazine June 16, 1967).
G $50   **VG $75**   **NM $100**

○ **764.** **Poster, "All the Beatles" (U.K.);** 19" x 52"; color poster with group and individual photos.
G $25   **VG $35**   **NM $50**

○ **765.** **Poster;** Mfd. by Dell; 19" x 52"; banner poster has B&W group and individual photos on color background; (not numbered, but referred to as Dell Poster #1).
G $25   **VG $35**   **NM $50**

○ **766.** **Poster;** Mfd. by Dell; 19" x 52"; banner poster has B&W individual photos on a red/pink background; (marked "Dell #2").
G $25   **VG $35**   **NM $50**

760   **761**

762

765

766

774

775

○ **767.** **Poster;** Mfd. by Fan Fotos (U.K.); 24" x 72"; life-size B&W photo posters; one of each Beatle; price is for set of four.
G $160   **VG $240**   **NM $325**

○ **768.** **Poster, John;** 6' x 2'; "Life-size" B&W poster of John with instrument marked "Beatles (USA) Ltd."; autograph at bottom.
G $40   **VG $60**   **NM $80**

○ **769.** **Poster, Paul;** (same as item #768.)

○ **770.** **Poster, George;** (same as item #768.)

○ **771.** **Poster, Ringo;** (same as item #768.)

○ **772.** **Poster, Life-size Poster Offer;** two-sided paper coupon from Heinz offering any one of items #768-771 posters for 75 cents and two labels from any two Heinz products; posters illustrated on coupon.
G $15   **VG $22**   **NM $30**

○ **773.** **Poster, Store Poster Offer Display;** 12" x 9"; Heinz cardboard display offering items #768-771 posters; held pad of item #772 coupons; the display pictures the Ringo poster; top of display folds back leaving the top part of the Ringo poster illustration displayed above offer; "Offer expires June 30, 1965."
G $150   **VG $225**   **NM $300**

○ **774.** **Poster;** Mfd. by Reveille (U.K.); 40" x 60"; color photo of the Beatles in old-fashioned swimsuits.
G $40   **VG $60**   **NM $80**

○ **775.** **Poster;** advertised in '60s teen magazines as "lifesize"; 42" x 58"; poster pictures the group posed in their collarless suits against an orange background.
G $40   **VG $60**   **NM $80**

The autobiography of the man who discovered the Beatles and other great British artists → **Brian Epstein**

A Cellarful of Noise

6

Books

This guide includes books published from 1963 to 1973. Values listed are for first editions unless otherwise noted. In most cases books published from the mid-1970s to 1990s are valued around cover price if in near mint condition. Some books which have been sold at discounts may be worth less than cover price.

The edition or printing of a book can be determined by looking at the copyright page. This page is usually the second or fourth page in a book. The year of publication will be listed on this page. Sometimes a first edition will be stated as such—*A Spaniard in the Works* hardcover book (item #796) is an exception. These first editions are not stated as such. Third to fifth printings are noted as such on the second to last page of the book.

Condition/Grading: Books with loose spines should be graded (G) or less. A short inscription or name on the first page does not reduce the value of a book greatly. (In some cases the inscriptions can themselves be interesting.) Books that have been sold or discarded by libraries (not stolen by over-zealous Beatle-fiends hopefully!) are valued at about the (G) value. Factors that must be considered with ex-library copies are stickers, stamps, or tears on the book from the library markings. We have noted if a hardcover was issued with a dustjacket. All values are for the hardcover with the dustjacket. Deduct 60% from the listed value if the dustjacket is missing.

This chapter is divided into two sections: hardcovers and paperbacks. Books are listed alphabetically by title. The author, publisher, and year of publication are listed after the title.

Hardcover Books

○ **776.** *The Beatles Book*; edited by Edward E. Davis; Cowles Publications; 1968; with dustjacket.
G $40   VG $60   NM $80

○ **777.** *The Beatles Illustrated Lyrics*; Alan Aldridge; Delacorte Press; 1969; with dustjacket.
G $20   VG $30   NM $40

○ **778.** *The Beatles Illustrated Lyrics, Volume 2*; Alan Aldridge; Delacorte Press; 1971; with dustjacket.
G $25   VG $35   NM $50

○ **779.** *The Beatles: The Authorized Biography*; Hunter Davies; McGraw Hill; 1968; 7" x 9$\frac{1}{4}$"; with dustjacket.
G $17   VG $25   NM $35

Book Club Edition; 5$\frac{3}{4}$" x 8$\frac{1}{2}$"; edges of pages are untrimmed.
G $12   VG $17   NM $25

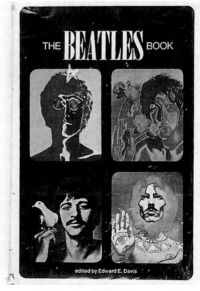
776

777

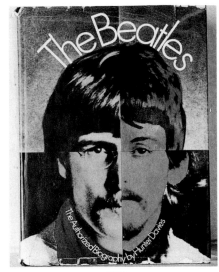

779

○ **780.** *The Beatles: The Authorized Biography Promo Poster;* Mfd. by McGraw Hill; 1968; 19" x 31"; an enlargement of the book dustjacket which was displayed in book stores to promote the book.
G $50   VG $75   NM $100

○ **781.** *The Beatles: The Real Story;* Julius Fast; Putnam and Sons; 1968; with dustjacket.
G $ 22   VG $ 35   NM $ 45

○ **782.** *Body Count;* Francine Schwartz; with dustjacket.
G $35   VG $50   NM $75

○ **783.** *A Cellarful of Noise;* Brian Epstein; Doubleday; 1964; with dustjacket.
G $30   VG $50   NM $75

○ **784.** *Dear Beatles;* compiled by Bill Adler; Laugh Books; 1966.
G $10   VG $15   NM $20

○ **785.** *En Flagrant Delire (In His Own Write En Francais);* John Lennon; Simon & Schuster; 1964.
G $35   VG $55   NM $75

○ **786.** *The Girl Who Sang With the Beatles and other stories;* Robert Hemenway; Alfred A. Knopf; 1970.
G $25   VG $35   NM $45

○ **787.** *Grapefruit;* Yoko Ono; Simon & Schuster; 1970; with dustjacket.
G $25   VG $35   NM $50

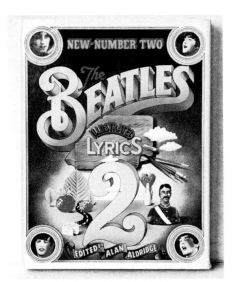

778

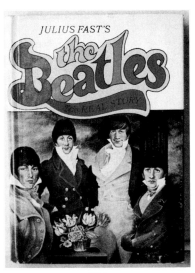

781

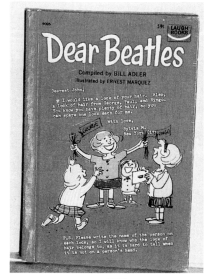

784

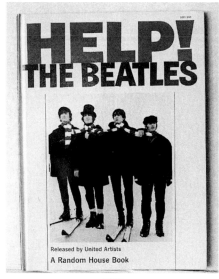

788

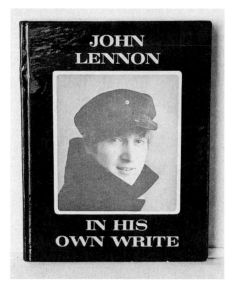

789

787

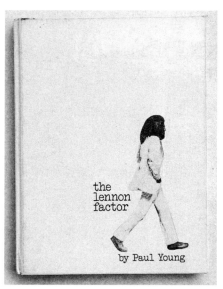

790

791

○ **788.** *Help!*; (no author listed); Random House; 1965.
G $25   VG $35   NM $50

○ **789.** *In His Own Write John Lennon*; Simon & Schuster; 1964; Note: Identifying a first edition of *In His Own Write*—the first edition has a $2^{1}/_{4}$" x $^{1}/_{2}$" red sticker with white printing on the front cover, the sticker states "THE WRITING BEATLE"; the back cover has "$2.50" printed in the lower left corner; "Printed in Great Britain" is on the copyright page; second through fifteenth printings are stated as such on the copyright page; the book was reprinted in the same form in 1996 (publisher listed on title page is not Simon & Schuster).

1st printing   G $75   VG $110   NM $150

2-15 printings   G $40   VG $60   NM $80

○ **790.** *The Lennon Factor*; Paul Young; Stein and Day; 1972.
G $30   VG $40   NM $60

○ **791.** *The Lennon Play: In His Own Write*; John Lennon, Adrienne Kennedy, and Victor Spinetti; Simon & Schuster; 1968.
G $35   VG $55   NM $75

○ **792.** *Lennon Remembers*; Jann Wenner; Straight Arrow Books; 1971; with dustjacket.
G $20   VG $30   NM $40

○ **793.** *The Longest Cocktail Party*; Richard DiLello; Playboy Press; 1972; with dustjacket.
G $20   VG $30   NM $40

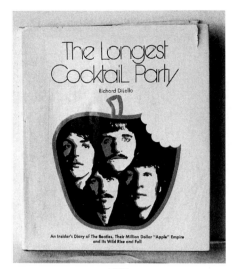

793

794

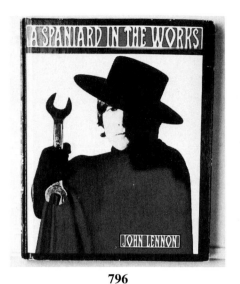

796

○ **794.** *Love Letters to the Beatles*; selected by Bill Adler; G.P. Putnam's Sons; with dustjacket (orange or green variation); green variation dustjacket is on 2nd printings.
G $10   **VG $15**   **NM $20**

○ **795.** *Love Letters to the Beatles* **Promo Poster;** Mfd. by G.P. Putnam's Sons; 12" x 11^1/$_2$"; poster is similar to the book dustjacket (orange variation).
G $75   **VG $110**   **NM $150**

○ **796.** *A Spaniard in the Works*; John Lennon; Simon & Schuster; 1965; price is for 1st-5th printings; Note: Identifying a first edition of A Spaniard in the Works—second through fifth printings are noted on the next to last page above "manufactured in the USA," first edition has nothing listed above "manufactured in the USA"; the book was reprinted in the same form in 1996 (publisher listed on title page is not Simon & Schuster).
G $40   **VG $60**   **NM $80**

○ **797.** *Spaniard in the Works* **Review Slip;** Mfd. by Simon & Schuster; 1965; 5" x 7"; Lennon drawing on photographic paper with "The book will be published by Simon & Schuster on July 1st for $2.50" printed with other info at bottom; this slip was included with books sent to book reviewers.
G $50   **VG $75**   **NM $100**

○ **798.** *Twilight of the Gods*; Wilfred Mellors; Viking Press; 1973; with dustjacket.
G $15   **VG $25**   **NM $35**

○ **799.** *We Love You Beatles*; Margaret Sutton; Doubleday & Co.; 1971; with dustjacket
G $20   **VG $35**   **NM $45**

Yellow Submarine (See item #450).

The Yellow Submarine Giftbook (See item #479).

Paperback Books

○ **800.** *All About the Beatles*; Edward DeBlasio; MacFadden Books; 1964.
G $5   **VG $8**   **NM $10**

○ **801.** *Apple to the Core*; Peter McCabe and Robert D. Schonfeld; Pocket Books; 1972.
G $3   **VG $5**   **NM $7**

○ **802.** *As Time Goes By*; Derek Taylor; Straight Arrow Books; 1973.
G $10   **VG $15**   **NM $20**

○ **803.** *The Beatle Book*; photos by Dezo Hoffmann; Lancer Special; 1964; with two page pullout poster.
G $5   **VG $7**   **NM $10**

○ **804.** *Beatlemania Hits the Bigwigs*; Stan Fine; Gem Publishing; 1964.
G $25   **VG $35**   **NM $50**

○ **805.** *The Beatles*; Aram Saroyan; Barn Dream Press; 1971.
G $30   **VG $45**   **NM $60**

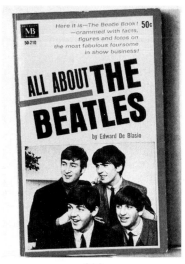

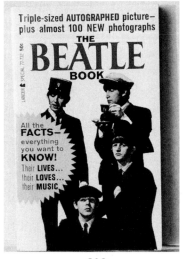

800   **803**   **804**

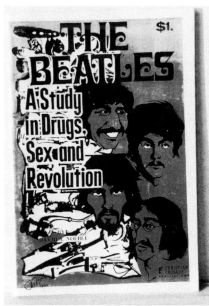

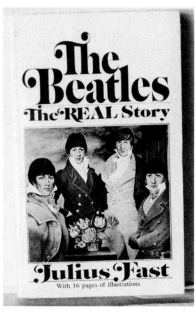

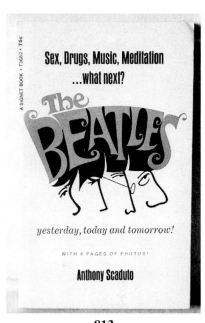

806   **810**   **813**

○ **806.** *The Beatles A Study in Drugs, Sex, and Revolution*; David Noebel; Christian Crusade Publications; 1969; second edition of ten thousand copies has a green cover and is valued the same.
| G $40 | VG $60 | NM $80 |

○ **807.** *The Beatles Get Back*; photographs by Ethan A. Russell, text by Jonathan Cott and David Dalton; Apple; 1969; included in the British, Canadian, and German editions of the "Let It Be" Box Set.
| G $40 | VG $65 | NM $80 |

○ **808.** *Beatles Quiz Book*; compiled by Jack House; William Collins Sons & Co., Ltd. (U.K.); 1964.
| G $20 | VG $35 | NM $45 |

○ **809.** *The Beatles: The Authorized Biography*; Hunter Davies; Dell; 1968.
| G $5 | VG $8 | NM $10 |

○ **810.** *The Beatles: The Real Story*; Julius Fast; Berkley Medallion Books; 1968.
| G $5 | VG $8 | NM $10 |

○ **811.** *The Beatles Up to Date*; (no author listed); Lancer Special; 1964.
| G $5 | VG $8 | NM $10 |

○ **812.** *The Beatles Words Without Music*; Rick Friedman; Grosset and Dunlap; 1968.
| G $6 | VG $8 | NM $12 |

○ **813.** *The Beatles Yesterday, Today and Tomorrow!*; Anthony Scaduto; Signet; 1968.
| G $5 | VG $7 | NM $10 |

○ **814.** *The Big Wigs*; Stan Fine; Gem Publishing; 1964; identical to item #804; Nixon or Goldwater cover.
G $15   **VG $25**   **NM $35**

○ **815.** *Body Count*; Francine Schwartz; Straight Arrow Books; 1972.
G $30   **VG $45**   **NM $60**

○ **816.** *A Cellarful of Noise*; Brian Epstein; Pyramid Books; 1965. ★ *Reprint Alert*
G $10   **VG $15**   **NM $20**

○ **817.** *Communism, Hypnotism, and the Beatles*; David Noebel; Christian Crusade Publications; 1965; 1st edition (blue and white cover) 10,000 copies; 2nd printing (25,000 copies); 3rd revised printing (10,000 copies); 4th printing (red and white cover) 10,000 copies.
G $40   **VG $60**   **NM $80**

○ **818.** *Die Beatles Kommen (Germany)*; 1964.
G $25   **VG $35**   **NM $50**

○ **819.** *Grapefruit*; Yoko Ono; Simon & Schuster; 1971.
G $20   **VG $30**   **NM $40**

○ **820.** *A Hard Day's Night*; John Burke; Dell; 1964.
G $7   **VG $10**   **NM $15**

○ **821.** *Help!*; Al Hine; Dell; 1965.
G $7   **VG $10**   **NM $15**

○ **822.** *Here Are The Beatles*; Charles Hamblett; Four Square Books (U.K.); 1964.
G $25   **VG $35**   **NM $50**

○ **823.** *How I Won The War*; Patrick Ryan; Ballantine Books; 1967.
G $7   **VG $10**   **NM $15**

○ **824.** *John Lennon: In His Own Write & A Spaniard in the Works*; John Lennon; Signet; 1968.
G $7   **VG $10**   **NM $15**

○ **825.** *The Kings of Rock*; edited by Bury Chan (Hong Kong); 1965; book title noted is loose translation of the Chinese title.
G $35   **VG $50**   **NM $75**

○ **826.** *Lennon Remembers*; Jann Wenner; Popular Library; 1971.
G $4   **VG $6**   **NM $8**

○ **827.** *The Longest Cocktail Party*; Richard DiLello; Playboy Press; 1972.
G $3   **VG $5**   **NM $8**

○ **828.** *Love Me Do! The Beatles Progress*; Michael Braun; Penguin (U.K.); 1964.
G $25   **VG $35**   **NM $50**

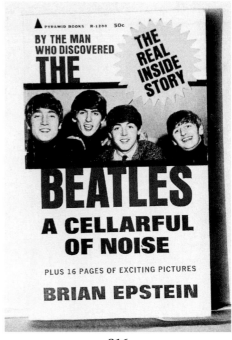

816

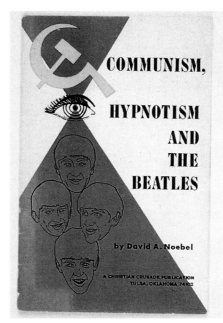

817

○ **829.** *The Magic Christian*; Terry Southern; Bantam Books; 1970.
G $5   **VG $7**   **NM $10**

○ **830.** *Out Of The Mouths of Beatles*; Adam Blessing; Dell; 1964.
G $10   **VG $15**   **NM $20**

○ **831.** *Over The Beatles*; Mike Hollaway; Dutch Palet Book Club (Holland); 1964.
G $15   **VG $25**   **NM $30**

818

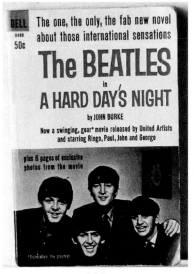

820

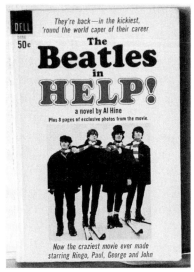

821

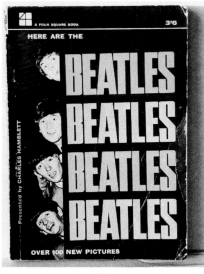

822

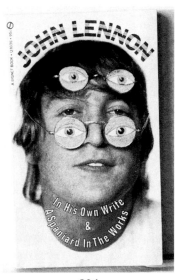

824

825

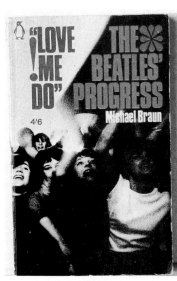

828

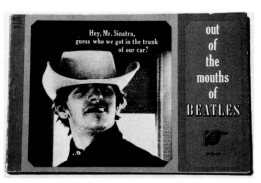

830

831

○ **832.** *The Penguin John Lennon*; John Lennon; Penguin (U.K.); 1966; 'Superman' cover.
G $25   **VG $35**   **NM $50**

○ **833.** *The Penguin John Lennon*; John Lennon; Penguin (U.K.); 1968; Lennon photo in voice balloon with drawing on John below.
G $25   **VG $35**   **NM $50**

○ **834.** *The True Story of the Beatles*; Billy Shepherd; Bantam Books; 1964.
G $6 VG $8   NM $12

○ **835.** *Turn Me On Dead Man*; J. Lancelot Turner; Stone Garden Press, Inc.; 1969.
G $35   **VG $50**   **NM $75**

○ **836.** *Up The Beatles Family Tree*; Cecil Humphrey-Smith, Michael Heenan, and Jennifer Mount; Achievements Ltd. (U.K.); 1966.
G $12   **VG $18**   **NM $25**

○ **837.** *The Writing Beatle*; John Lennon; Signet Books; 1967.
G $7   **VG $10**   **NM $15**

Yellow Submarine; (See item #451).

○ **838.** *Zo Zijn de Beatles*; Meyden and Langereis; Strenghold (Holland); 1964.
G $15   **VG $25**   **NM $30**

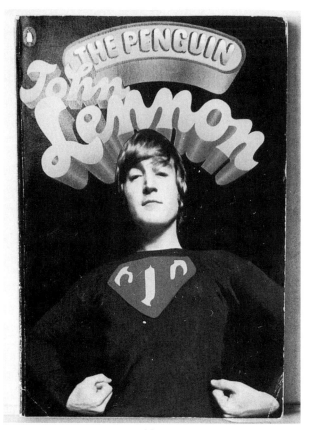

832

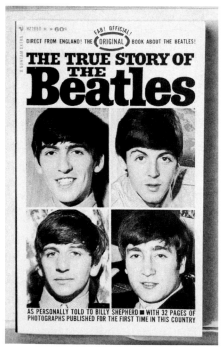

834

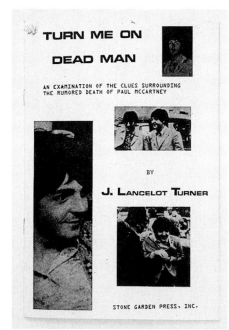

835

838

7

Magazines

In the period from 1963 to 1973 there were thousands of magazines which had photos and articles on the Beatles. Coverage ranged from a small photo or article to a cover story or even a special edition totally on the Beatles. We have separated this chapter into five sections: Magazines Exclusively on the Beatles, Teen and Rock Magazines, National/Mainstream Magazines, Newspaper & Magazine Supplements/Tabloids, and Comic Books. The Magazines Exclusively on the Beatles section and the Comic Books section list every item. The Teen and Rock Magazines section lists a general price range for most magazines and mentions a few special issues. The National/Mainstream Magazine section and the Newspaper & Magazine Supplements/Tabloids section lists general price ranges.

Other paper items of interest to some collectors are newspaper clippings and scrapbooks. Groups or collections of newspaper clippings have some value, while individual clippings generally have little value. The value of a scrapbook depends on the quality of the contents. Local newspaper clippings have greater value than magazine clippings. Other items of interest in a scrapbook would be concert stubs, memorabilia ads or flyers, wrappers or packaging from memorabilia, etc. A scrapbook of newspaper clippings can be worth between $15 and $40 depending on the size and quality of the contents. Scrapbooks which contain special items such as concert stubs would have the value of the stub added to the scrapbook value. Some collectors may be looking for articles on specific group members, while other collectors may be looking for articles or ads from concert appearances.

Condition/Grading: Magazines in all grades must be complete. No clips, missing pages, or missing covers are allowed. Deduct these percentages for each listed defect.

Defect	Deduct
No front cover	75%
No back cover	50%
1 to 2 pages gone	60%
2 to 3 small clips	40%
Tape on cover or spine	40%
Small coupon clipped out	10%

Magazines with multiple defects or missing numerous pages have little collectible value.

Grading Guidelines

(NM) Near Mint Condition: Magazines should have very little wear; cover and pages should be crisp with no defects or browning of pages; cover and interior should not have any creases or writing.

(VG) Very Good Condition: Magazine can have a little wear; cover should not have any writing or major creases.

(G) Good Condition: Magazine has wear; spine may be slightly rolled or slightly loose.

Magazines in each section of this chapter are listed alphabetically by title and then by date. We have noted where magazines vary from the usual 8½" x 11" format in these sections: Magazines Exclusively on the Beatles and Teen and Rock Magazines.

Magazines Exclusively on the Beatles

○ **839.** *All About The Beatles*; Yopu Press; 1964.
  G $10   **VG $15**   **NM $20**

○ **840.** *All About Us*; Sixteen magazine; 1965; sold by mail order.
  G $14   **VG $20**   **NM $25**

○ **841.** *American Vs. Beatles: Battle of the Groups*; Country Wide Publications; 1964.
  G $10   **VG $15**   **NM $20**

○ **842.** *Around the World With the Beatles* (U.K.); 1964; 11 1/4" x 17".
  G $17   **VG $25**   **NM $35**

○ **843.** *The Beatle Album*; K.G. Murray Publishing (Australia); 1964.
  G $30   **VG $45**   **NM $60**

○ **844.** *Beatle Biografie*; *Humo* magazine (Holland); 1968; 8 1/4" x 10 3/4"; collection of newsprint articles from *Humo* magazine in special folder.
  G $40   **VG $60**   **NM $80**

○ **845.** *The Beatle Book No. 1*; Warsons Printing (New Zealand); 1964.
  G $30   **VG $45**   **NM $60**

○ **846.** *Beatle Fun Kit*; Deidre Publications (*DIG* magazine); 1964; 11" x 14"; a difficult magazine to find intact because many items in it were designed to be removed; recently found in quantity.
  G $25   **VG $35**   **NM $50**

○ **847.** *Beatle Hairdos & Setting Patterns*; Dell; 1964.
  G $30   **VG $45**   **NM $60**

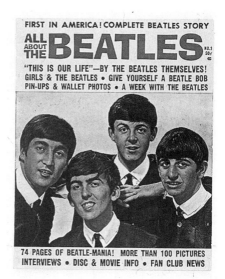

839

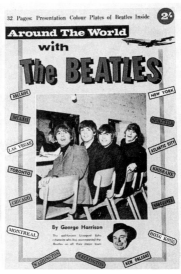

842

843

844

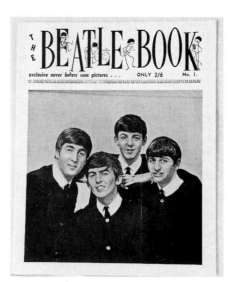

845

846

848. **Beatlebox;** *Jukebox* magazine (Belgium); 1964; special all-Beatle issue printed in either Dutch or French language.
G $30   VG $45   NM $60

849. **Beatledom;** *Twin Hits*; 1964.
G $10   VG $15   NM $20

850. **Beatlemania (Australia);** 1964.
G $25   VG $35   NM $50

851. **Beatlemania #1;** SMP Publishing Ltd.; 1964.
G $12   VG $18   NM $25

852. **Beatlemania Collector's Item;** SMP Publishing; 1964; 10 ½" x 14".
G $15   VG $25   NM $35

853. **Beatleopaedia;** Romeo (U.K.); 1964; 48 pages of newsprint articles in a heavy cardboard cover.
G $35   VG $50   NM $75

854. **The Beatles;** Charlton; sixteen-page booklet printed on various colors of paper; includes photos, stories and lyrics to songs; #1 spring 1964, #2 summer 1964, #3 fall 1964, #4 winter 1964-65, #5 spring 1965, #6 summer 1965, #7 fall 1966; value is per issue.
G $6   VG $9   NM $12

855. **The Beatles;** Music Makers, Inc.; 1964; 5½" x 7½".
G $20   VG $30   NM $40

847

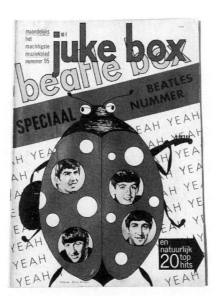

848

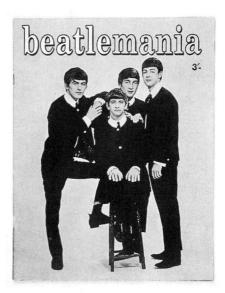

850

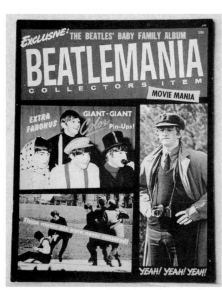

852

853

854

○ **856.** *The Beatles*; N.V. Drukkerij de Spaarnestad (Holland); 1964.
G $25   **VG $35**   **NM $50**

○ **857.** *The Beatles* **(Japan)**; 1966; 7" x 10"; 134 pages.
G $40   **VG $60**   **NM $80**

○ **858.** *The Beatles*; Music Life (Japan); 1966; 9" x 12".
G $40   **VG $60**   **NM $80**

○ **859.** *The Beatles*; PYX Production; 1964; 7" x 9¹/₂"; printed on heavy paper stock; sold by mail; add 50% to value if there are radio station call letters on the cover.
G $10   **VG $15**   **NM $20**

○ **860.** *The Beatles* **(Japan)**; 1967; 10" x 14¹/₄".
G $35   **VG $50**   **NM $75**

○ **861.** *The Beatles Are Back*; MacFadden-Bartell Corp.; 1964.
G $9   **VG $12**   **NM $18**

○ **862.** *The Beatles Are Here*; MacFadden-Bartell Corp.; 1964.
G $9   **VG $12**   **NM $18**

○ **863.** *Beatles Around The World*; George Newnes (U.K.); 1964.
G $15   **VG $25**   **NM $30**

○ **864.** *The Beatles At Carnegie Hall*; Hamilton Co. (U.K.); 1964; 7" x 9".
G $25   **VG $35**   **NM $50**

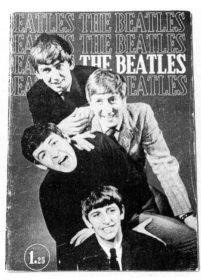

856

858

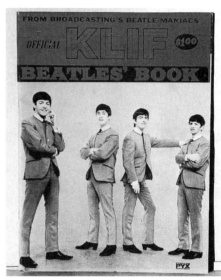

859

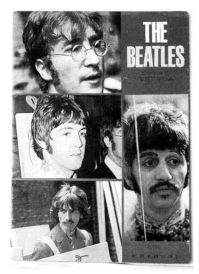

860

862

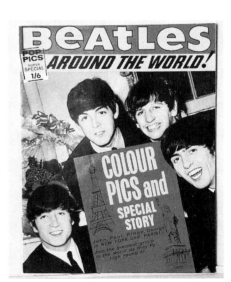

863

○ **865.** *Beatles, Beatles, Beatles*; J.L.D. Publishing; 1964.
　　G $12　　　　VG $18　　　　NM $25

○ **866.** *The Beatles Book*; Beat Publications (Japan); 1965; 8³/₈" x 10 ³/₄"; nearly identical text to the *Beatle Monthly Book Christmas Extra 1965*, but with many different photos.
　　G $30　　　　VG $45　　　　NM $60

○ **867.** *The Beatles Book Monthly*; Beat Publications (U.K.); 6" x 8¹/₄"; 32 pages with black and white cover photos; (issues #47, 53, 58 through 68, and the Christmas Extras have color photo covers); published from August 1963 (#1) until December 1969 (#77). ★ *Repro Alert*

We have listed prices for original editions. Starting in mid-1976 the original publisher began reprinting the *Beatles Book Monthly* #1-77. The reprints were the same as the originals except that four new pages were added. These four pages could easily be removed, making it hard to distinguish originals from reprints. The easiest way to determine if an issue is a reprint is to compare it side by side to an original. The color background on the top of the reprint cover is usually a slightly different shade than on the original. Look at the B&W cover and interior photos. The photos on the originals will look clear and dark portions will look black. Certain photos on the reprints will lack clarity and definition and dark portions can appear gray instead of black. In some cases the reprint will vary in size from the standard 6" x 8¹/₄" format. The reprint will be a little taller, shorter, or narrower.

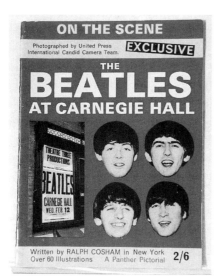

864

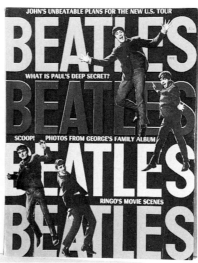

865

866

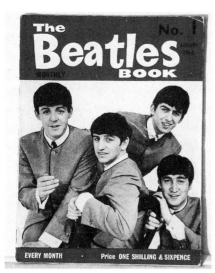

867—#1

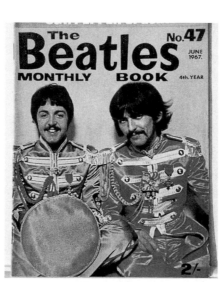

867—#47

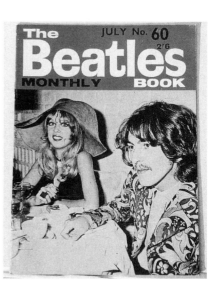

867—#60

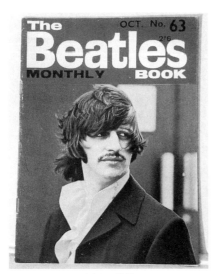

867—#63

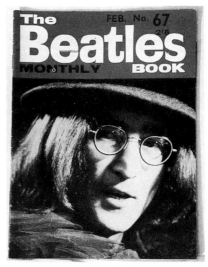

867—#67

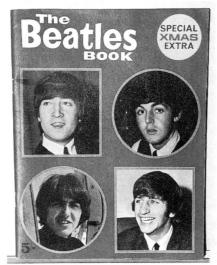

867—1965 Xmas Extra

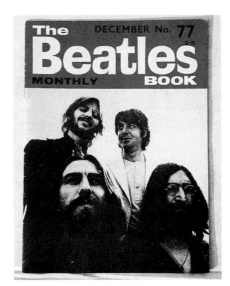

867—#77

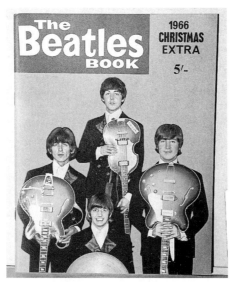

867—1966 Xmas Extra

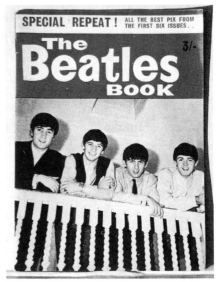

867—SR

Prices

	(G)	(VG)	(NM)
#1	$45	$70	$90
#2-5 each	$10	$15	$20
#6-9	$7	$10	$15
#10-77	$6	$9	$12
1965 Christmas Extra	$30	$45	$60
1966 Christmas Extra	$30	$45	$60
Special Repeat! (1966)	$15	$25	$35

Beatles Book Monthly Checklist

⭕ 1 ⭕ 12 ⭕ 23 ⭕ 34 ⭕ 45 ⭕ 56 ⭕ 67
⭕ 2 ⭕ 13 ⭕ 24 ⭕ 35 ⭕ 46 ⭕ 57 ⭕ 68
⭕ 3 ⭕ 14 ⭕ 25 ⭕ 36 ⭕ 47 ⭕ 58 ⭕ 69
⭕ 4 ⭕ 15 ⭕ 26 ⭕ 37 ⭕ 48 ⭕ 59 ⭕ 70
⭕ 5 ⭕ 16 ⭕ 27 ⭕ 38 ⭕ 49 ⭕ 60 ⭕ 71
⭕ 6 ⭕ 17 ⭕ 28 ⭕ 39 ⭕ 50 ⭕ 61 ⭕ 72
⭕ 7 ⭕ 18 ⭕ 29 ⭕ 40 ⭕ 51 ⭕ 62 ⭕ 73
⭕ 8 ⭕ 19 ⭕ 30 ⭕ 41 ⭕ 52 ⭕ 63 ⭕ 74
⭕ 9 ⭕ 20 ⭕ 31 ⭕ 42 ⭕ 53 ⭕ 64 ⭕ 75
⭕ 10 ⭕ 21 ⭕ 32 ⭕ 43 ⭕ 54 ⭕ 65 ⭕ 76
⭕ 11 ⭕ 22 ⭕ 33 ⭕ 44 ⭕ 55 ⭕ 66 ⭕ 77

⭕ **1965 Christmas Extra;** $8^{1}/_{2}$" x $10^{3}/_{4}$"

⭕ **1966 Christmas Extra;** $8^{1}/_{2}$" x $10^{3}/_{4}$"

⭕ **Special Repeat! (1966);** "64 pages of all the best pix from the first six issues."

See items #30 (Binder) and #63 (Calendar) in the General Memorabilia chapter for related items made by Beat Publications.

⭕ **868.** *The Beatles By Royal Command*; Daily Mirror Publications (U.K.); 1964.
　　G $20　　**VG $30**　　**NM $40**

⭕ **869.** *Beatles Color Pinup Album*; Teen Screen; 1964.
　　G $10　　**VG $15**　　**NM $20**

⭕ **870.** *The Beatles Coming* **(Japan);** 1966; 7" x 10"; 120 pages; B&W Photos with text in Japanese.
　　G $40　　**VG $60**　　**NM $80**

⭕ **871.** *The Beatles Complete Coverage*; Beatle Publishing Corp.; 1964; covered New York appearance.
　　G $10　　**VG $15**　　**NM $20**

⭕ **872.** *The Beatles Complete Life Story*; *Teen Screen*; 1964.
　　G $10　　**VG $15**　　**NM $20**

⭕ **873.** *Beatles Complete Story From Birth Till Now*; *Sixteen* magazine; 1965.
　　G $10　　**VG $15**　　**NM $20**

868　　　　**871**

870

○ **874.** *The Beatles Forever*; Lamplight Enterprises; 1973.
   G $4   **VG $6**   **NM $8**

○ **875.** *The Beatles From Beatlemania to Bangla Desh*; Lamplight Enterprises; 1973.
   G $6   **VG $9**   **NM $12**

○ **876.** *The Beatles From The Beginning*; Magnum-Royal Publications; 1970.
   G $6   **G $9**   **NM $12**

○ **877.** *The Beatles in America*; *Daily Mirror* (U.K.); 1964. ★ *Repro Alert*
   G $15   **VG $25**   **NM $35**

○ **878.** *The Beatles in Cincinnati*; WSAI Good Guys; 1964.
   G $35   **VG $50**   **NM $75**

○ **879.** *The Beatles Make a Movie*; Magnum Publications; 1964.
   G $10   **VG $15**   **NM $20**

○ **880.** *The Beatles Meet the Dave Clark 5*; Kahn Communications; 1964.
   G $10   **VG $15**   **NM $20**

○ **881.** *The Beatles 96 Fotos* (**Brazil**); 1965; unusual magazine which came with sheets with 96 photos to separate and attach.
   G $35   **VG $50**   **NM $75**

○ **882.** *The Beatles on Broadway*; Whitman; 1964; 8½" x 11¾".
   G $9   **VG $12**   **NM $18**

○ **883.** *The Beatles Personality Annual*; County Wide Publications; 1964.
   G $9   **VG $12**   **NM $18**

○ **884.** *The Beatles Picture Book*; K.G. Murray Publishing (Australia); 1964; 7½" x 10½".
   G $30   **VG $45**   **NM $60**

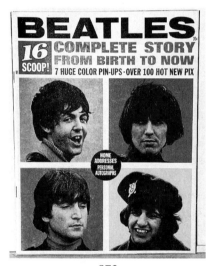

873

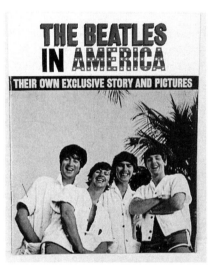

877

878

879

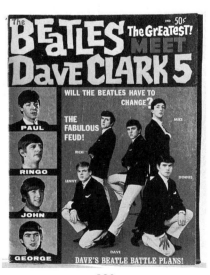

880

881

885. *The Beatles Pictures For Framing*; Pocket Books Inc.; 1964; also found with cover variation that has a banner on the cover stating "Pictures Suitable For Framing."
G $9   **VG $12**   **NM $18**

886. *Beatles 'Round The World #1*; Acme; 1964; 10" x 13"; issued with a color centerfold.
G $10   **VG $15**   **NM $20**

887. *Beatles 'Round The World #2*; Acme 1964; 10" x 13"; issued with a fold-out poster.
G $15   **VG $25**   **NM $35**

888. *Beatles 'Round The World #3: Elvis vs. The Beatles*; Acme; 1965; $8^1/_4$" x $10^3/_4$".
G $40   **VG $60**   **NM $80**

889. *The Beatles Starring in A* **Hard Day's Night**; Whitman; 1964; $8^1/_2$" x $11^3/_4$".
G $10   **VG $15**   **NM $20**

890. *The Beatles Starring in A* **Hard Day's Night Display Bin**; Mfd. by Whitman; 1964; 12" x $8^1/_2$" x $4^1/_4$" box which held copies of item #889; bin would have been placed on countertops in stores.
G $175   **VG $250**   **NM $350**

891. *Beatles Started The Big Sound*; Par Publishing; 1964.
G $10   **VG $15**   **NM $20**

892. *The Beatles Talk!*; *DIG* magazine; 1964.
G $10   **VG $15**   **NM $20**

893. *The Beatles Talk!* **(Souvenir Theatre Edition)**; DIG magazine; 1964.
G $15   **VG $25**   **NM $30**

894. *Beatles U.S.A.*; Jamie Publications; 1964; 11" x 14".
G $20   **VG $30**   **NM $40**

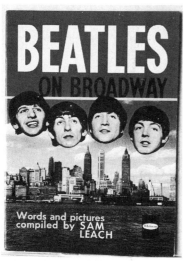

882

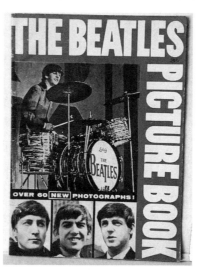

884

887

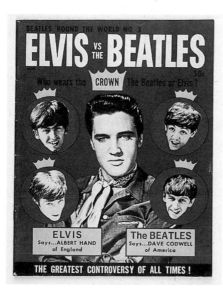

888

890

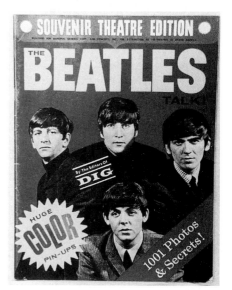

893

○ **895.** *Beatles Whole True Story*; *Sixteen* magazine; 1966.
G $10   **VG $15**   **NM $20**

○ **896.** *Best of the Beatles*; MacFadden-Bartell Corp.; 1964; issued with three-page fold-out pinup.
G $10   **VG $15**   **NM $20**

○ **897.** *Best of the Beatles From Fabulous*; Fabulous magazine; (U.K.) - 1964; 10" x 13"
G $15   **VG $25**   **NM $35**

○ **898.** *Bravo—das sind die Beatles*; Kindler + Schiermeyer (Germany); 1965; 1965 Special Christmas Extra; 7^1/$_2$" x 9^3/$_4$".
G $30   **VG $45**   **NM $60**

○ **899.** *Das Sind die Beatles*; Neuer Tessloff Verlag (Germany); 1964; 7" x 10".
G $25   **VG $35**   **NM $50**

○ **900.** *Das Sind die Beatles Zwei (#2)*; Neuer Tessloff Verlag (Germany); 1964; 7" x 10".
G $25   **VG $35**   **NM $50**

○ **901.** *Dave Clark 5 vs. The Beatles*; Tempest Publication Inc.; 1964.
G $10   **VG $15**   **NM $20**

○ **902.** *Fabulous Goes All Beatles*; *Fabulous* magazine (U.K.); February 15, 1964; 10" x 13".
G $15   **VG $25**   **NM $35**

○ **903.** *Fabulous Goes Filming With The Beatles*; Fabulous Magazine (U.K.); June 13, 1964; 10" x 13".
G $15   **VG $25**   **NM $35**

○ **904.** *Help!*; *Sixteen* magazine; 1965.
G $10   **VG $15**   **NM $20**

○ **905.** *Jill Meets The Beatles*; WTRY Radio; 1965 WTRY Radio contest winner named Jill wins a contest and gets to meets the Beatles!
G $25   **VG $35**   **NM $50**

○ **906.** *John and Yoko Their Love Book*; M.F. Enterprises; 1970.
G $15   **VG $25**   **NM $30**

896

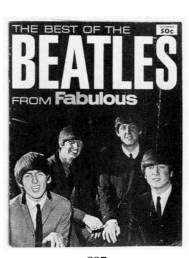

897

898

901

902

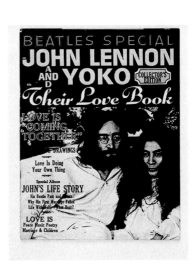

906

○ **907.** *Les Beatles*; Le Semaine Radio-Tele (France); 1964; 6" x 8$^{1}/_{4}$"; similar design to the *Beatles Monthly* books.
G $25   **VG $35**   **NM $50**

○ **908.** *Los Beatles* (**Mexico**); May 1964; 8$^{5}/_{8}$" x 11$^{1}/_{4}$"; 36 pages.
G $25   **VG $35**   **NM $50**

○ **909.** *Los Beatles* (**Spain**); 1965; 6$^{1}/_{4}$" x 8$^{1}/_{2}$"; 20 pages; includes photos from Barcelona and Madrid concerts.
G $30   **VG $45**   **NM $60**

○ **910.** *Meet The Beatles*; MacFadden-Bartell Corp.; 1963
G $15   **VG $22**   **NM $30**

○ **911.** *Meet The Beatles*; World Distributors (U.K.); 1963; 7" x 9".
G $17   **VG $25**   **NM $35**

○ **912.** *Meet The Beatles Nummer To* (**#2**); illustrerte Klassikere (Sweden); 1964; same contents as the German *Das Sind die Beatles Zwei* (item #900).
G $25   **VG $35**   **NM $50**

○ **913.** *New Beatles: The Fab Four Come Back*; Highlight Publications; 1964.
G $10   **VG $15**   **NM $20**

○ **914.** *The Original Beatles Book*; Petersen Specialty Publications; 1964; heavy paper centerfold.
G $9   **VG $12**   **NM $18**

○ **915.** *The Original Beatles Book Two*; Petersen Specialty Publications; 1964; heavy paper centerfold.
G $9   **VG $12**   **NM $18**

○ **916.** *Paul McCartney Dead—The Great Hoax*; Country Wide Publications; 1969; cover price is 60 cents. ★ *Repro Alert*
G $25   **VG $35**   **NM $50**

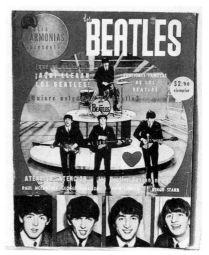

908

909

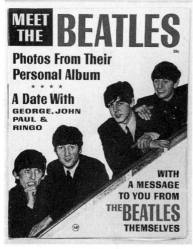

910

911

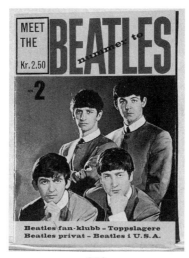

912

913

○ **917.** *Pop Pics Super, Beatle John Lennon*; George Newnes Ltd. (U.K.); 1964; 5$^1/_2$" x 8$^1/_2$"; 14 pages; price of (35 cents) or (1£ 6s) on cover; set of all four (#917-920) were also sold together in a clear plastic bag with pockets; "all 4 for 5£" printed on the bag, add 50% to value if this bag is present.
G $10   **VG $15**   **NM $20**

○ **918.** *Pop Pics Super, Beatle Paul McCartney*; (same as above).

○ **919.** *Pop Pics Super, Beatle George Harrison*; (same as above).

○ **920.** *Pop Pics Super, Beatle Ringo Starr*; (same as above).

○ **921.** *Pop Pics Super Special, The Beatles Film*; Sun Printers Ltd. (U.K.); 1964; 9" x 11$^3/_4$".
G $7   **VG $10**   **NM $15**

○ **922.** *The Real True Beatles*; Fawcett Publications; 1964.
G $15   **VG $22**   **NM $30**

○ **923.** *Ringo's Photo Album*; Jamie Publications; 1964; all photos taken by Ringo.
G $10   **VG $15**   **NM $20**

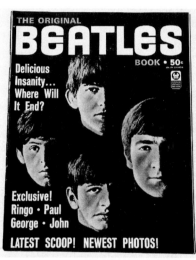

914

916

917

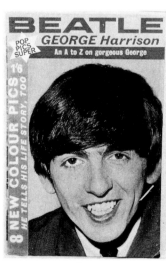

919

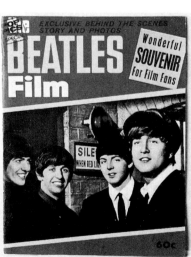

921

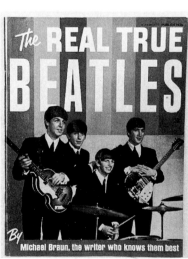

922

○ **924.** *Talking Pictures #1: The Beatles*; Herald House Inc.; 1964.
G $9   VG $12   NM $18

○ **925.** *Teen Pix Album*; Celebrity Publications; 1964.
G $15   VG $22   NM $30

○ **926.** *Teen Screen Life Story, John*; S.M.H. Publications; 1964.
G $12   VG $18   NM $25

○ **927.** *Teen Screen Life Story, Paul*; (same as above).

○ **928.** *Teen Screen Life Story, George*; (same as above).

○ **929.** *Teen Screen Life Story, Ringo*; (same as above).

○ **930.** *Teen Talk*; Sabre Publishing; 1964 (marked May or June); 64 pages; cover price of 35 cents.
G $12   VG $18   NM $25

○ **931.** *Teen Talk*; Sabre Publishing; 1964; 32 pages; no cover price; similar to above item; this magazine was issued with the album "The American Tour with Ed Rudy #2."
G $15   VG $22   NM $30

○ **932.** *Teeners Special Beatles #1*; SVZ Publishing; 1964.
G $25   VG $35   NM $50

○ **933.** *Uncut Official Version: Beatles Movie* (**A Hard Day's Night**); *Sixteen* magazine; 1964.
G $10   VG $15   NM $20

○ **934.** *Who Will Beat The Beatles*; Magnum Publications; 1964.
G $10   VG $15   NM $20

Yellow Submarine Magazine; (see item #505 and 506).

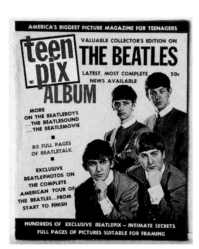

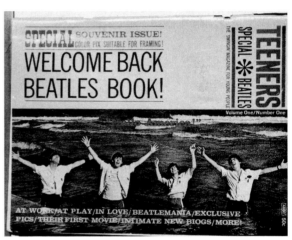

923   925   932

926   927   933   934

Teen and Rock Magazines

We have listed the different titles of teen and rock magazines available in the 1960s. It would be very difficult to list every issue that the Beatles appeared in, as almost every issue from 1964 to 1970 had something on the Beatles. The Beatles dominated these magazines from 1964 to 1966. Value ranges have been listed for the magazines. The value depends on the amount on the Beatles in a particular issue. A magazine with only one or two pages on the Beatles would be at the low end. A magazine with ten or twenty pages on the Beatles would be at the high end. Issues with a Beatle or the Beatles on the cover are the most in demand. Issues with multiple color photographs have a higher value as many of the 1960s magazines had only black and white interior photos. First issues of a title are collectible and

command a premium. We have noted some #1 issues of certain titles. Some of the British magazines had early (pre-1964) coverage and these are sought after. A few of the British magazines, such as *Rave* and *Fabulous*, had limited distribution in the United States. Some British magazines also were very high quality. For all these reasons British magazines generally command higher values than many of the U.S. publications. At the end of this section we have listed individual values for the most collectible teen and rock magazines. Issues with other collectible artists such as Jim Morrison, the Rolling Stones, Janis Joplin, Jimi Hendrix, etc. on the cover can be valued in the same value range as magazines with a Beatle on the cover.

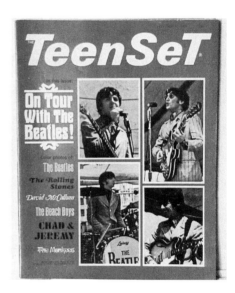

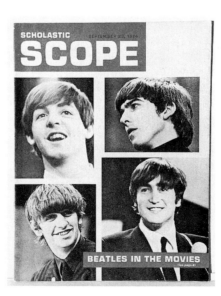
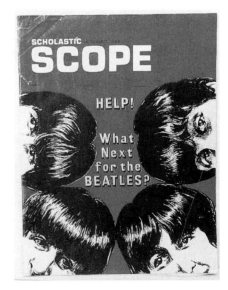

A selection of Teen and Rock Magazines.

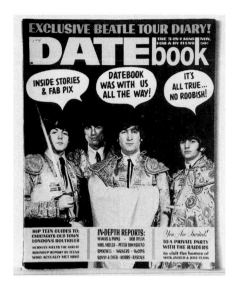

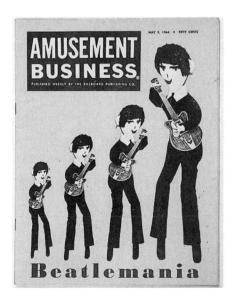

A selection of Teen and Rock Magazines.

A selection of Foreign Magazines.

Value Ranges:	G	VG	NM
Complete magazine with an article on the Beatles	**$4 to $6**	**$6 to $9**	**$8 to $12**
Complete magazine with a Beatle or Beatles on the cover	**$4 to $6**	**$7 to $10**	**$9 to $16**

(Please refer to Condition/Grading guidelines at the beginning of the chapter for adjustments to values.)

U.S. Publications

Beat (WCFL Radio edition; #1, March 25, 1967)
Beat (KRLA Radio edition; #1, March 10, 1965)
Beat (WHOO Radio edition; #1, May 1967)
Best Songs
Billboard
Boxoffice
Cashbox
Circus (titled *Hullabaloo* prior to March 1969)
Crawdaddy (#1, September 1966)
Creem
Datebook (#1, September 1957)
Dig (#1, November 1955)
Discoscene (later became *Scene*)
Eye (#1, March 1968)
Fabulous Teen (#1, April 1966)
Fave (#1, September 1967)
Fifteen
Flip Teen (#1, September 1964)
For Teens Only
Freak Out USA (#1, Fall 1967)
Go (#1, April 1, 1966)
Hit Parader
Hullabaloo (#1, October 1966; becomes *Circus March* 1969)
Jazz & Pop
Keen Teen (#1, December 1964)
Modern Teen (#1, June 1957)
National Blast (newspaper; #1, August, 22, 1965)
Outasite (#1, February 1968)
Pop Teen's a Go Go Pinups (#1, March 1966)
Popular Teen (#1, April 1966)
Record Beat (newspaper)
Rock & Roll Songs
Rolling
Stone (newspaper; #1, November 1967)
Shindig (#1, 1965)
Sixteen (#1, May 1957)
Song Hits
Startime
Swing Teen Newspaper
Teen
Teen Album
Teen Circle (#1, October 1965)
Teen Life (#1, July 1961)
Teen Pinups
Teen Scoop

Teen Scrapbook (#1, October 1964)
Teen Screen (#1, December 1959)
Teen Set (#1, 1965)
Teen Stars
Teen Talk
Teen Trends (#1, November 1965)
Teen Tunes & Pinups (#1, July 67)
Teen World
Teen's Top Ten (#1, Summer 1965)
Teenville (#1, November 1964)
Tiger Beat (#1, September 1965)
Today's Teens (#1, October 1965)
Top Teen Stars
Words and Music
Young Miss

British Publications

Beat Monthly (#1, May 1963; later becomes *Beat Instrumental Monthly*)
Big Beat (#1, 1963)
Boyfriend
Disc
Fabulous
Jackie
Hit Parade (merges into *Rave* after September 1964)
Melody Maker (newspaper)
Mersey Beat (newspaper)
New Musical Express (newspaper)
Pop Pics (#1, February 1963)
Pop Star Pictorial
Pop Ten Teenbeat (#1, October 1963)
Pop Weekly (#1, Sept 1962)
Rave (#1, February 1964)
Ready, Steady, Go!

German Publication
Bravo

Japanese Publications
Music Life
Teen Beat

Spanish Publication
Fans

Noteworthy Teen/Rock Magazines

○ **935.** *Datebook*; September 1966; Paul on the cover plus story which quotes John's famous statement "I don't know which will go first—rock-n-roll or Christianity!"
  G $15   **VG $25**   **NM $30**

○ **936.** *Datebook*; October 1966; Paul on the cover plus eight-page story by the editor protested the furor over Lennon's statement; add 20% to price if the 3" x 5" protest banner is still on the cover.
  G $10   **VG $15**   **NM $20**

○ **937.** *Eye*; September 1968; John Lennon on the cover; issued with a Bob Dylan poster inside; deduct 40% if the poster is missing.
  G $30   **VG $45**   **NM $60**

○ **938.** *National Record News*; "Special Beatles Issue"; 1964; four-page newspaper with headline "Beatlemania Sweeps U.S."; issued in January 1964 just before the "invasion"; issued by Capitol Records (but that's not mentioned in the issue!); supposedly one million of these were distributed free across the U.S.
  G $8   **VG $12**   **NM $16**

○ **939.** *Rolling Stone #1*; November 1967; first issue of this historic music magazine; John Lennon on the cover. ★ *Reprint Alert*
  G $150   **VG $225**   **NM $300**

○ **940.** *Rolling Stone #3*; December 14, 1967; the Beatles are on the cover plus an article about *Magical Mystery Tour*.
  G $30   **VG $45**   **NM $60**

○ **941.** *Rolling Stone #9*; April 27, 1968; the Beatles are on the cover.
  G $20   **VG $30**   **NM $40**

○ **942.** *Rolling Stone #20*; October 26, 1968; Beatles cover story.
  G $15   **VG $22**   **NM $30**

○ **943.** *Rolling Stone #24*; December 21, 1968; the Beatles are on the cover.
  G $15   **VG $22**   **NM $30**

○ **944.** *Rolling Stone #46*; November 15, 1969; Beatles cover story.
  G $15   **VG $22**   **NM $30**

○ **945.** *Teen Set (Yellow Submarine Special Issue)*; 1968; *Yellow Submarine* cover plus twenty-page color insert section on the movie and two-page story on John and Cynthia.
  G $10   **VG $15**   **NM $20**

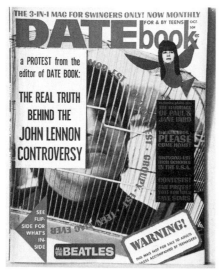

936

937

945

National/Mainstream Magazines

This section deals with all those magazines that are not teen or rock related. Most magazines listed in this section have a Beatle or the Beatles on the cover with an article inside. We gave listed a selection of the most collectible magazines. Here are value ranges for magazines not listed individually:

Complete magazine with an article on the Beatles
     G $2 to $4   **VG $4 to $6**   **NM $6 to $10**

Complete magazine with a Beatle or Beatles on the cover
     G $4 to $9   **VG $6 to $12** **NM $8 to $18**

(Please refer to Condition/Grading guidelines at the beginning of the chapter for adjustments to values.)

○ **946.** *Avante-Garde* **#11;** March 1970; cover story on Lennon' Bag One drawings; can be found with black or red cover variation.
    G $15   **VG $25**   **NM $35**

○ **947.** *Cosmopolitan;* December 1964; cover story on John "Beatle with a future."
    G $20   **VG $30**   **NM $40**

○ **948.** *Down Beat;* November 16, 1967; cover story on the Beatles.
    G $10   **VG $15**   **NM $20**

○ **949.** *Down Beat;* January 23, 1969; Ringo is on the cover.
    G $6   **VG $9**   **NM $12**

○ **950.** *Down Beat;* January 22, 1970; Paul and John on the cover plus a review of "Abbey Road."
    G $10   **VG $15**   **NM $20**

○ **951.** *Jet;* July 1, 1965; the Beatles and Mary Wells cover plus story on "What the Beatles learned from Negroes."
    G $15   **VG $25**   **NM $35**

○ **952.** *Jet;* October 26, 1972; John, Yoko, and Dick Gregory cover story.
    G $15   **VG $25**   **NM $30**

*** A note on *Life* magazines. Most issues were sold by mail subscriptions. In some cases newsstand copies had a paper $3^1/_2$" x 14" banner attached on the left edge of the cover. This banner would list features in that weeks issue. Add 35% to the value if the banner is present.

○ **953.** *Life;* August 28, 1964; Beatles cover story; "They're here again and what a ruckus!"
    G $20   **VG $30**   **NM $40**

○ **954.** *Life;* July 24, 1967; Australian edition; Beatles cover story; "The new far-out Beatles."
    G $25   **VG $35**   **NM $50**

○ **955.** *Life;* September 13, 1968; Beatles cover story; part one of the 44-page serialization of *The Beatles Authorized Biography* by Hunter Davies.
    G $12   **VG $20**   **NM $25**

○ **956.** *Life;* September 20, 1968; part two of the 44-page serialization of *The Beatles Authorized Biography* by Hunter Davies.
    G $6   **VG $9**   **NM $12**

○ **957.** *Life;* November 7, 1969; "Paul is still with us" cover story; article about the death hoax.
    G $10   **VG $15**   **NM $20**

○ **958.** *Life;* April 16, 1971; Paul cover story; "The ex-Beatle tells his story."
    G $9   **VG $12**   **NM $18**

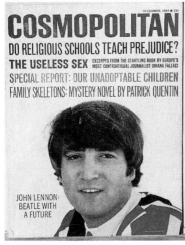

947

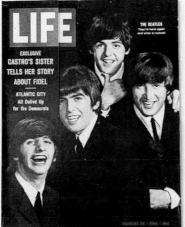

953

957

○ **959.**   *Look*; December 13, 1966; John cover story; "A shorn Beatle tries it on his own."
G $10   **VG $15**   **NM $20**

○ **960.**   *Look*; January 9, 1968; John by Avedon on the cover; eight-page pullout of the Beatles by Avedon.
G $20   **VG $30**   **NM $40**

○ **961.**   *Look*; March 18, 1969; John and Yoko cover story; "Beatle John & his girlfriend join forces and POW!"
G $10   **VG $15**   **NM $20**

○ **962.**   *Newsweek*; February 24, 1964; Beatles cover story; "Bugs about the Beatles."
G $20   **VG $30**   **NM $40**

○ **963.**   *Playboy*; February 1965; candid interviews of the Beatles by Jean Sheperd.
G $12   **VG $18**   **NM $25**

○ **964.**   *Post*; March 21, 1964; Beatles cover story plus original fiction by John; "The secret of the Beatles."
G $17   **VG $25**   **NM $35**

○ **965.**   *Post*; August 8, 1964; Beatles cover story; "Summer madness—the Beatles are back."
G $17   **VG $25**   **NM $35**

○ **966.**   *Post Display Poster*; for August 8, 1964 issue; 10" x 13 $^{1}/_{2}$"; cardboard poster advertises the August 8th issue of the (*Saturday Evening*) *Post*; the Beatles are pictured (as on the cover of the issue.)
G $50   **VG $75**   **NM $100**

○ **967.**   *Post*; August 27, 1966; Beatles as matadors cover; "Here they are again—the Beatles" article.
G $15   **VG $22**   **NM $30**

○ **968.**   *Post*; May 4, 1968; Beatles and Guru cover story.
G $9   **VG $12**   **NM $18**

960

964

965

966

967

968

969. ***Post***; May 18, 1968; Part 2 of the Beatles and Guru story; "There once was a guru from Rishikesh."
     G $5   **VG $7**   **NM $10**

970. ***Ramparts***; October 1967; cover story on John from *How I Won the War*.
     G $20   **VG $30**   **NM $40**

971. ***Ramparts***; July 1971; cover story on John and Yoko; "Inside Lennon: Interview with the radical Beatle"
     G $15   **VG $25**   **NM $35**

972. ***Science Digest***; November 1969; Ringo on the cover.
     G $5   **VG $8**   **NM $10**

973. ***Screw*** **#18**; June 27, 1969; John and Yoko cover and interview.
     G $15   **VG $22**   **NM $30**

974. ***Time***; September 22, 1967; Beatles cover story; "The Beatles/Their new incarnation."
     G $20   **VG $30**   **NM $40**

975. ***TV Junior*** **#2**; July 1964; Beatles cover story.
     G $15   **VG $22**   **NM $30**

976. ***TV Junior***; September 1964; Beatles cover story.
     G $15   **VG $2**   **NM $30**

977. ***Yale Literary Magazine***; March 1968; *Yellow Submarine* front and back cover; 24-page story about the movie.
     G $25   **VG $35**   **NM $50**

970

974

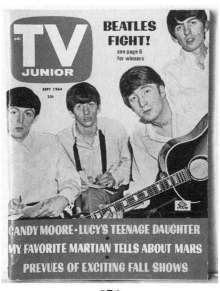

976

977

Newspaper & Magazine Supplements/Tabloids

Many magazines and newspapers ran special articles on the Beatles to attract readers. These were often found in the Sunday newspaper magazines, such as *Parade,* or included as a bonus with the regular paper in the form of a pull-out section. Magazines also used special supplements as a bonus with their regular issues, or as an item that could be ordered by mail.

The magazine and regional or nationally distributed newspaper supplements usually covered topics of a general nature, such as a Beatles' concert tour, new movie, etc. Of much more interest to collector's are supplements produced by local newspapers. These usually covered local appearances, and often included pictures taken by the paper's own photographers as well as interviews obtained by local reporters. Some of these photos, interviews, press conferences, etc. were not picked up by the wire services and remain unique to these supplements.

Tabloids are the newsprint magazines usually found near the checkout counters of grocery stores. The Beatles, both collectively and individually, were good copy for these wildly sensational and speculative publications.

Value is dependant upon the content of the article, in terms of both text and photos. At the lower end of the scale would be a Sunday supplement with only a short article inside. The highest value would be an eight- to sixteen-page special covering a local Beatle appearance with unique photos and interesting interviews and sidebars.

Value ranges for Newspaper & Magazine Supplements/ Tabloids:

	G	VG	NM
Nationally distributed supplement or tabloid with article and photos	$5 to $10	$7 to $15	$10 to $20
Mail order only supplement	$7 to $12	$10 to $18	$15 to $25
Local supplement with original photos and text	$10 to $15	$15 to $20	$20 to $35

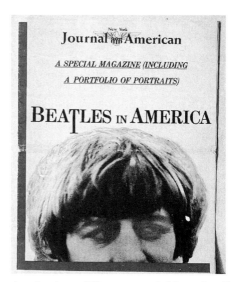 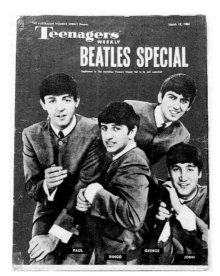 

A selection of Newspaper & Magazine Supplements/Tabloids.

A selection of Newspaper & Magazine Supplements/Tabloids.

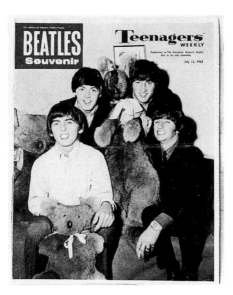

A selection of Newspaper & Magazine Supplements/Tabloids.

Comic Books

○ **978.** *Batman #222;* June 1970; D.C. Comics; Paul death hoax take-off.
G **$15**   VG **$22**   NM **$30**

○ **979.** *The Beatles Complete Life Stories;* 1964; Dell Comics; Note: As with other cross-over collectibles, the price on this item has been driven up, in this case by comic book collectors. The comic must be near perfect to command a price over $100.
G **$35**   VG **$75**   NM **$150**

○ **980.** *Girls' Romance #109;* June 1965; D.C. Comics; Beatles on cover.
G **$20**   VG **$30**   NM **$40**

○ **981.** *Go-Go #2;* 1966; Charlton Comics; Beatle cover photo and story.
G **$10**   VG **$15**   NM **$20**

○ **982.** *Go-Go and Animal #8;* March 1968; Tower Comics; Beatles on front and back cover.
G **$9**   VG **$12**   NM **$18**

978

979

980

983

985

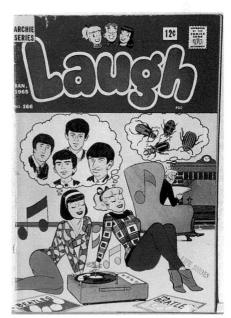

986

○ **983.** *Heart Throbs* **#101;** May 1966; D.C. Comics; Beatles on the cover.
G $20   **VG $30**   **NM $40**

○ **984.** *Herbie* **#5;** October 1964; American Comics; "Herbie, Boy Beetle" story.
G $12   **VG $18**   **NM $25**

○ **985.** *Jimmy Olsen* **#79;** September 1964; D.C. Comics "The Red-Headed Beatle of 1,000 B.C." story.
G $9   **VG $12**   **NM $18**

○ **986.** *Laugh* **#166;** January 1965; Archie Comics Beatles on the cover.
G $9   **VG $12**   **NM $18**

○ **987.** *My Little Margie* **#54;** November 1964; Charlton Comics; Beatles on the cover plus story titled "Beatlemania."
G $30   **VG $45**   **NM $60**

○ **988.** *Smile* **#1;** 1970; Drawing of John and Nixon on the cover.
G $15   **VG $22**   **NM $30**

○ **989.** *Strange Tales* **#130;** March 1965; Marvel Comics "The Thing Meets The Beatles" story.
G $ 10   **VG $ 15**   **NM $ 20**

○ **990.** *Summer Love* **#46;** October 1965; Charlton Comics; Beatles on the cover and one story is titled "The Beatles were my downfall."
G $20   **VG $30**   **NM $40**

○ **991.** *Summer Love* **#47;** October 1966; Charlton Comics; Beatles on the cover and one story is titled "The Beatles saved my romance."
G $20   **VG $30**   **NM $40**

○ **992.** *Teen Confessions* **#31;** December 1964; Charlton Comics; Beatles on the cover.
G $20   **VG $30**   **NM $40**

○ **993.** *Teen Confessions* **#37;** January 1966; Charlton Comics; Beatles on the cover and one story is titled "Bring on the Beatles."
G $20   **VG $30**   **NM $40**

○ **994.** *Tippy Teen* **#5;** June 1966; Tower Comics; Beatle gag on front cover and Beatle pinup inside.

G $10   **VG $15**   **NM $20**

Yellow Submarine; (see item #472).

987

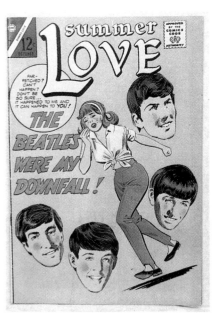

990

991

8

Sheet Music
and Music Books

SHEET MUSIC

Sheet music was issued for many of the songs recorded by the Beatles. Most sheets had photos of the Beatles on the cover. Some of the earliest sheets were issued by the Gil Music Corp. ("I Saw Her Standing There," "From Me To You," and "She Loves You"); the Duchess Music Corp. ("I Want To Hold Your Hand"); Concertone Songs Inc. ("Please Please Me" on VJ 581); and the Jobete Music Co. Inc. ("Money"). The majority of sheets were issued by three Charles Hansen subsidiaries: Keys, Charles Hansen Publications, and the Sheet Music Institute. From March 1964 to August 1967 many of the sheets were issued by Keys; from October 1965 to May 1970 many of the sheets were issued by Charles Hansen Publications; and from October 1967 to September 1969 many were issued by the Sheet Music Institute. After 1970 most of the Beatles sheet music was issued with plain covers by Warners Brothers.

On most of the Keys, Hansen, and Sheet Music Institute sheets there is a five-digit number in the lower left-hand corner of the cover. These numbers generally run in sequence from year to year. A copyright date inside the sheet music would be the original date the song was copyrighted (not necessarily the date the sheet music was printed). The date of issue on most Keys, Hansen, and Sheet Music Institute sheet music can be determined by looking on the back cover in the lower right-hand corner at a group of letters and numbers which were a date code. From 1964 to late 1966 the code looking like this: F25M 166. The number 166 translated to January 1966. The last three digits of the code were the month and year of issue. From late 1966 to 1970 the code looking like this: 267/S/13381. The number 267 translated to February 1967. The first three digits of the code were the month and year of issue. A similar formula can be applied to music books.

We have listed value ranges for original 1960s issues of sheet music with the Beatles pictured on the cover:

(G)	(VG)	(NM)
$5-12	$8-$20	$10 - $25

Some of the nicer sheets are those with color covers of the group. Earlier sheets which credit the Beatles as playing on Vee Jay, Atco, etc. are also in the higher range.

Another factor which makes collecting sheet music interesting is the different variations of sheet music available. Here is a list of some of the variations that can be found.

1. Different songwriter credits. For example, the first issue of the sheet for "Flying" from February 1968 credits Lennon and McCartney. The sheet was reissued in March 1968 crediting all four Beatles.

2. Different color covers.

3. Different paper stock. Sometimes changing from glossy to flat.

4. Different cover photos. For example, the December 1965 sheet for "We Can Work It Out" had the cover photo printed reversed. It was reissued in January 1966 with the photo printed correctly. The photo on "Let It Be" was reduced approximately 75% from the February 1970 edition to the March 1970 edition. These are just a few of the many variations. Undoubtedly there are many more.

Here is a partial listing of sheet music that we know is available from 1963-1970. Note: some were not necessarily issued the same year that the song was first recorded.

All of these are 8$\frac{1}{2}$" x 11"

"All I've Got to Do"
"All My Loving"
"All You Need is Love"
"And I Love Her"
"Another Girl"
"Ask Me Why"

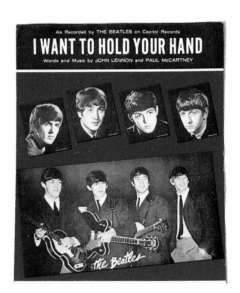
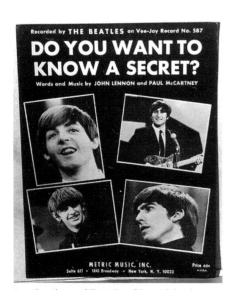

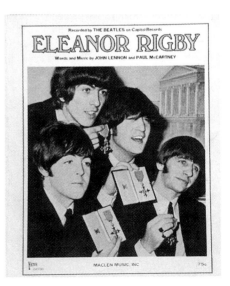

A selection of Beatles Sheet Music.

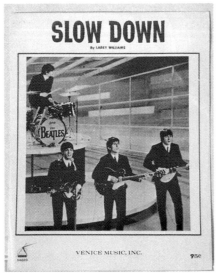  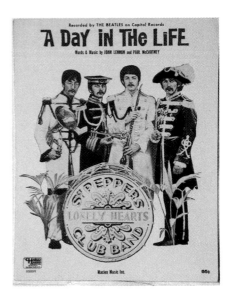

A selection of Beatles Sheet Music.

"Baby, You're A Rich Man"
"Back in The U.S.S.R."
"Bad Boy"
"The Ballad of John and Yoko"
"Because"
"Birthday"
"Blackbird"
"Blue Jay Way"
"Boys"
"Can't Buy Me Love"
"Carry That Weight"
"Chains"
"Come Together"
"The Continuing Story of Bungalow Bill"
"Cry Baby Cry"
"Cry For A Shadow"
"A Day in The Life"
"Day Tripper"
"Dear Prudence"
"Dizzy Miss Lizzie"
"Do You Want to Know A Secret?"
"Don't Bother Me"
"Don't Let Me Down"
"Don't Pass Me By"
"Drive My Car"
"Eight Days A Week"
"Eleanor Rigby"
"Everybody's Got Something to Hide"
"Flying"
"For You Blue"
"Get Back"
"Glass Onion"
"Good Night"
"Happiness is A Warm Gun"
"A Hard Day's Night"

"Hello, Goodbye"
"Help!"
"Helter Skelter"
"Here Comes The Sun"
"Here, There and Everywhere"
"Hey Jude"
"Hold Me Tight"
"Honey Pie"
"I Am the Walrus"
"I Don't Want to Spoil the Party"
"I Feel Fine"
"I Me Mine"
"I Should Have Known Better"
"I Wanna Be Your Man"
"I Will"
"I'll Cry Instead"
"I'll Follow the Sun"
"I'll Get You"
"I'm A Loser"
"I'm Down"
"I'm Happy Just to Dance With You"
"I'm So Tired"
"If I Fell"
"The Inner Light"
"It Won't Be Long"
"Julia"
"Kansas City"
"Lady Madonna"
"Let It Be"
"Little Child"
"Long, Long, Long"
"Long Tall Sally"
"Lovely Rita"
"Lucy in the Sky with Diamonds"
"Magical Mystery Tour"

"Maxwell's Silver Hammer"
"Michelle"
"Misery"
"Mr. Moonlight"
"My Bonnie"
"The Night Before"
"Not A Second Time"
"Nowhere Man"
"Ob-La-Di, Ob-La-Da"
"Octopus's Garden"
"Oh! Darling"
"Old Brown Shoe"
"P.S. I Love You"
"Paperback Writer"
"Penny Lane"
"Piggies"
"Please Mr. Postman"
"Rain"
"Revolution"
"Ringo's Theme"
"Rocky Raccoon"
"Rock and Roll Music"
"Roll Over Beethoven"
"Savoy Truffle"
"Sexy Sadie"
"Sgt. Pepper's Lonely Hearts Club Band"
"She Came in Through The Bathroom Window"
"She's A Woman"
"Slow Down"
"Something"
"Strawberry Fields Forever"
"Take Out Some Insurance on Me"
"A Taste of Honey"
"Taxman"
"Tell Me What You See"
"Thank You Girl"
"There's A Devil in Her Heart"
"Ticket to Ride"
"Twist and Shout"
"We Can Work it Out"
"What Goes On"

"When I'm Sixty-Four"
"While My Guitar Gently Weeps"
"Yellow Submarine"
"Yer Blues"
"Yes It Is"
"Yesterday"
"You Can't Do That"
"You Know My Name (Look up the Number)"
"You're Going to Lose That Girl"
"You've Got to Hide Your Love Away"
"You've Really Got A Hold on Me"
"Your Mother Should Know"

All of these are 9" x 12"

"Do You Want to Know A Secret?"
"My Bonnie Lies Over the Ocean"
"From Me to You"
"I Saw Her Standing There"
"I Want to Hold Your Hand"
"Money"
"Please Please Me"
"Rock & Roll Music"
"Roll Over Beethoven"
"She Loves You"

(NOTE: "She Loves You" and "From Me to You" were reprinted in 1981. The reprints are almost identical to the originals.)

All of these are 7" x 10¹/₂"

An unusual variation were the "5-Way Hansenork (Instrumentation)" issued by Hansen in 1969. The photo was printed sideways and wrapped around the front and back of the sheet. Six titles were available:
H-91 "Hey Jude"
H-93 "(The) Fool on the Hill"
H-99 "Glass Onion"
H-116 "Don't Pass Me By"
H-145 "While My Guitar Gently Weeps"
H-296 "Yesterday"

MUSIC BOOKS

"Music books" were issued for Beatle albums starting with *Something New*. Some albums would have different books issued for Vocals, Piano, etc. For example there were six different music books issued for "A Hard Day's Night". The six different were: 1A-Vocal; 1B-Guitar; 1C-All Organ; 1D-Combo; 1E-Accordian Book; and 1F-Home Players Book. Many music books would have photo insert sections. (Values reflect complete music books. Music books missing photo insert sections would be valued at 50% of values listed.)

Price Ranges for Music Books:

(G)	(VG)	(NM)
$7 to $12	$10 to $18	$15 to $25

There were other Beatle-related music books not issued specifically on one album. Some examples are: *The Beatle Book of Recorded Hits* (1964); *New Beatle Guitar Hits* (1964); *The Beatles 4 Way Fake Combo Book* (1964); *The Golden Beatles* (1965); *Everybody Plays the Beatles* (1970), etc. These type of music books sell for approximately $10 to $15 in NM shape.

○ **995.** *The Apple Songbook* is the music book with the highest value. The *Apple Songbook* was issued in 1973 and has 216 pages. The book includes music by many Apple artists including: George Harrison, Ringo Starr, Badfinger, Mary Hopkin, Yoko Ono, Lon & Derrek Van Eaton, Billy Preston, Jackie Lomax and the Radha Krishna Temple.

G $40   **VG $60**   **NM $80**

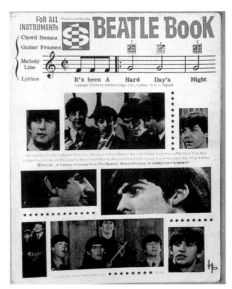

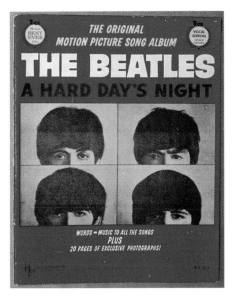

A selection of Beatles Music Books.

9

Movie Items

Most items in this chapter were sent to theater owners to promote the movie. The items were supposed to be returned to the National Screen Service or destroyed after being used to promote the movie. Many times the items gathered dust in theater basements or were taken home by patrons or employees. We have listed some of the terms used when discussing movie memorabilia.

Posters

One Sheet: 27" x 42" (a standard movie poster).

Three Sheet: 41" x 77" (actually in two pieces).

Six sheet: 72" x 72" (actually in two pieces).

The above three posters are on paper stock and normally were sent to the theater pre-folded.

The posters listed below were made of a thicker (heavy paper) stock. These posters were sent to the theaters flat or rolled.

Window Card: 14" x 22"; there was a blank space at the top for the theater owner to print its name and play-dates.

Insert: 14" x 36"

Half Sheet/Jumbo Lobby Card: 22" x 28"

Title Display/Banner Poster: 24" x 82" (displayed horizontally); other sizes: 30" x 40" and 40" x 60"

Definitions

Lobby Cards: 11" x 14" set of eight; each card is numbered at the bottom (1 through 8); sent to theaters flat.

Movie Number: A two-part number issued by the National Screen Service to every movie in the U.S. For example, the number for *A Hard Day's Night* is 64/261. The first number (64) is the year of release—1964. The second number (261) is the unique number issued to a movie that year. An "R" placed before the first number (i.e., R84/261) denotes a re-release from 1984. The movie number can be found in the lower right-hand corner of posters, lobby cards, and stills. The number is sometimes stamped on the reverse of a pre-folded poster.

Pressbook: A six- to sixteen-page booklet sent to theater owners prior to booking a movie. The booklet gives movie synopsis, radio, TV and merchandising tie-ins, ad mats, etc. The booklet describes the different posters available for the theater owner to order.

Stills: 8" x 10" photos used to promote the movie; movie title and movie number should be on the bottom of still.

Grading Guidelines

Small tac holes in the corners of movie posters do not greatly reduce their value. Tears (mended or unmended) do negatively affect the price. Most one-sheet, three-sheet, and six-sheet movie posters were sent pre-folded. Other sizes of posters were sent rolled or flat. If one of these other sizes of posters has been folded, then it would be valued at or below the VG price depending on the size of the crease and the effect it has on the poster's appearance.

NOTE: Values have been listed for the ONE SHEET style of poster.

Apply the following percentages for the listed size

Three Sheet—125%
Six Sheet—125%
Window Card—60%
Insert—75%
Half Sheet—75%
30" x 40"—100%
40" x 60"—100%

A Hard Day's Night 1964 (Movie number 64/261)

○ **996.** **Lobby Cards**; set of eight different cards; value is for each. ★ *Repro Alert*
G $30   VG $55   NM $75

○ **997.** **Poster;** one sheet. ★ *Repro Alert*
G $150   VG $250   NM $350

○ **998.** **Poster;** title display/banner.
G $200   VG $300   NM $400

○ **999.** **Poster;** 11" x 14"; advertising the paperback book tie-in and the movie; on heavy stock paper; red, white and black.
G $200   VG $300   NM $400

○ **1000.** **Premiere Menu;** special menu for supper party at the Dorchester in London, following the Royal Premiere.
G $125   VG $190   NM $250

○ **1001.** **Premiere Program (U.K.);** at the London Pavilion July 6, 1964; a benefit sponsored by the Variety Club of Great Britain.
G $125   VG $190   NM $250

○ **1002.** **Premiere Program (U.K.);** Northern premiere in Liverpool on July 10, 1964 to benefit the Liverpool Boys Association.
G $125   VG $190   NM $250

○ **1003.** **Press Information Kit;** envelope contains folder which includes four 8" x 10" B&W stills and several informational sheets on United Artists letterhead.
G $150   VG $225   NM $300

○ **1004.** **Press Show Invitation (U.K.);** 4½" x 6"; invitation to a morning screening of the movie at the Leicester Square Theater prior to the premiere July 6, 1964.
G $100   VG $150   NM $200

○ **1005.** **Pressbook;** 13" x 18"; twelve pages; some pressbooks came with an insert page advertising supplement; add 15% to value if present.
G $35   VG $55   NM $75

○ **1006.** **Preview Ticket;** unused: 9" x 3¼"; used: 7½" x 3¼"; advance or preview souvenir ticket made of cardboard with die-cut Beatle photo; various colors; add 50% to value if unused; there were also other variations of preview tickets for this movie.
G $10   VG $15   NM $20

○ **1007.** **Program;** made by Program Publishing Co.; 8¼" x 10½"; sold at the theater; two cover variations: one has red borders, other has blue borders.
G $25   VG $35   NM $50

996—#2

996—#8

998

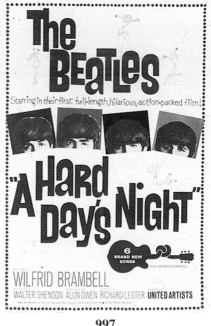

997

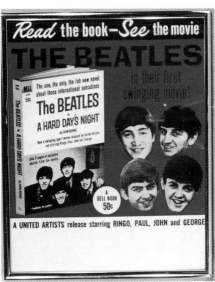

999

1000

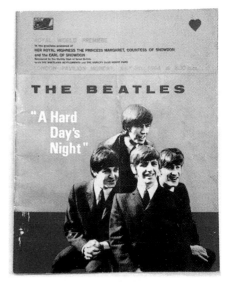

1001

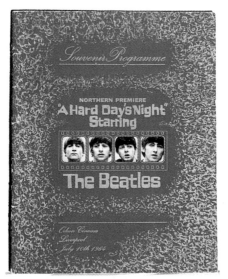

1002

1004

○ **1008.** **Souvenir Badge;** 3³/₄" diameter; cardboard with B&W photo; "I've Got My Beatle Movie Ticket Have You?" printed in red; some have hole at top for string.
G $6   **VG $9**   **NM $12**

○ **1009.** **Stills;** B&W; various issued; value is for each still.
G $5   **VG $7**   **NM $10**

The Beatles Come To Town 1964 (Movie Number 64/517)

○ **1010.** **Ad Mat;** 8¹/₂" x 14"; B&W flyer sent to the theater owner.
G $25   **VG $35**   **NM $50**

○ **1011.** **Poster;** one sheet; yellow and pink day-glo colors; "Ya Ya Ya" at top with song titles on bottom.
G $150   **VG $300**   **NM $400**

○ **1012.** **Poster;** one sheet; yellow and pink day-glo colors; "She Loves You, Yea Yea Yea!" at top.
G $150   **VG $300**   **NM $400**

○ **1013.** **Poster;** one sheet; group photo at top with red and white background.
G $175   **VG $325**   **NM $425**

○ **1014.** **Poster (Canada);** half sheet; gold with red and black print; B&W group photo in corner.
G $125   **VG $200**   **NM $300**

Note: The above four posters are the only sizes that were available for this short feature.

○ **1015.** **Stills;** B&W; value is for each still.
G $9   **VG $12**   **NM $18**

1006a

1006b

1007

1008

1011

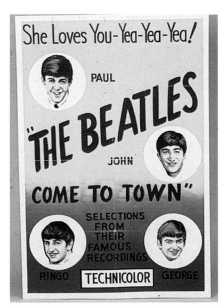

1012

Help! 1965
(Movie Number 65/293)

○ **1016.** **Lobby Cards;** set of eight different cards; value is per card.
   G $30   VG $55   NM $75

○ **1017.** **Poster;** one sheet ★ *Repro Alert*
   G $160   VG $275   NM $375

1016—#1

1013

1016—#5

1014

1016—#6

1017

1016—#7

1019

1020

1021

1022

○ **1018.** **Poster, Advance;** 40" x 60"; similar art to one sheet; "Get your tickets in advance for Special Gala Premiere Performances _____ " and "First Come First Served! Tickets go on sale _____ . These Special Tickets will guarantee you a seat. A Souvenir Tag will be presented to each ticket buyer" printed on the poster, with space left for the theater owner to fill in dates.
  G $200 **VG $325** **NM $450**

○ **1019.** **Poster;** Title Display/Banner.
  G $200 **VG $300** **NM $400**

○ **1020.** **Premiere Program (U.K.);** a Variety Club of Great Britain benefit at the London Pavilion on July 29, 1965.
  G $110 **VG $175** **NM $225**

○ **1021.** **Press Information Kit;** over 20 B&W photos, over 50 pages of information in a 10" x 13" envelope with movie logo.
  G $150 **VG $225** **NM $300**

○ **1022.** **Pressbook;** 13" x 18"; sixteen pages.
  G $35 **VG $55** **NM $75**

○ **1023.** **Preview Ticket;** unused: $8^1/_2$" x $3^3/_4$"; used: 7" x $3^3/_4$"; made of cardboard in various designs; add 50% if unused.
  G $10 **VG $15** **NM $20**

○ **1024.** **Souvenir Badge;** $3^3/_4$" diameter; cardboard with B&W photo; "I Needed Help! So I Got my Beatles Movie Ticket!" printed in red; some had hole at top for string.
  G $9 **VG $12** **NM $15**

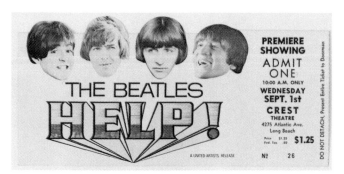

1023a

1024

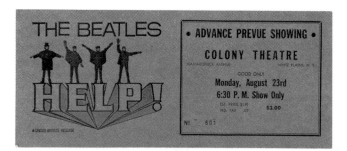

1023b

○ **1025.   Stills**; B&W; various issued; value is per still.
　　　　G $6　　　　　　VG $9　　　　　　NM $12

Combo *A Hard Day's Night/Help!* 1965 (Movie Number 64/261 65/293) Movie Number 65/384 stamped on back of one sheets.

○ **1026.   Poster;** one sheet or 40" x 60" size; a special poster for this special double feature; billed as "UN-BEATLE-BLE!"; these are the only two poster sizes available for this special double feature release.
　　　　G $200　　　　　VG $325　　　　　NM $450

Yellow Submarine 1968 (Movie Number 68/310)

○ **1027.   Lobby Cards**; set of eight different cards; value is per card.
　　　　G $35　　　　　VG $60　　　　　NM $80

1027—#1

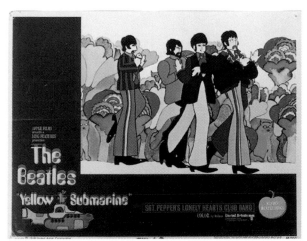

1027—#6

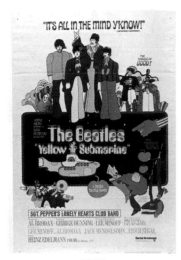

1028

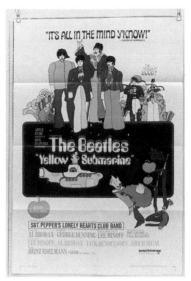

1029

1033

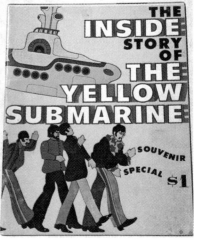

1034

○ **1028. Poster;** one sheet; "A dozen Beatle songs" in apple plus Sgt. Pepper's Band on poster.
G $200   **VG $350**   **NM $450**

○ **1029. Poster;** one sheet; "Eleven Beatle Songs" in apple; no Sgt. Pepper's Band on poster.
★ *Repro Alert*
G $175   **VG $300**   **NM $400**

○ **1030. Poster;** Title Display/Banner.
G $200   **VG $300**   **NM $400**

○ **1031. Premiere Ribbon;** 7" x 2³/₄"; two color ribbon worn at the premier of the movie.
G $45   **VG $70**   **NM $90**

○ **1032. Press Information Kit;** 8¹/₂" x 11"; yellow envelope with portholes; fact sheet inside; two of the Beatles look out portholes when the fact sheet is inserted.
G $75   **VG $150**   **NM $200**

○ **1033. Pressbook;** 13" x 18"; eight pages; of special interest because two of the pages list various companies licensed to produce Yellow Sub products.
G $30   **VG $45**   **NM $60**

○ **1034. Program;** 8¹/₂" x 11"; theater program titled "The Inside Story of The Yellow Sub"
G $35   **VG $55**   **NM $75**

○ **1035. Stills;** B&W; various issued; value is per still; one set is numbered in the lower right-hand corner "YS-M-1" through "YS-M-30"; some of this set had a description of the scene on a piece of paper glued to the back of the still.
G $6   **VG $9**   **NM $12**

○ **1036 Stills;** color set of eight different stills; featuring the same scenes as on the lobby cards; value is per still.
G $15   **VG $25**   **NM $35**

1039

Let It Be 1970
(Movie Number 70/169)

○ **1037.** **Lobby Cards;** set of eight different color cards; value is per card.
　　G $25　　　VG $35　　　NM $50

○ **1038.** **Poster**; one sheet.
　　G $75　　　VG $135　　　NM $175

○ **1039.** **Poster;** Title Display/Banner.
　　G $175　　　VG $260　　　NM $350

○ **1040.** **Pressbook;** 11" x 17"; six pages.
　　G $20　　　VG $30　　　NM $40

○ **1041.** **Preview Ticket;** 4" x 9"; B&W; Beatles faces shown as on album cover; various size variations.
　　G $25　　　VG $35　　　NM $50

○ **1042.** **Stills**; B&W; various issued; value is per still.
　　G $4　　　VG $6　　　NM $8

○ **1043.** **Stills;** color set of eight different; featuring the same scenes as the lobby cards; value is per still.
　　G $10　　　VG $15　　　NM $20

1037

1038

1041a

1041b

Magical Mystery Tour
(Early 1970s release)

Note: *Magical Mystery Tour* was given a limited release in the early 1970s. These items were not from the National Screen Service. These items were made by Carson Entertainment Group which promoted the release.

1044

○ **1044.   Poster;** 23" x 29"; featured artwork from the album cover.
G $75   VG $110   NM $150

○ **1045.   Pressbook;** 8$\frac{1}{2}$" x 11"; four pages.
G $20   VG $30   NM $40

Go Go Mania 1965
(Movie Number 65/195)

American International produced this teen film which featured numerous groups including the Animals, Billy J. Kramer, Peter and Gordon, and the Beatles. Posters feature artwork with five long-haired lads.

○ **1046.   Lobby Card;** according to the pressbook one of the cards features Paul and George singing at microphone; value is for this card.
G $35   VG $50   NM $75

○ **1047.   Poster;** one sheet.
G $25   VG $35   NM $50

○ **1048.   Stills;** B&W; various issued; there are at least four which feature the Beatles; value is for stills featuring the Beatles.
G $7   VG $10   NM $15

How I Won The War 1968
(Movie Number 68/13)

○ **1049.   Lobby Cards;** color set of eight different card; John is featured on cards #1, 2, and 5; value is for set.
G $75   VG $110   NM $150

○ **1050.   Poster;** one sheet.
G $30   VG $45   NM $60

○ **1051.   Poster;** Title Display/Banner.
G $75   VG $110   NM $150

○ **1052.   Pressbook;** 11" x 17"; six pages.
G $15   VG $22   NM $30

○ **1053.   Stills;** B&W; various issued; value is per still that features John.
G $4   VG $6   NM $8

○ **1054.   Stills;** color set of eight different; value is for the set.
G $35   VG $55   NM $75

Candy 1969
(Movie Number 69/37)

○ **1055.   Lobby Cards;** set of eight different color cards; value is for cards that feature Ringo.
G $12   VG $1   NM $25

○ **1056.   Poster;** one sheet.
G $15   VG $25   NM $35

○ **1057.   Pressbook**
G $10   VG $15   NM $20

○ **1058.   Stills;** B&W; various issued.
G $3   VG $4   NM $6

○ **1059.   Stills;** color set of eight different cards; value is for stills that feature Ringo.
G $6   VG $9   NM $12

The Magic Christian 1970
(Movie Number 70/57)

○ **1060.   Lobby Cards;** set of eight different color cards; all cards feature a small picture of Ringo in border art; value is for these cards which feature Ringo in the scene photo: card #1, 3, 6, and 7; other cards are valued at $15 each in NM shape.
G $12   VG $18   NM $25

○ **1061.** **Poster;** one sheet.
G $15   VG $25   NM $35

○ **1062.** **Pressbook;** 10" x 15"; 28 pages.
G $10   VG $15   NM $20

○ **1063.** **Stills;** B&W; various issued; value is per still with Ringo.
G $3   VG $4   NM $6

○ **1064.** **Stills;** color set of eight different cards; value is for stills that feature Ringo.
G $5   VG $8   NM $12

200 Motels 1971
(Movie number 71/344)

○ **1065.** **Lobby Card;** Ringo appears on card #5 (this is only card in set which Ringo appears on).
G $10   VG $15   NM $20

○ **1066.** **Poster;** one sheet.
G $20   VG $30   NM $40

○ **1067.** **Pressbook**
G $10   VG $15   NM $20

○ **1068.** **Stills;** B&W; various issued; value is for stills featuring Ringo.
G $3   VG $5   NM $6

○ **1069.** **Stills;** color; value is for still featuring Ringo.
G $6   VG $9   NM $12

Blindman 1972
(Movie number 72/109)

○ **1070.** **Lobby Cards;** color set of four different cards; Ringo is only on card #1; value is for set.
G $25   VG $35   NM $50

○ **1071.** **Poster;** one sheet.
G $15   VG $22   NM $30

○ **1072.** **Poster;** Title Display/Banner.
G $45   VG $70   NM $95

○ **1073.** **Pressbook**
G $10   VG $15   NM $20

○ **1074.** **Stills;** B&W; various issued stills; value is for stills that feature Ringo.
G $3   VG $4   NM $6

○ **1075.** **Stills;** color set of eight different; value is for stills that feature Ringo; Ringo is featured on still #1, 6, and 7.
G $5   VG $7   NM $10

Concert for Bangladesh 1972
(Movie number 72/135)

○ **1076.** **Lobby Cards;** color set of eight different cards; value is for cards that feature George and/or Ringo.
G $15   VG $25   NM $35

○ **1077.** **Poster;** one sheet; A or B style; "A" style has photo similar to cover of the LP; "B" style has photos of George, Dylan, and Russell; add 25% for "B" style.
G $25   VG $35   NM $50

○ **1078.** **Poster;** Title Display/Banner; day-glo colors
G $60   VG $90   NM $125

○ **1079.** **Pressbook;** 8$\frac{1}{2}$" x 14".
G $10   VG $15   NM $20

○ **1080.** **Stills**; B&W; various issued; value is for stills that feature Ringo or George.
G $3   VG $5   NM $6

○ **1081.** **Stills;** color set of eight different; value is for stills that feature Ringo or George.
G $6   VG $9   NM $12

Another movie item available is 16 and 35 millimeter film of the Beatles' movies and cartoons. It is possible to purchase theater and TV prints of the Beatles' movies and cartoons through film collector's newspapers and at film conventions. Coming attractions trailers can also be found. Trailers are three-to-five-minute coming attractions films shown between movies at the theater. Television spots (ads) for movies are generally shorter, found in 30-second and 60 second lengths. A collector will need special equipment, including a projector, to view these films. The collector will also need to become versed in film-collecting terminology. Film quality varies; prints can be worn, have colors that are changing, be missing footage, be bad dupes, etc. So let the buyer beware, unless you can view the entire film prior to purchase. Or better yet, find a reputable dealer who stands behind his merchandise.

10

Record Promotion Items

This chapter lists some of the many promotional items which were manufactured to help sell Beatle records. These items were sent to record stores and radio stations to promote new releases. Some were nationally distributed; others only regionally. The majority of items were from Capitol Records beginning, with the "Meet The Beatles" album in January 1964.

The posters, displays, etc. were to be used for the duration of a promotion and then destroyed. Most other types of memorabilia were available for purchase to the general public. To get record promotion items you had to know someone "in the business" or be lucky enough to have the record store give you a poster when the promotion was over. It is difficult to place a value on some posters and displays because of their rarity. Values can vary widely on some of these items because they are seldom seen for sale. Large displays and motion displays are difficult to find in excellent shape because of their size and number of parts. Complete displays bring the highest price. Only half of a display will not necessarily bring half of the price of the complete display. A word of caution: as with other Beatle memorabilia, there are reproductions of some of these promo posters on the market. A repro is not always easy to detect without having an original to compare it to. Original promo posters have photographs and Capitol logos which are clear and detailed.

Items in this chapter are listed chronologically by the date of release of the album they promoted.

○ **1082.** **"The Beatles Are Coming!" Sticker;** 2" x 3"; peel and stick; white with orange print; four wigs shown along with above slogan; add 100% if sticker is unused; (this is one of the earliest U.S. memorabilia items).
  G $15   **VG $22**   **NM $30**

○ **1083.** **"Meet The Beatles" LP Bin Divider;** 12" x 14½"; B&W on cardboard; pictures the album with "Beatles!" above it.
  G $200   **VG $300**   **NM $400**

1082

1083

○ **1084.** **"Meet The Beatles" Poster;** $20\frac{1}{2}$" x $14\frac{1}{2}$"; white background with B&W photo of group, the "Meet the Beatles" album, and the "I Want to Hold Your Hand" 45-rpm picture sleeve with printing in red.
G $400   **VG $600**   **NM $800**

○ **1085.** **"Meet The Beatles" Standee;** similar to above, but made of cardboard with an easel on the back. ★*Repro Alert*
G $500   **VG $750**   **NM $1,000**

○ **1086.** **"Meet The Beatles" Motion Display;** 31" x 26"; made of cardboard; resembles the "I Want to Hold Your Hand" 45-rpm picture sleeve; the Beatles' heads rock back and forth powered by a battery operated motor.
G $4,000   **VG $6,000**   **NM $10,000**

○ **1087.** **"The Beatles Are Here!" Poster;** 25" x 11"; white with red print reads "The Beatles Are Here! Available on Capitol 45's and Lp's."
G $250   **VG $375**   **NM $500**

○ **1088.** **Second Album Poster;** 25" x 10"; orange poster with black print reads "The Beatles Second Album is Here On Capitol Records Now!"
G $250   **VG $375**   **NM $500**

○ **1089.** **Second Album Poster;** 42" x 54"; an enlargement of the album cover with song titles; a small picture of the "Meet The Beatles" album is at the bottom; "The Beatles on Capitol Are The Greatest!" is printed on bottom.
G $700   **VG $1,100**   **NM $1,400**

○ **1090.** **Second Album Display;** B&W cardboard heads of John, Paul, and George (4" to $5\frac{1}{2}$" tall); Ringo's head is printed on a 12"-tall piece of cardboard with the word balloon "Just Out! The Beatles Second Album"; all attach to the album cover.
G $1,000   **VG $1,500**   **NM $2,000**

○ **1091.** *A Hard Day's Night* **Poster;** 1964; $12\frac{1}{4}$" x $14\frac{1}{4}$"; album cover shown with "NOW IN STOCK" in white print above it.
G $250   **VG $375**   **NM $500**

1086

1088

1087

1089

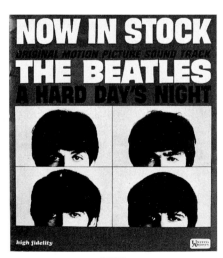

1091

○ **1092.** **"Something New" LP Bin Divider;** 1964; 12" x 14^1/$_2$"; B&W on cardboard; "Something New" album cover shown with "This Browser Box Reserved For The Beatles' New Capitol Album! Look For It Here About July 29th" written above.
G $200   **VG $300**   **NM $400**

○ **1093.** **"Something New" Poster;** 1964; 12^3/$_4$" x 11^3/$_4$"; pre-release poster pictures album cover, sticker reads "Available About July 20! Worth Waiting for!"
G $200   **VG $300**   **NM $400**

○ **1094.** **"Something New" Poster;** 1964; 20" x 39"; album cover shown on right; "Here Now! The Beatles Newest and Greatest!" printed on left.
G $700   **VG $1,100**   **NM $1,400**

○ **1095.** **Vee Jay Records Poster;** 1964; 12" x 25"; a poster mounted on cardboard with color artwork of the group's faces; a cropped version of the poster was included in The Beatles vs. The Four Seasons album.
G $200   **VG $300**   **NM $400**

○ **1096.** **"The Beatles Story" Display;** a 50" x 34" top with a 39^1/$_2$" x 12" bottom; a display with a record bin to hold "The Beatles' Story" album and their first three albums; the color cardboard display was released at Christmas time in 1964; the Beatles are shown wearing Santa Claus outfits; "Happy Holidays from the Beatles" is printed below their photos.
G $2,000   **VG $3,000**   **NM $4,000**

○ **1097.** **"Beatles '65" Display;** 1964 - 20" x 20"; cardboard enlargement of album cover; bottom three photos project out as do the umbrellas the Beatles are holding; has two side flaps and easel for support.
G $700   **VG $1,100**   **NM $1,400**

○ **1098.** **"Beatles '65" Display;** 1964; 20" x 20"; cardboard enlargement of album cover; easel on back.
G $500   **VG $750**   **NM $1,000**

1093

1092

1095

1096

○ **1099.** **"Beatles '65" Poster;** 1964; 18" x 24"; pictures album cover; "Yeah, Yeah, We've Got It" printed at top; "And we have the gift of the year, too" with an arrow pointing to the Beatles Story album on bottom of poster.
G $500   VG $750   NM $1,000

○ **1100.** **"Beatles VI" Display;** 1965; 45½" x 23½"; three sections, made of cardboard; an enlargement of the album cover in the center section; the five previous Capitol album covers are pictured on the two side sections.
G $1,500   VG $2,200   NM $3,000

○ **1101.** **"Beatles VI" Poster;** 1965; 27" x 21"; an enlargement of the record jacket with small photos of the five previous Capitol albums under it; top reads "The Perfect Gift For The June Grad! Beatles VI is Here!"
G $700   VG $1,100   NM $1,400

○ **1102.** *Help!* **Bandage;** 1965; 3½" long; a white Curad bandage with "HELP BEATLES" printed in red numerous times; OP: came in a wrapper with "BEATLES HELP BEATLES" and "CAPITOL" printed in red; add 100% to value if bandage is in original wrapper; Note: The HELP! bandage dispenser was not made in the 1960s and is of recent vintage!
G $7   VG $10   NM $15

○ **1103.** *Help!* **Bandage;** 1965; 18" x 5"; adhesive sticker shaped like a bandage has "Ask for the Beatles HELP! Soundtrack" printed in red, pink, and black on a white background.
G $100   VG $150   NM $200

1099

1101

1100

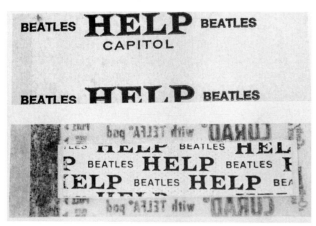

1102

1103

○ **1104.** *Help*! **Motion Display;** 1965; 24" x 24"; cardboard box-shaped display; the lid opens and four paper hands with the letters "H-E-L-P" come out; one of the hands has a paper ring; battery operated motor controls the lid and hands; OP: mailed in a brown cardboard box with "Beatles Help Display" and Capitol Records logo printed on it.
G $1,700   VG $2,500   NM $3,500

○ **1105.** *Help*! **Poster;** 1965; 23" x 48"; reads "Gift Problems?" in blue at top, suggests *Help*! and other Capitol and Angel gift ideas; pictures LP cover in black and white in center.
G $600   VG $900   NM $1,200

○ **1106.** **"Rubber Soul" Display;** 1965; 22$^{1}/_{2}$" x 22$^{1}/_{2}$"; cardboard enlargement of album cover with an easel on the back; some also came with a 6" x 22$^{1}/_{2}$" side flap; flap reads "The Beatles Sing 12 Brand New Songs!"; add 100% to price if it has flap.
G $400   VG $600   NM $800

○ **1107.** **"Rubber Soul" Poster;** 1965; 22" x 34$^{1}/_{4}$"; brown and white enlargement of album cover; "Great for Giving! Or Just Groovy Listening!" printed at bottom.
G $150   VG $225   NM $300

○ **1108.** **"Yesterday and Today" Poster;** 1966; 18" x 22"; "Butcher" cover photo; "INCREDIBLE!" printed at top. ★ *Repro Alert*
G $400   VG $600   NM $800

○ **1109.** **"Yesterday and Today" Poster;** 1966; 18" x 21"; "Trunk" cover photo; "Buy Beatles Here!" printed at top.
G $400   VG $600   NM $800

○ **1110.** **"Revolver" Poster;** 1966; 25" x 32"; enlargement of album cover with "BANG!" printed at top; "Including Yellow Submarine and Eleanor Rigby" printed at bottom. ★ *Repro Alert*
G $400   VG $600   NM $800

1106

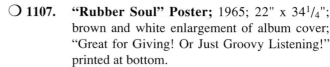

1107

1108

1109

1110

○ **1111.** **"Revolver" Poster;** 1966; $34\frac{1}{2}$" x $44\frac{1}{2}$"; reads "Welcome John Paul George Ringo" at top, album cover enlargement below.
G $500   **VG $750**   **NM $1,000**

○ **1112.** **"Sgt. Pepper" Display Kit;** 1967; consisted of the following items: six album jackets, four side panel inserts, four accessory tags, and misc. clips, etc.; two album covers used to make a hanging unit; side panel inserts have either a heart, Sgt. stripes, drum logo or arrow with "Sgt. Pepper's Lonely Hearts Club Band" or "New Beatle Portrait! Sgt. Pepper Cutouts! Printed Lyrics! and 13 New Beatle Songs!" printed on them; the side panels slide into the album jackets to make a countertop display.
G $600   **VG $900**   **NM $1,200**

○ **1113.** **"Sgt. Pepper" Poster;** 1967; 25" x $31\frac{1}{2}$"; poster shows album cover (front, rear and part of inside) and cutout sheet insert from album.
G $600   **VG $900**   **NM $1,200**

○ **1114.** **Capitol Letter Opener and Magnifying Glass Set;** letter opener is $9\frac{5}{8}$" long, magnifying glass is $8\frac{1}{4}$" long; the letter opener had a plastic handle with the Capitol logo and Capitol LP covers pictured inside, including "Sgt. Pepper"; the magnifying glass had a plastic handle with the Capitol logo and Capitol LP covers including one by the Beach Boys; set came in a Capitol gift box.
G $500   **VG $750**   **NM $1,000**

○ **1115.** **"Magical Mystery Tour" Poster;** 1967; 36" x 48"; album cover pictured on red background; "New! For Christmas!" printed in white on top.
G $600   **VG $900**   **NM $1,200**

○ **1116.** **"White Album" Poster;** 1968; 23" x 38"; similar to the poster included with the album; "It's Here!" printed at the top in red $3\frac{1}{2}$" tall letters.
G $100   **VG $150**   **NM $200**

1115

1113

1111

1116

○ **1117.** **"Yellow Submarine" Balloon;** 1969; 6" long; pictures a submarine; "Yellow Submarine," "The Beatles," "SW153," and Capitol Records logo printed on balloon.

G $35   **VG $55**   **NM $75**

○ **1118.** **"Yellow Submarine" Display;** 1969; 14" square x 33" high; cardboard bin; a 22"-long cardboard Yellow Submarine rests atop a 52"-long cardboard tube which fits into the bin; the bin is decorated with colorful *Yellow Submarine* graphics.

G $1,700   **VG $2,500**   **NM $3,500**

○ **1119.** **"Yellow Submarine" Poster;** 1969; 20" x 37"; large Yellow Sub on poster; "The Beatles" written on the left above sub; "Yellow Submarine" written on right above sub; back is blank except for the four Beatles each looking through their own porthole.

G $400   **VG $600**   **NM $800**

○ **1120.** **A is for Apple Counter Browser Box;** 1969; 15" wide x 26^1/$_2$" tall; cardboard display which held two tiers of 45-rpm records side by side; 11^1/$_2$" apple shown on top.

G $500   **VG $750**   **NM $1,000**

○ **1121.** **"Abbey Road" Bin;** 1969; 14" tall x 10" diameter; cardboard octagon-shaped "waste basket" with photo similar to the album cover; held 8-tracks or cassettes; could also be hung as a mobile.

G $225   **VG $350**   **NM $450**

○ **1122.** **"Abbey Road" Counter Display;** 1969; 12" x 19"; made of cardboard with die-cut figures of the group crossing the street.

G $250   **VG $375**   **NM $500**

○ **1123.** **"Abbey Road" Floor Display;** 1969; 11^1/$_2$" x 27^1/$_2$" (top), 27" high (bottom); two-piece cardboard display; top half has an enlargement of the album cover with die-cut figures of the Beatles crossing the road; top piece attaches to bottom with a pole; bottom half is a record bin which is black with "The BEATLES" printed on it in green on the front; a green apple is on the side; a white arrow, with a crack in it, points up on base.

G $1,750   **VG $2,500**   **NM $3,500**

1118   **1121**

1123

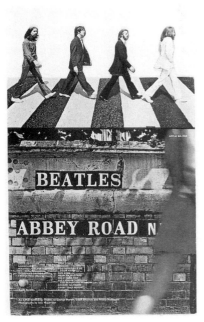

1122

○ **1124.** **"Abbey Road" Poster;** 1969; 23" x 33"; enlargement of the rear of the album cover; "Record and Tape" printed in lower left corner.
G $300   **VG $450**   **NM $600**

○ **1125.** **Christmas Mobile;** 1969; 9¹/₂" x 9¹/₂"; cardboard album covers; album covers from "Rubber Soul" to "Abbey Road" are on the mobile; top has "Hung up for a gift? Give the Beatles!" printed on it; there are Apple logos on top sides of album covers.
G $400   **VG $600**   **NM $800**

○ **1126.** **"Something/Come Together" Poster;** 1969; 17" x 23"; B&W group photo with "The Beatles Something/Come Together OUT NOW Apple Records" printed at top; this poster was also sold through the fan club.
G $150   **VG $225**   **NM $300**

○ **1127.** **"Hey Jude" Album Display;** 1970; 27" x 15"; gold cardboard with black and white photo and print; "New From The Beatles!" printed on top; group photo on bottom; display holds albums.
G $400   **VG $600**   **NM $800**

○ **1128.** **"Hey Jude" Counter Display;** 1970; 12" x 16"; cardboard display which pictures the album cover with the song titles listed at top.
G $250   **VG $375**   **NM $500**

○ **1129.** **The Beatles Computer;** 1970; 4" x 9"; slide chart with Beatle bios, important dates in Beatle history, discography, etc. listed on pull-out chart.
G $50   **VG $75**   **NM $100**

○ **1130.** **"Let It Be" Poster;** 1970; 19" x 27"; album cover on right side; "Now Available" on top; black background with white print.
G $250   **VG $375**   **NM $500**

○ **1131.** **"Let It Be" Poster;** 1970; 22" x 22"; album cover enlargement; the only print on the poster is "Printed in USA" in lower left corner.
G $40   **VG $60**   **NM $80**

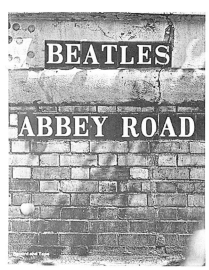

1124

1130

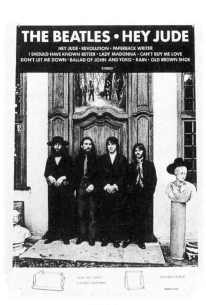

1128

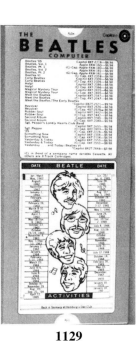

1129

1127

11

Apple Memorabilia

The Beatles own company, Apple, produced a number of promotional items for their employees, business associates, wholesalers, and retailers. They also sold a line of clothing and miscellaneous items through the Apple Boutique in London.

This chapter lists a selection of items produced by Apple with the exception of promotional posters and displays, and fan club material, each of which are included in Chapter 10 and Chapter 12, respectively. The Apple material was issued between 1968 and 1973.

○ **1132.** **Apple, Foam Rubber;** 6" tall; green apple with cardboard leaf that reads "Merry Christmas from Apple"
G $200   **VG $300**   **NM $400**

○ **1133.** **Box;** 4" square; lucite box with silver Apple on lid.
G $75   **VG $110**   **NM $150**

○ **1134.** **Bumpersticker;** black with green apple; reads "A is for Apple Records."
G $10   **VG $20**   **NM $30**

○ **1135.** **Business Card, with Apple logo;** used by company employees.
G $8   **VG $10**   **NM $12**

1134

1133

1135

❍ **1136.**   **Catalogue;** 1972; $8^3/_4$" x $11^3/_4$"; side-bound heavy paper binder contains listings of all Apple releases to date.
  G $50   **VG $75**   **NM $100**

❍ **1137.**   **Catalogues;** from the record division; various catalogues listed Apple record releases.
  G $10   **VG $15**   **NM $20**

❍ **1138.**   **Clothing;** from the Apple Boutique; usually identifiable by tags or labels.
  G $75   **VG $110**   **NM $150**

❍ **1139.**   **Cube;** $3^1/_2$" square; cardboard apple shown with bites out of it; "A Merry Christmas & a Happy New Year From Apple" printed on top; sent, unassembled in a flat 8"x 8" cardboard mailer with Apple logo on it; add 50% if mailer is present.
  G $100   **VG $150**   **NM $200**

❍ **1140.**   **Dartboard;** 18" diameter; heavy round dartboard with green apple at bullseye, marked "Apple Records" at top.
  G $300   **VG $450**   **NM $600**

❍ **1141.**   **Key Ring;** $2^1/_2$" diameter; clear lucite disk with green and red Apple design, and metal key ring attached.
  G $40   **VG $60**   **NM $80**

❍ **1142.**   **Lighter;** chrome Zippo lighter with Apple logo on side.
  G $100   **VG $150**   **NM $200**

❍ **1143.**   **Matchbook;** 2" x $2^1/_4$"; black matchbook with Apple logo on front, address on back.
  G $15   **VG $22**   **NM $30**

1143

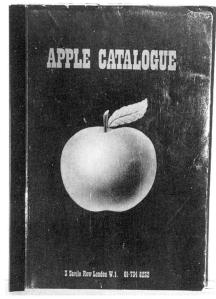

1136

1137

1139

1140

1141

1142

○ **1144. Mirror;** 9" x 9"; two-piece glass mirror with Apple logo in center.
G $125   **VG $185**   **NM $250**

○ **1145. Money Clip;** stainless steel money clip with green and red Apple in center.
G $50   **VG $75**   **NM $100**

○ **1146. Mug;** white pottery mug with Apple logo and "Apple Boutique" on side.
G $50   **VG $75**   **NM $100**

○ **1147. Paperweight;** clear round domed lucite paperweight with green and red Apple logo inside.
G $100   **VG $150**   **NM $200**

○ **1148. Paperweight;** 3" tall; brass apple with "Apple" engraved on side.
G $225   **VG $340**   **NM $450**

○ **1149. Postcard;** black and white postcard pictures the Apple Headquarters.
G $7   **VG $10**   **NM $15**

○ **1150. Postcard;** black with green apple.
G $7   **VG $10**   **NM $15**

○ **1151. Postcard;** 3½" x 5½"; multi-color photo of the "Fool" mural from the side of the Apple Boutique; reverse reads "Apple Card."
G $7   **VG $10**   **NM $15**

○ **1152. Poster;** 22" x 28"; reads "A is for..."; the "Fool" mural is shown; marked "Apple Publishing."
G $40   **VG $60**   **NM $80**

○ **1153. Press Book 1969;** titled *Beatles Press Book*; contains biographies, discography, tour info, and history of the group through June 1969; 32 pages.
G $50   **VG $75**   **NM $100**

○ **1154. Press Book;** 7½" x 10¾"; titled B*eatles—a little book*; includes biographies, discographies, etc.
G $20   **VG $30**   **NM $40**

1145

1146

1147

1149

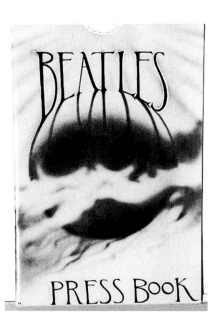

1153

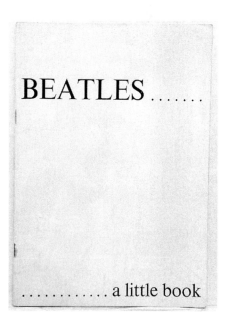

1154

○ **1155. Radio;** 8" diameter; green velour apple with green cardboard leaves which read "Apple Records"; radio inside of apple.

G $250   **VG $375**   **NM $500**

○ **1156. Record Box;** 7¹/₄" x 7¹/₄" x 2¹/₄"; cardboard box with Apple logo; box held twenty-five 45-rpm records on the Apple label; space on end flap to write in record number.

G $15   **VG $22**   **NM $30**

○ **1157. Record Crate;** 14" x 14" x 18"; wooden crate designed to hold albums; Apple labels on each end, engraved "Apple Records, London" on sides; came with dividers listing various Apple artists.

G $225   **VG $340**   **NM $450**

○ **1158. Stationery;** numerous sizes and styles were available; used for in-house and promotional purposes; some include Apple logo, address, etc.; valued at $10 to $20 per piece in NM shape.

○ **1159. Stickers;** 6" x 8"; sheet of adhesive stickers showing various vegetables; "Stick a garden on something you love" in bottom left corner; Apple logo on right.

G $20   **VG $30**   **NM $40**

○ **1160. Wristwatch;** 1¹/₂" square dial; heavy watch with black leather or suede band; green apple on watch face; no numbers on watch face; marked "Old England" on back or watch face.

G $425   **VG $650**   **NM $850**

1155

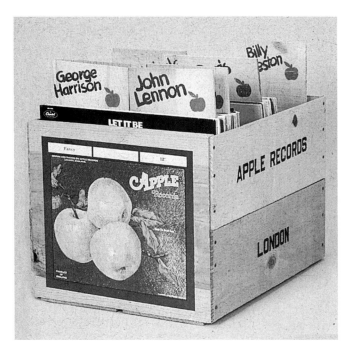

1157

1159

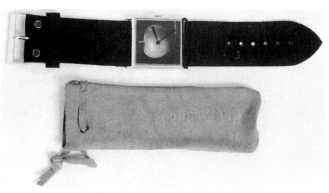

1160

12

Fan Club Items

The Beatles had thousands of fan clubs all over the world. Many of these fan clubs sent out magazines, newsletters, photos, etc. This chapter lists items issued by "The Official Beatles Fan Club" (U.K.) and "Beatles (U.S.A) Limited." All items are from the U.S. fan club unless U.K. is noted. The booklets, bulletins and yearly Christmas Records were sent free to members of the club, while other items were offered for sale to members at various times. In an August 1971 letter to fan club members it was announced that the name of the club was changing from "The Official Beatles Fan Club" to "The Apple Tree." The items listed in this chapter are listed alphabetically, and then chronologically or numerically, as appropriate.

○ **1161.** *Apple Scruffs Monthly Book* **(U.K.);** 1970; produced by Beatle fans and sold outside Apple headquarters; B&W contents; value is for each
    G $20   **VG $30**   **NM $40**

○ **1162.** **Booklet;** 1969; 8^1/$_2$" x 11"; 24 pages; booklet has a color photo of the group on the cover; "Beatles (U.S.A.) Ltd." on cover.
    G $15   **VG $25**   **NM $30**

○ **1163.** **Booklet;** 1970; 8^1/$_2$" x 11"; 20 pages; booklet has a B&W cover photo of the group; "The Official Beatles Fan Club" on cover.
    G $12   **VG $20**   **NM $25**

○ **1164.** **Booklet;** 1971; 8^1/$_2$" x 11"; 20 pages; booklet has a plain green cover with "Official Beatles Fan Club, 1971" on front.
    G $10   **VG $15**   **NM $20**

○ **1165.** **Bulletin;** August 1964; 8^1/$_2$" x 11"; 40 pages; this issue features the script to *A Hard Day's Night*.
    G $20   **VG $35**   **NM $45**

1162

1165

○ **1166.** **Bulletin;** May 1965; 8¹/₂" x 11"; 40 pages; titled "Special Anniversary Album"; inside the flap on the back cover is a pen and ink sketch of one of the Beatles (attached with perforations on one end); each bulletin came with only one Beatle attached, so there are four variations; deduct 35% from listed values if the sketch has been removed from the booklet.
G $20   **VG $30**   **NM $40**

○ **1167.** **Bulletin;** April 1966; 7" x 11"; 16 pages; titled "Special International Album."
G $20   **VG $30**   **NM $40**

○ **1168.** **Bulletin/Poster;** Summer 1967; 7¹/₄" x 10" (folded); bulletin lists info on the "Sgt. Pepper" LP; bulletin unfolds into a 20" x 29" color Sgt. Pepper poster.
G $20   **VG $30**   **NM $40**

○ **1169.** **Bulletin/Poster;** Summer 1968; 7¹/₄" x 10" (folded); bulletin unfolds into a 20" x 29" color poster of the Beatles just before they left for India to see the guru.
G $15   **VG $25**   **NM $35**

○ **1170.** **Bulletin/Poster;** Summer 1969; 7¹/₄" x 10" (folded); bulletin unfolds into a 20" x 29" color photo of the group titled "Revelation!"
G $12   **VG $18**   **NM $25**

1166

1167

1168

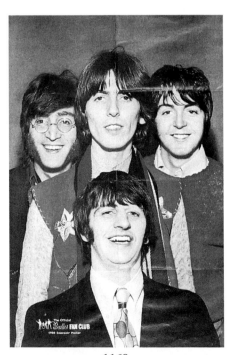

1169

1170

○ **1171.** **Christmas Record;** 1964; 7" square; a tri-fold item that has the record, bulletin and photos on three attached sections; value is for the undetached tri-fold; record alone (detached) is worth $30 in NM.
G $100   **VG $175**   **NM $250**

Christmas Record; 1965; none issued in U.S.; according to the *Beatle Bulletin* from April 1966 the club did not send out a 1965 Christmas record because they received the material much too late to prepare one.

○ **1172.** **Christmas Record;** 1966; 7" x 8½" postcard; price is for uncut postcard; deduct 70% if record is cut from postcard.
G $60   **VG $90**   **NM $120**

○ **1173.** **Christmas Record;** 1967; 7" x 8½" postcard; price is for uncut postcard; deduct 70% if record is cut from postcard.
G $60   **VG $90**   **NM $120**

○ **1174.** **Christmas Record;** 1968; 7" flexi-disc with picture sleeve; this picture sleeve used the same design as on the 1967 U.K. Christmas Record, though the printing on the back of the sleeve is different; deduct 50% if picture sleeve is missing.
G $45   **VG $70**   **NM $90**

○ **1175.** **Christmas Record;** 1969; 7" flexi-disc with picture sleeve; the picture sleeve issued on both the U.S. and U.K. Christmas Records for 1969 were the same; the disk has drawings of the Beatles' faces and is a product of Americom Corp.; deduct 50% if picture sleeve is missing.
G $40   **VG $60**   **NM $80**

○ **1176.** **Christmas Album;** a collection of all the Beatles Christmas messages from 1963 to 1969 on one album which was offered to members for $2.50 in 1970. ★ *Repro Alert*
G $50   **VG $125**   **NM $225**

○ **1177.** **Christmas Record (U.K.);** 1963; 7" flexi-disc with a picture sleeve that opens up; Newsletter #2 is printed on inside of sleeve; deduct 75% if picture sleeve is missing.
G $125   **VG $190**   **NM $250**

○ **1178.** **Christmas Record (U.K.);** 1964; 7" flexi-disc with a B&W picture sleeve; issued with a newsletter insert; (see also item #1194); add $10 for insert; deduct 60% if picture sleeve is missing.
G $75   **VG $110**   **NM $150**

○ **1179.** **Christmas Record (U.K.);** 1965; 7" flexi-disc with a B&W picture sleeve; issued with a newsletter insert; (see also item #1196); add $10 for insert; deduct 60% if picture sleeve is missing.
G $70   **VG $100**   **NM $140**

○ **1180.** **Christmas Record (U.K.);** 1966; 7" flexi-disc with a color picture sleeve designed by Paul; issued with a newsletter insert which is worth $10; deduct 60% if picture sleeve is missing.
G $50   **VG $75**   **NM $100**

1171

1176

1177

1179

○ **1181.** **Christmas Record;** (U.K.); 1967; 7" flexi-disc with a color picture sleeve designed by Julian & John Lennon and Ringo; issued with a newsletter insert which is worth $10; deduct 60% if picture sleeve is missing.
G $45   **VG $70**   **NM $90**

○ **1182.** **Christmas Record (U.K.);** 1968; 7" flexi-disc with a color picture sleeve; deduct 60% if picture sleeve is missing.
G $45   **VG $70**   **NM $90**

○ **1183.** **Christmas Record (U.K.);** 1969; 7" flexi-disc with a color picture sleeve designed by Richard and Zak Starkey; deduct 60% if picture sleeve is missing.
G $40   **VG $60**   **NM $80**

○ **1184.** **Christmas Album (U.K.);** a collection of all the Beatles' Christmas messages from 1963 to 1969 on one album titled "From Them to You"; offered to U.K. club members in 1970.
★ *Repro Alert*
G $75   **VG $150**   **NM $300**

○ **1185.** **Concert Booklet;** 1964; 12" x 12"; Souvenir Publishing and Distributing; color cover with B&W photos inside.
G $15   **VG $22**   **NM $30**

○ **1186.** **Concert Booklet;** 1965; 12" x 12"; Souvenir Publishing and Distributing; color cover with B&W photos inside.
G $15   **VG $22**   **NM $30**

○ **1187.** **Concert Booklet;** 1966; 12" x 12"; Raydell Publishing; color cover with B&W photos inside.
G $30   **VG $45**   **NM $60**

○ **1188.** **Cube;** a cardboard cube which was mailed flat in a white mailing envelope (envelope is $7^{1}/_{2}$" x $12^{1}/_{2}$") with fan club logo; assembles into a 5"-square cube with color photos of the Beatles

and an apple; sent as a fan club gift "poster' in 1970; add 50% if envelope is present.
G $15   **VG $25**   **NM $35**

○ **1189.** **Folder;** $8^{3}/_{4}$" x $11^{3}/_{4}$"; green folder with two pockets contains last newsletter announcing end of fan club, several glossy photos and small "War is Over" poster.
G $50   **VG $75**   **NM $100**

○ **1190.** **(Beatle) Guardian Angel Club Packet;** Mfd. by *Teen Screen* magazine; 1965; contents include satin ribbon, welcome letter, and advertising flyer for Beatle magazines.
G $45   **VG $70**   **NM $90**

○ **1191.** **Membership Cards;** cards were issued from 1964 to 1971; price is per card.
G $7   **VG $10**   **NM $15**

1180

1190

1181

1182

1189

This is to Certify that

☆ JEANETTE SPEAKER ☆

is a member in good standing of the

BEATLEMANIAC FAN CLUB

№ 6995

№ 4658

Be A BEATLE Booster!

This certifies that

is a registered member
of the Intermountain

Beatle Fan Club

Julie N. Mc Clelland
President
219 East Broadway

KNAK KGEM KEEP KLO KUPI KSNN KOVO

The Beatles Fan Club

C/o Miss R. BROWN,
90 BUCHANAN ROAD,
WALLASEY,
CHESHIRE.

PAUL   GEORGE

MEMBERSHIP CARD

The "especially George" fan club
ORGANIZED 1964

Motto: Think George, or don't think at all.

Barb Thompson
NAME OF MEMBER

PRES *Penny Rehak*

RINGO   JOHN

OFFICIAL MEMBERSHIP CARD

BEATLES FAN CLUB

Name

Address

Trudy Midcalf   *Dawne Hester*

PRESIDENT   VICE-PRESIDENT

ONTARIO'S OFFICIAL BEATLES FAN CLUB
Compliments of CHUM-1050

KCbQ
1170 in San Diego

BEATLE FEVER

This is to certify that

Tom Miller

is a member of the

KCBQ GOOD GUY BEATLE FAN CLUB

WSAI   CHARTER MEMBER   WSAI

DUSTY RHODES' BEATLES BOOSTERS

☆ ☆ NORTH AMERICA'S FIRST BEATLES FAN CLUB ☆ ☆

Name

Dusty —
Chief
Beatle
Bug!

BEATLEMANIA UNLIMITED!

BEATLE NUMBER 10046

KRLA **BEATLES FAN CLUB**
OF SOUTHERN CALIFORNIA

DAVE HULL
President

№ 2319

NAME

ADDRESS

is a member in good standing and a confirmed
Beatle Maniac

Official
Beatle Fan Club
OF GREATER CLEVELAND

Karen Diallafiora
is an Official Member of Beatle Fan Club No. 144

President *Carol King*

Exec. Sect. *Scott Burton*

WHK Radio

THIS IS TO CERTIFY THAT

Debby Johnson

IS AN OFFICIAL MEMBER OF THE

N. A. A. B. P.

NATIONAL ASSOCIATION for the
ADVANCEMENT of BEATLE PEOPLE

NANCY MARREN
&
MOLLY GARDNER
CO-PRESIDENTS

SUE MAGUIRE
&
DEE-DEE SMITH
SECRETARIES

THE BEATLES FAN CLUB
of Massachusetts
6 BEACON ST., BOSTON 8, MASS.

MEMBERSHIP CARD

This is to certify that

Miss Carlene Estes

is a member in good standing for the year 1964

KQV BEATLES FAN CLUB

Chuck Brinkman

Shirley Clark
SIGNATURE

BEATLES FAN CLUB

BEATLES I.U.S.A / LIMITED
P.O. BOX 505
RADIO CITY STATION
NEW YORK N.Y. 10019

This is to certify that

JEFF AUGSBURGER

Name

is an official member of our Fan Club.

Ringo Starr   *George Harrison*

Paul McCartney   *John Lennon*

Be it known that

MELANIE McDOWELL is

an **OFFICIAL MEMBER** of the

I.B.B.B. CLUB

Tom Clay - Pres.

"We don't like them
WE LOVE THEM"

THE OFFICIAL BEATLES FAN CLUB of AMERICA
92 N. POCONO ROAD, MOUNTAIN LAKES, N. J.

Member's Name *COLLETTE DOLAC*

Membership Number *4095*

Member's Signature *Collette Dolac*

P. T. O. For Area Secretary's Name and
Address

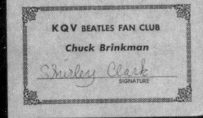

The Official
Beatles FAN CLUB

First Floor, Service House,
13 Monmouth Street, London W.C.2.
Telephone: COVent Garden 2332

THIS IS TO CERTIFY THAT

IS AN OFFICIALLY ENROLLED MEMBER
OF THE FAN CLUB AND HAS BECOME
BEATLE PERSON NUMBER   155101

Anne Collingham

ANNE COLLINGHAM
National Secretary of The Official Beatles Fan Club

○ **1192.** **Newsletter #2 (UK);** printed on inside of 1963 Christmas Record sleeve; (see also item #1177).

○ **1193.** **Newsletter #3 (UK);** Summer 1964; 8¹/₂" x 5¹/₂"; 32-page booklet.
G $20   **VG $30**   **NM $40**

○ **1194.** **Newsletter #4 (UK);** 7" x 7"; issued with the 1964 Christmas Record; (see also item #1178).
G $7   **VG $10**   **NM $15**

○ **1195.** **Newsletter #5 (UK);** Summer 1965; 8" x 5"; twelve pages with photos from *Help!*.
G $15   **VG $25**   **NM $35**

○ **1196.** **Newsletter #6 (UK);** 7" x 7"; issued with the 1965 Christmas Record; (see also item #1179).
G $5   **VG $7**   **NM $10**

○ **1197.** **Newsletter #7 (UK);** Summer 1966; 8" x 5"; twelve pages with photos from Shea Stadium Concert.
G $15   **VG $22**   **NM $30**

○ **1198.** **Newsletter #8 (UK);** 7" x 7"; Super Pix sales brochure.
G $5   **VG $7**   **NM $10**

○ **1199.** **Photo Album, John;** June 1965; 8¹/₂" x 11"; an eight-page booklet with B&W photos of John; originally cost 35 cents.
G $12   **VG $18**   **NM $25**

○ **1200.** **Photo Album, Paul;** (same as above).

○ **1201.** **Photo Album, George;** (same as above).

○ **1202.** **Photo Album, Ringo;** (same as above).

○ **1203.** **Photos;** 3³/₄" x 5¹/₂"; B&W on paper; one of each Beatle with autograph.
G $2   **VG $4**   **NM $5**

○ **1204.** **Photos;** 8" x 10"; B&W; numerous photos were issued from 1964 to 1971; all should be marked at the bottom as being issued by "Beatles (U.S.A) Ltd." and "Copyright Beatles Fan Club - 1969," etc.
G $2   **VG $3**   **NM $5**

○ **1205.** **Postcards;** 3¹/₂" x 5"; color postcards from 1969; four different—one of each Beatle with his wife; price is per postcard.
G $2   **VG $3**   **NM $4**

○ **1206.** **Poster;** 1971; 21" x 28"; montage of drawings/art by Patti Randall; copyright by The Apple Tree; Summer 1971 gift from the fan club.
G $12   **VG $18**   **NM $25**

Poster, Life Size; (see items #768-771).

1200

1201

13

Trading Cards

Rare isn't a word usually associated with Beatle trading cards. Demand was so great for the cards in early 1964 that Topps, the major producer of baseball cards, had to delay production of their 1964 baseball set to satisfy orders for Beatle cards! Topps Chewing Gum made all the Beatle trading cards (gum cards) in the U.S. The cards were marked T.C.G. which stood for Trading Card Guild. Any collector content to obtain the basic 344 cards made in the U.S. in 1964 should be able to put sets together in decent condition at a reasonable cost. Once you get beyond the basic sets, there awaits enough of a challenge for even the most advanced collector, as this overview of the various aspects of card collecting will demonstrate.

Most of the cards are not that difficult to find, but their wrappers, boxes, and cartons can be hard to locate. Everybody saved the cards; some saved the wrappers. But only a few saved the boxes and cartons, so they are quite valuable. Most packs contained five trading cards. So, there were five cards for every one wrapper. The display box held twenty-four packs of cards. So, there were 120 cards for every one display box. The shipping carton held twenty-four display boxes. So, there were 2,888 for every one shipping carton!

All of the Beatle trading cards produced in the U.S. were made by Topps, the major player in both sports and non-sports cards in the 1960s. The first set of cards was numbered from 1-60, and had black and white photos on the front, with the numbers at the bottom of the mostly blank back. These were followed by two more series (or sets) of the same design. The second series, from 61-115, and the third series from 116-165. The third series cards seem to be the easiest set to complete of all the trading cards sold in the U.S.

All the black and white cards series and the *A Hard Day's Night* series of cards were sold in a pack with a stick of gum and five cards. The two color photo sets, the Color Series and the Diary Series, were sold in a pack with a stick of gum and four cards.

All three series of black and white cards were sold using the same yellow wrapper. The store display box was the key for the buyer to know what cards they were getting. The first series cards were sold from a 24-pack orange/red store display box. When the second series was issued, the same box was used, with a large sticker on the box top reading "2nd Series." The third series had its own display box, a blue one with a prominent "New Series" marking.

Topps also produced a set of cards based on the movie *A Hard Day's Night*. These cards are numbered 1-55 and have sepia-colored photos, a brownish tone often used for card sets that were based on movies. The back of the "Beatle Movie" cards have text corresponding to the photos on the fronts. This card set has perhaps the most attractive display box and wrapper of the Topps set.

The Beatles Color cards were Topps' first set utilizing color photos, and were numbered from 1-64. The orange backs were a "question and answer" text format, based on questions the Beatles had been asked in interviews and press conferences. The display box and wrapper both feature an attractive design.

The Beatles Diary cards appear to be a continuation of the color card set, with blue backs containing a fantasy text based on what the Beatles may have written in their diaries. These cards are numbered 1A-60A, there is a variation on card number 21A, with either a John or a George signature on the bottom. The Diary series utilized the same wrapper and display box as the color set. A "New Series" sticker was affixed to the box top.

Topps produced one other set of Beatle cards, a 55-card set of Beatle "Plaks," which were oversized $4^3/_4$" x $2^1/_2$" cards with Beatle photos, apparently cut out from previous issues, and positioned on simulated wood-grained backgrounds, with slogans dominating the cards. The cards are perforated with "hooks" on each end, which allow them to be attached end to end to create "chains" of cards. Many collectors have never seen these cards because they were a Topps test set. It was released only in a few cities so that Topps could gauge the public's reaction. For whatever reason, the cards never received widespread distribution, and are considered the most difficult set to complete. The wrapper and display box are also rarities and seldom seen, even at Beatle conventions and major card shows. Assembling this 55-card set, card by card, is a quest that usually takes years of diligent searching, utilizing major non-sports card dealers and every other avenue available where cards might be obtained.

In addition to the card sets, wrappers and display boxes, collectors can pursue several other associated items. Uncut sheets of cards occasionally surface. Topps printed their cards in 132-count sheets, but half-sheets of 66-cards are more common and generally contain all the cards in the set. Uncut sheets are often unfinished, with either the backs of the cards not printed, or a color missing from the color card sets.

Shipping cartons were used to send the display boxes to the retailers. These containers can be considered a rare item, seldom offered for sale.

Also of interest to collectors are the card sets produced in Britain. A, B and C was the company manufacturing the early sets, and was affiliated with Topps in the U.S. The first set released in Britain was a 60-card black and white set with identical photos to the Topps first series set. The British second series cards are numbered 61-105 and all the photos are different than the U.S. second series. A, B

and C also produced a color set numbered from 1-40, with many photos differing from the U.S. issues, and a 50-card set of color cards featuring many British acts. Cards 1-23 of this 50-card set are all Beatles.

The British cards that garner the most interest are the two sets that were released in conjunction with the movie *Yellow Submarine*. Primrose Confectionary inserted single cards of their small sized 50-card set in boxes of candy sticks. Fortunately for collectors, complete sets of 50 cards were available by mail order and these cards are usually sold in complete sets today.

Anglo Gum produced the most sought-after British set, a 66-card issue based on *Yellow Submarine*. The backs of this colorful set were puzzle pieces that provided a "giant picture" of the *Yellow Submarine* characters when assembled. This "giant picture" was also available by mail order in the form of a poster, which could be obtained by sending in Yellow Submarine wrappers. In actuality, the poster is an uncut 66-card sheet, with only the card backs printed. The wrappers for this set are quite desirable, in that they come in four different colors, each featuring a different Beatle.

GRADING

Proper grading is very important when pricing cards. Here are some grading guidelines:

(NM) Near mint: Cards cannot have creases, tears, writing, tape or rounded corners; cards must look and feel very clean with no wear.

(VG) Very good: Cards cannot have creases, tears, writing or tape; some minor wear at the corners is okay.

(G) Good: Cards cannot have tears, writing or tape; cards can have rounded corners or light creases.

When grading cards also check for uniform size. Sometimes a card will look near mint, but further inspec-

tion will reveal that a fan trimmed an edge so it would fit into a wallet or frame. The centering of cards is also a factor that must be considered. Sometimes a factory defect of an off-center card is found. If the photo on the card is slightly off-center (borders not square), its value is not diminished greatly. Cards that have part of the photo or writing cut off because they are off-center are valued at the good price. Topps trading cards (with the exception of the Beatle Plaks) which have multiple creases, tears, writing, tape or other imperfections are generally worth less than 25 cents each. Cards which have been glued or taped into scrapbooks also fall into this category.

U.S. Trading Cards

All cards in this section were made by T.C.G. (Topps). All cards in this section measure $2^1/_2$" x $3^1/_2$", unless otherwise noted. The three wrappers (#1210, 1218, and 1224) measure 5" x 6" when open. Cards printed in Canada have slight variations. The B&W series of cards from Canada have dark backs instead of white backs.

○ **1207.** **B&W First Series** #1-60; photo and autograph on front; number on back in green or blue ink.
Set

G $50	VG $75	NM $100

Single Cards

G 60 cents	VG 90 cents	NM $1.50

○ **1208.** **B&W Second Series** #61-115; photo and autograph on front; number on back in orange or green ink.
Set

G $50	VG $70	NM $90

Single Cards

G 60 cents	VG 90 cents	NM $1.50

○ **1209.** **B&W Third Series** #116-165; photo and autograph on front; number on back in green ink.
Set

G $40	VG $60	NM $80

Single Cards

G 60 cents	VG 90 cents	NM $1.50

★ *Repro Alert* No B&W series were made after the third series. The B&W fourth through sixth series were not manufactured in the 1960s and are of recent vintage.

○ **1210.** **B&W Series Wrapper;** held items #1207-1209; held five cards and a stick of gum; add 100% to value for an unopened pack of cards; two different variations of wrapper can be found; Big Twin Chews ad on right or left side of wrapper; Canada wrapper has "Bubble Gum with picture cards" printed on it.
G $10   **VG $15**   **NM $20**

○ **1211.** **B&W Series Rack Pack;** held items #1207-1209; $10^1/_2$" x 4"; held 30 cards; marked "3/10 cent packs for 29 cents"; clear cellophane wrapping with header card; value is for sealed item; value for header card only is $40 in NM.
G $80   **VG $120**   **NM $160**

○ **1212.** **B&W Series Box;** 8" x $3^3/_4$" x $1^7/_8$"; held 24 packs of item #1207; illustrated cardboard box with box top that flips open for display; red box.
G $150   **VG $220**   **NM $280**

○ **1213.** **B&W Second Series Box;** 8" x $3^3/_4$" x $1^7/_8$"; held 24 packs of item #1208; same as above box with paper sticker with "2nd Series" printed on it affixed to box lid.
G $150   **VG $220**   **NM $280**

○ **1214.** **B&W New Series Box;** 8" x $3^3/_4$" x $1^7/_8$"; held 24 packs of items #1209; illustrated cardboard box with box top that flips open for display; blue box.
G $100   **VG $150**   **NM $200**

○ **1215.** **B&W Series Shipping Carton;** $15^1/_2$" x 8" x $11^1/_2$"; held 24 of items #1212-1214; corrugated cardboard carton illustrated in red and black.
G $250   **VG $375**   **NM $500**

1210

1214

1211

1215

○ **1216.** **Color Series** #1-64; color photo on front with questions and answers on back.

Set
G $50   **VG $75**   **NM $100**

Single Cards
G 60 cents   **VG 90 cents**   **NM $1.50**

○ **1217.** **Diary Series** #1A-60A; color photo on front with "Dear Diary" entries on back; card #21A can be found with either a John or a George autograph on the back.

Set
G $50   **VG $75**   **NM $100**

Single Cards
G 60 cents   **VG 90 cents**   **NM $1.50**

○ **1218.** **Color Photos Wrapper;** held items #1216 and 1217; held four cards and a stick of gum; add 100% to value for an unopened pack of cards; wrapper can be found with five variations; variations include "Big Twin Chews" on right or left side and three different premium offers.
G $10   **VG $15**   **NM $20**

1216 front of un-cut sheet

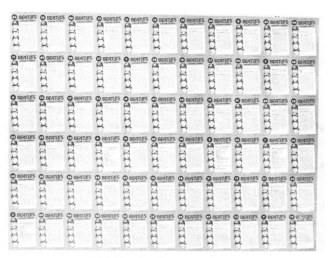

1216 back of un-cut sheet

○ **1219.** **Color Photos Rack Pack;** held items #1216 or 1217; 10$\frac{1}{2}$" x 4"; held 30 cards; marked "3/10 cent packs for 29 cents"; clear cellophane wrapping with header card; value is for sealed item; header card alone valued at $40 in NM shape.
G $90   **VG $120**   **NM $175**

1218

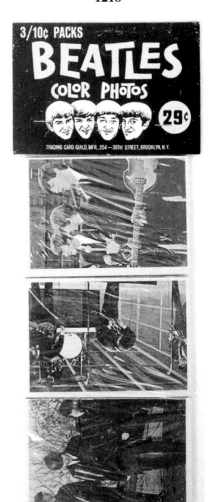

1219

○ **1220.** **Color Photos Box;** 8" x 3³/₄" x 1⁷/₈"; held 24 packs of item #1216; illustrated cardboard box with box top that flips open for display.
G $100   **VG $150**   **NM $200**

○ **1221.** **Color Photos Shipping Carton;** 15¹/₂" x 8" x 11¹/₂"; held 24 of item #1220; corrugated cardboard carton illustrated in yellow and black.
G $250   **VG $375**   **NM $500**

○ **1222.** **Diary Series Box;** held 24 packs of item #1217; same box as item #1220, but has paper sticker affixed to top of lid; sticker has "NEW SERIES" printed on it.
G $100   **VG $150**   **NM $200**

○ **1223.** **Beatles Movie** *A Hard Day's Night* Series #1-55; sepia-tone picture on front with the scene described on back.
Set
G $50   **VG $75**   **NM $100**

Single Cards
G 60 cents   **VG 90 cents**   **NM $1.50**

○ **1224.** **Beatles Movie HDN Wrapper;** held item #1223; held five cards and a stick of gum; add 100% to value if pack is unopened; two variations of wrapper with minor color variations on edge.
G $15   **VG $25**   **NM $30**

○ **1225.** **Beatles Movie HDN Rack Pack;** held item #1223; 10¹/₂" x 4"; held 30 cards; marked "3/10 cent packs for 29 cents"; clear cellophane wrapping with header card; value is for sealed item; header card alone valued at $40 in NM shape.
G $100   **VG $150**   **NM $200**

○ **1226.** **Beatles Movie HDN Box;** 8" x 3³/₄" x 1⁷/₈"; held 24 packs of item #1223; illustrated cardboard box with box top that flips open for display.
G $140   **VG $220**   **NM $280**

○ **1227.** **Beatles Movie HDN Shipping Carton;** 15¹/₂" x 8" x 11¹/₂"; corrugated cardboard carton which held 24 of item #1226.
G $250   **VG $375**   **NM $500**

○ **1228.** **Beatles Plaks Series** #1-55; these cards measure 2¹/₂" x 4³/₄" and were a test set; they were only marketed in certain cities for a short time; the cards have perforations which when torn form hooks and slots for cards to fasten to one another; fifty of the cards have Beatle photos with a slogan; the remaining five cards have a slogan only; there are instructions for hooking up plaks on the back of the card.
Set
G $325   **VG $475**   **NM $650**

Single Cards
G $5   **VG $10**   **NM $15**

1220

1221

1225

1224

1226

○ **1229.** **Beatles Plaks Wrapper;** 6¹/₂" x 6"; held item #1228; add 30% for an unopened pack.
| G $150 | VG $225 | NM $300 |

○ **1230.** **Beatles Plaks Box;** 8" x 5" x 2"; held 24 packs of #1228; illustrated cardboard box.
| G $800 | VG $1,200 | NM $1,600 |

U.K. Trading Cards

○ **1231.** **B&W Series #1-60;** 3¹/₄" x 2¹/₄"; photo and autograph on front with number in blue on back.
Set
| G $50 | VG $60 | NM $90 |

Single Cards
| G 75 cents | VG $1.00 | NM $1.50 |

○ **1232.** **B&W Series #1-60 Wrapper;** 6³/₄" x 4¹/₄"; red and black on white background; add 50% for unopened pack; held two cards and piece of gum.
| G $15 | VG $25 | NM $35 |

○ **1233.** **B&W Series Box;** 7" x 5" x 2"; orange cardboard box which held 72 packs of item #1231
| G $200 | VG $300 | NM $400 |

○ **1234.** **B&W Series #61-105;** 3¹/₄" x 2¹/₄"; photo and autograph on front with number on back; photos different than on any U.S. set.
Set
| G $75 | VG $120 | NM $180 |

Single Cards
| G $1.00 | VG $2.00 | NM $3.00 |

○ **1235.** **B&W Series #61-105 Wrapper;** 6³/₄" x 4¹/₄"; yellow on white background; add 100% for unopened pack.
| G $20 | VG $30 | NM $40 |

1235

1232

1229

1230

1233

○ **1236.**   **B&W Series Store Poster;** 10" x 12" paper poster; reads "A & B C BEATLES BUBBLE GUM AUTOGRAPHED WALLET-SIZED PHOTOS!" with color picture of group.

G $125	VG $190	NM $250

○ **1237.**   **Color Series #1-40;** 3$^1/_4$" x 2$^1/_4$".
Set

VG $60	NM $90	G $120

Single Cards

G $1.50	VG $2.25	NM $3.00

○ **1238.**   **Color Series Wrapper;** 6$^3/_4$" x 4$^1/_4$"; add 50% for unopened pack.

G $15	VG $25	NM $35

○ **1239.**   *Yellow Submarine* **Series #1-50;** issued by Primrose Confectionary; 1$^1/_4$" x 2$^1/_2$"; color scene on front; description of scene on back.
Set

G $75	VG $110	NM $150

Single Cards

G $1.50	VG $2.00	NM $3.00

1239   **1240**

○ **1240.**   *Yellow Submarine* **Box;** Primrose Confectionary; 1$^1/_2$" x 2$^3/_4$"; one card (item #1239) came in each box of ten sweet cigarettes; box is red and pictures Beatles and the sub.

G $60	VG $90	NM $120

○ **1241.**   *Yellow Submarine* **Series #1-66;** issued by Anglo Confectionary; 2$^1/_2$" x 3$^1/_2$"; color scene on front with a puzzle back; backs of 66 cards form a color picture.
Set

G $375	VG $500	NM $750

Single Cards

G $6	VG $12	NM $15

1241

1236

1241b

○ **1242.** *Yellow Submarine* **Wrapper;** Anglo Confectionary; 5¼" x 5⅞"; held item #1241; there are four different wrappers; one of each Beatle; on the back of the wrapper there is a premium offer (see item #1113); add 50% for an unopened pack; price is per wrapper.

G $60	VG $90	NM $125

○ **1243.** *Yellow Submarine* **Box;** Anglo Confectionary; 7½" x 5½" x 2"; colorful box which held 40 packs of cards (item #1241)

G $400	VG $600	NM $800

○ **1244.** *Yellow Submarine* **Complete Giant Picture;** Anglo Confectionary; 27½" x 21"; color cardboard picture which was offered by mail order; ten wrappers (item #1242) and 3 shillings had to be sent in to receive it.

G $150	VG $225	NM $300

Australian Trading Cards

○ **1245.** **Happy-Ade Cards;** eight different cards; 2⅜" x 3¼"; B&W photos; two of each Beatle—one with instrument and one with close-up; included in packages of Happy-Ade Drink mix, one card per package; back of card lists which Beatle photos are included with each flavor; value is per card.

G $6	VG $9	NM $12

Swedish Trading Cards

○ **1246.** **Swedish Trading Cards;** 1¾" x 2¾"; many were "colorized" photos with pastel backgrounds; value is per card.

G $3	VG $5	NM $6

1242a

1242c

1242b

1245

1243

1244

SOUVENIR PROGRAM

THE BEATLES

MANILA, PHILIPPINES
RIZAL MEMORIAL
FOOTBALL STADIUM
JULY 4, 1966

14

Concert tickets, Programs, and Related Ephemera

Seeing the Beatles perform live in person was undoubtedly the highlight of any fan's involvement with the group during the years they were touring. Momentos of the Beatles' concerts are a challenge for the collector to obtain, due to the fact that they were of a fragile nature (usually paper), available for only a short time, and usually available only in the locality where the concert took place. These items can make for a very interesting collection in a minimum of space. The Beatles performed hundreds of times before audiences, so the variety of material available is endless and can be a lifetime pursuit.

TICKETS

Tickets from Beatle concerts worldwide are quite varied in size and appearance. In their home country of Great Britain, many of the concerts were held in movie theaters and other small venues, especially in the 1962 to 1963 era. The tickets from these shows often are of similar design on thin paper. Some of the tickets from television appearances and award shows are more colorful and impressive. Other parts of the world produced tickets which were sometimes quite large, such as the 1966 Tokyo ticket, 1965 Barcelona ticket, and the 1966 Manila ticket. Australian tickets are small and simple in design. Of interest to most North American collectors are the many varied tickets produced for the Beatles' tours here in 1964, 1965, and 1966.

The Beatles played 72 shows in North America at 52 different sites between February 11, 1964 and August 29, 1966. On numerous occasions, they performed both an afternoon and evening show at the same venue. On one occasion, August 21, 1966, they played an afternoon show in Cincinnati, followed by an evening show in St. Louis. This twin bill was necessitated by a rainout in Cincinnati the previous day.

Tickets from the 1960s exhibit much more variety in size, design, and color than those computer tickets of today. In the pre-computer printer-era most concert promoters contracted with local or regional printers. Thus the size, design, and color of the tickets often varies widely from city to city. Several venues used different colors of tickets to differentiate seat location and thus ticket price.

While a mediocre seat to see a major artist today can cost upwards of $40, a cheap seat at the Beatles' first U.S. concert in Washington, D.C. in 1964 could be had for a mere $2! If you were lucky enough to get a spot close to the stage, it set you back $4. With refreshments and a couple of souvenirs, a group of four fans could easily spend $20-$30 between them at a Beatles concert.

Charles Finley's huge payment to lure the Beatles to Kansas City resulted in the highest ticket prices for the 1964 tour. Seats in Kansas City ranged from $4.50 to $8.50, possibly part of the reason the show was not well attended. However, the tickets for this show are one of the classics, as the reverse side of the ticket pictures Charles Finley in a Beatle wig with the slogan "Today's Beatle fans are tomorrow's baseball fans."

There are several approaches to take when collecting Beatles tickets. Some fans may look for tickets from historic shows, such as Shea Stadium (1965) or Candlestick Park (1966), their last show, while others may focus on shows from nearby venues, or a show they actually attended.

Condition of ticket stubs varies widely. Many fans preserved them in scrapbooks, often attaching them with glue or tape. Back damage is generally less important than front damage or creases. Removing tape from ticket fronts is not always practical or advisable, as the ticket surface is usually removed with the tape. Minor creases are of less importance when collecting stubs than when collecting unused tickets, as some wear is natural, considering that the stub usually spent the concert in someone's pocket.

Values of Beatles concert tickets vary widely, depending on a number of factors. One is current demand for the ticket. Washington, D.C. (their first U.S. concert), Shea Stadium (1965, their biggest concert), and Candlestick Park (1966, their last concert) are the top attractions of each year, as they are of special historic interest. Stubs from Montreal, Las Vegas, and New Orleans have proven elusive for many advanced collectors, although these may be of less interest to beginning collectors

Size and design of a ticket also affects value. A large ticket with a picture of the group is more desirable than one of small size with no picture, if all other factors are equal. Unused tickets are generally at the top of the heap in value. Unused tickets are most common from dates on the 1966 tour, as the Beatles failed to sell-out some stadiums as they almost always did in 1964 and 1965. The two most common unused tickets are Suffolk Downs (near Boston) and the 1966 Shea Stadium show. Both are somewhat easy to find due to quantities retained by the original promoters, and offered for sale in recent years. The third most common unused ticket is the 1966 Candlestick Park show.

Unused tickets were often retained for other reasons. Atlantic City required a minimum purchase of four tickets through mail-order sales, so extra tickets were sometimes bought and not used. Rain kept some people away at outside stadium shows. Some people drove long distances to the show and left their tickets at home. Other fans won tickets in radio station contests and didn't use them. Often the unused tickets that turn up are the furthest from the stage, as they would be the last to sell.

Values for ticket stubs are quite variable due to the enormous differences in size of the stub retained by the concert-goer, often because of the policy of the promoter or venue. Tickets that have a perforation where the ticket was to have been torn are less desirable if the tear removes more of the ticket than necessary. At some venues the patron received the large ticket portion, while at others, the small end was retained by the concert-goer. Often the small end contains only the seat number and date, while the large portion is the attractive section. Sometimes tickets without a perforation were torn roughly in the middle, and either end may turn up in old collections.

Special tickets were printed for specific uses at some concerts. Tickets earmarked for use by members of the media may be marked "press box." Even ushers had tickets printed for them at several shows. These types of tickets would, of course, be quite limited and hence more valuable than the usual ones.

A collector of tickets faces several hurdles in search that collectors of records or other memorabilia do not have to deal with. First, most tickets turn up in the general vicinity of where the concert took place. Thus, a collector in New York is unlikely to come across tickets from western or southern locations. If you want a ticket from Memphis, you are unlikely to find it in Seattle! If you live near a city where the Beatles played, you may find duplicates that you can trade to collectors in other cities. Trading is a viable activity among collectors.

The other problem in collecting tickets is that they are often attached to a scrapbook. Although the ticket stub may be the only item of value in the scrapbook, the owner of the scrapbook may recall the hours of work assembling it, and assign a value somewhat in excess of the ticket value, and may be reluctant to sell the ticket separately.

What is the value of a Beatles concert ticket? There is no one answer that can cover all the variables previously discussed, but the following values fit the majority of tickets. Tape, creases, and other damage can, of course, lower the value.

Concert Ticket Value Guidelines

Small stub without the word "Beatles" on it	$30-$50
Stub with the word "Beatles" on it	$50-$100
Stub with photo of the Beatles	$100-$200
Unused ticket	$200-$350
(Suffolk Downs valued at $60-$100)	
Unused ticket with photo of the Beatles	$200-$400
(Shea Stadium 1966 valued at $175-$225)	

Pre-1963 tickets can have a greater value than these guidelines.

★ *Repro Alert*

An excellent book for Beatle concert ticket collectors is *The Beatles Live!* by Mark Lewisohn. (Published by Henry Holt and Company, Inc., 1988). This book lists every Beatle gig from 1957-1966, including anecdotes about certain appearances. This book also includes photographs of tickets, programs and concert posters. Unfortunately this book is out of print, but check for used copies or with the publisher for a new edition.

Tickets from concerts outside North American.

Tickets from 1964 North American concerts.

Tickets from 1965 North American concerts.

Tickets from 1966 North American concerts.

Concert-Related Ephemera

Collectors of tickets and programs often find that businesses, radio stations, and newspapers had ties to the concerts in many cities. These usually involved such things as ticket contests, giveaways, or other promotions. Many radio stations provided disc jockeys as masters of ceremonies at the concerts. Some of these activities resulted in material (usually paper) that enhances a collection. Types of items found include, but are not limited to: product inserts, store posters, concert handouts, ticket order forms and envelopes, radio station surveys, and letters. We have pictured some of the many concert-related items that are available. Values are somewhat dependent on size, content, and interest in the piece.

Parking Pass

Chicago Pamphlet

Saharan **Magazine**

Royal Crown Ticket Offer

Chicago Ticket Contest

Closed-Circuit Telecast Tickets

7-Up Ticket A

7-Up Ticket B

Closed-Circuit Flyer

Programs

Programs from Beatle concerts fall into two major categories. The most plentiful are those which were distributed at a number of different venues over a period of days or weeks, such as the Australian Tour program or the 1965 U.K. Tour program. The support acts were usually under contract for the entire tour, so changes were usually not necessary in the program format. One notable exception was the Beatles-Roy Orbison 1963 Tour where the cover was changed to reflect that the Beatles had assumed top billing midway through the tour.

More scarce and usually more valuable are programs from "one-off" shows, such as The Royal Variety Show, their Carnegie Hall appearance, Night of One Hundred Stars show, etc. Their higher value is usually the result of smaller print runs, and also the historical significance of the shows.

The programs content often includes, but is not limited to, advertisements, biographies of the artists, order of performance, and photos. The design ranges from the very elaborate to very simple, which also may affect value.

○ **1247. Albany Cinema, Liverpool (10-15-61);** Variety Matinee Fundraiser; the Beatles are pictured inside wearing leather jackets.
  G $400　　　**VG $600**　　　**NM $800**

○ **1248. Tower Ballroom, New Brighton (10-12-62);** Beatles were second billing to Little Richard in this Epstein-produced show.
  G $250　　　**VG $375**　　　**NM $500**

○ **1249. Empire Theatre, Liverpool (10-28-62);** Another NEMS show with Little Richard headlining; Little Richard on program cover.
  G $250　　　**VG $375**　　　**NM $500**

○ **1250. Embassy Cinema, Peterborough (12-2-62);** Frank Ifield headlined the show.
  G $150　　　**VG $275**　　　**NM $400**

○ **1251. Helen Shapiro Tour (2-2-63 to 3-3-63);** Beatles were one of six acts on this, their first national tour; Helen Shapiro on the cover.
  G $125　　　**VG $250**　　　**NM $350**

○ **1252. Royal Hall, Harrogate (3-8-63);** the Beatles topped the bill and appeared on the program cover.
  G $200　　　**VG $300**　　　**NM $400**

1247

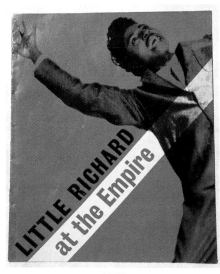

1249

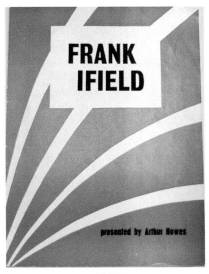

1250

1251

○ **1253.** **Roe/Montez Tour (3-9-63 to 3-31-63);** Beatles second tour of Britain with Tommy Roe and Chris Montez headlining the tour and appearing on the cover.

G $100   VG $175   NM $275

○ **1254.** **Royal Albert Hall, London (4-18-63);** this show was broadcast live by the BBC; titled "Swinging Sounds, 63."

G $200   VG $300   NM $400

○ **1255.** **Empire Pool, Wembley (4-21-63);** New Musical Express Poll Winners Concert.

G $125   VG $200   NM $300

○ **1256.** **Beatles-Roy Orbison Tour (5-18-63 to 6-9-63);** the Beatles third tour of Britain; cover is black with "Roy Orbison" over "The Beatles"; soon after the tour started the cover was changed to give the Beatles top billing.

G$75   VG $150   NM $225

○ **1257.** **Odeon Theatre, Romford (6-16-63);** last of the Mersey Beat Showcase concerts; red and white striped cover; Gerry & the Pacemakers and Billy J. Kramer among supporting acts.

G $150   VG $225   NM $300

○ **1258.** **ABC Cinema, Yarmouth (6-30-63);** The first of the Beatles summer seaside concerts.

G $75   VG $125   NM $225

○ **1259.** **Winter Gardens, Margate (7-8-63 to 7-13-63);** two shows nightly with Billy J. Kramer.

G $150   VG $225   NM $300

○ **1260.** **Odeon Theatre, Weston Super-Mare (7-22-63 to 7-27-63);** with Gerry & the Pacemakers; Orange tinted cover.

G $150   VG $225   NM $300

○ **1261.** **Urmston Show, Urmston (8-5-63);** August Bank holiday appearance at this annual fair with Brian Poole and the Tremeloes also on the bill.

G $175   VG $250   NM $350

1252

1253

1254

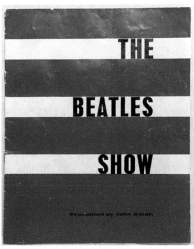

1257

1259

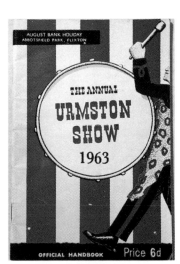

1261

○ **1262.** **Odeon Cinema, Llandudno (8-12-63 to 8-17-63);** with Billy J. Kramer and Tommy Quickly; purple-tinted cover.
G $150   **VG $225**   **NM $300**

○ **1263.** **Princess Theatre, Torquay (8-18-63);** the Fourmost were also on the bill; orange cover with B&W photo of each Beatle.
G $150   **VG $200**   **NM $300**

○ **1264.** **Gaumont Theatre, Bournemouth (8-19-63 to 8-24-63);** with Billy J. Kramer and the Dakotas; blue-tinted cover.
G $150   **VG $225**   **NM $300**

○ **1265.** **Odeon Theatre, Southport (8-26-63 to 8-31-63);** with the Pacemakers, Fourmost, and Tommy Quickly; red-tinted cover.
G $150   **VG $225**   **NM $300**

○ **1266.** **Worcester, Taunton, Luton & Croydon (9-4-63 to 9-7-63);** "The Beatles Show" presented by John Smith; group photo on red cover; four different towns in four nights
G $150   **VG $225**   **NM $300**

○ **1267.** **ABC Theatre, Blackpool (9-8-63);** generic theatre cover; Beatles pictured inside; the Countrymen were the main supporting act.
G $100   **VG $150**   **NM $200**

○ **1268.** **Royal Albert Hall, London (9-15-63);** the Beatles topped the bill at the "Great Pop Prom"; purple cover.
G $200   **VG $300**   **NM $400**

○ **1269.** **Scottish Tour (10-5-63 to 10-7-63);** appearances in Glasgow, Kirkcaidy, and Dundee.
G $175   **VG $250**   **NM $350**

○ **1270.** **Beatles Fall Tour (11-1-63 to 12-13-63);** the Beatles fourth tour of Britain; silver or gold foil cover; Peter Jay & the Jaywalkers was the main supporting act.
G $75   **VG $125**   **NM $175**

1264

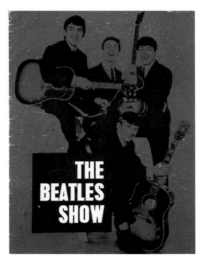
1265

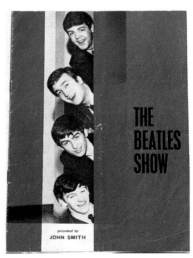
1266

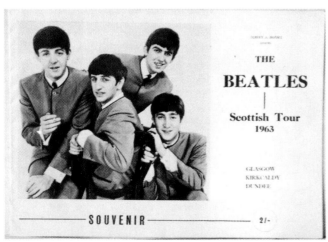
1269

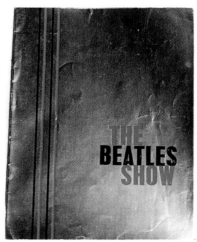
1270

○ **1271.** **Prince of Wales Theatre, London (11-4-63);** The Royal Variety Show where John made his "rattle your jewelry" statement.
G $250   VG $375   NM $500

○ **1272.** **Empire Theatre, Liverpool (12-7-63);** the Northern Fan Club appearance, including filming of the "Juke Box Jury" television show.
G $175   VG $250   NM $350

○ **1273.** **Wimbledon Palais, London (12-14-63);** the Southern Fan Club concert, including a personal meeting with all 3,000 fans!
G $175   VG $250   NM $350

○ **1274.** **Astoria Cinema, London (12-24-63 to 1-4-64);** the Beatles Christmas show; Group pictured on blue and yellow cover. ★ *Repro Alert*
G $75   VG $125   NM $200

○ **1275.** **Olympia Theatre, Paris (1-16-64 to 2-4-64);** with Trini Lopez and others.
G $150   VG $225   NM $300

○ **1276.** **Carnegie Hall, New York (2-12-64);** two evening shows at this prestigious venue.
G $250   VG $375   NM $500

○ **1277.** **Empire Pool, Wembley (4-26-64);** The New Musical Express 1963-64 Annual Poll Winners All-Star Concert.
G $100   VG $175   NM $250

○ **1278.** **ABC Cinema, Edinburgh and Odeon Cinema, Glasgow, Scotland (4-29 & 4-30-64);** "Mop-tops" on cover.
G $200   VG $300   NM $400

1271

1272

1274

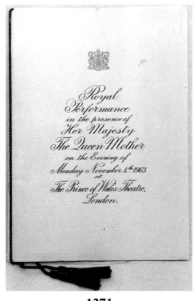

1275

1276

1278

○ **1279. Prince of Wales Theatre, London (5-31-64);** the Beatles only appearance in the Brian Epstein produced "Pops Alive" concert series.
G $200   VG $300   NM $400

○ **1280. Veilinghal, Blokker, Holland (6-6-64);** two shows at this venue; 6" x 9½"; 24 pages.
G $200   VG $300   NM $400

○ **1281. Princess Theatre, Hong Kong (6-9-64);** "The Beatles Show" on the cover with drawings of the group at bottom; Maori Hi-Five main supporting act
G $200   VG $300   NM $400

○ **1282. Australian Tour (6-12-64 to 6-20-64);** red cover with B&W photos of each Beatle; Sounds Incorporated was the main supporting act.
G $100   VG $150   NM $250

○ **1283. New Zealand Tour (6-22-64 to 6-27-64);** "The Beatles Show" with concert photo on cover
G $175   VG $250   NM $350

○ **1284. Hippodrome Theatre, Brighton (7-12-64);** Jimmy Nicols band, The Shubdubs, were a backup band at this show (Jimmy Nicol had stood-in for an ill Ringo at concerts during the first half of June 1964).
G $150   VG $225   NM $300

○ **1285. Palladium Theatre, London (7-23-64);** "Night of 100 Star" charity show; Lennon drawing on the cover.
G $150   VG $225   NM $300

1279

1280

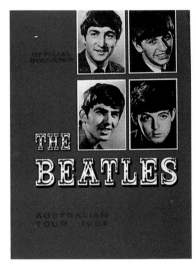

1282

1283

1284

1285

○ **1286.** **Isstadion, Stockholm, Sweden (7-28 & 7-29-64);** four shows in two days.
G $200   VG $300   NM $400

○ **1287.** **Gaumont Cinema, Bournemouth (8-2-64);** The Kinks, a new group, were among the supporting acts.
G $150   VG $225   NM $300

○ **1288.** **Futurist Theatre, Scarborough (8-9-64);** the group is pictured around a statue on the cover; same cover photo as item #1284.
G $150   VG $225   NM $300

○ **1289.** **Opera House, Blackpool (8-16-64);** orange cover with the Beatles pictured; the Kinks and the High Numbers (The Who) were also on the bill.
G $150   VG $225   NM $300

○ **1290.** **1964 North American Tour (8-19-64 to 9-20-64);** a 12" x 12" booklet with purple cover was sold during the tour; "Beatles (U.S.A.) Ltd." is printed at top of the cover; this booklet was also available from the fan club.
G $15   VG $22   NM $30

○ **1291.** **Arena, Milwaukee (9-4-64);** this Triangle Theatrical Productions' program switched the names under the photos of John and George.
G $50   VG $75   NM $100

○ **1292.** **International Amphitheatre, Chicago (9-5-64);** very similar to the program from the Arena concert the night before; the names were again switched under the photos of John and George; a version with the names corrected has been verified and is worth 25% more.
G $50   VG $75   NM $100

1286

1288

1289

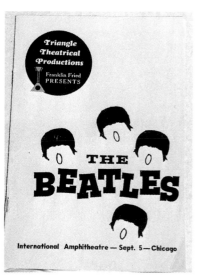

1292

○ **1293.** **Paramount Theatre, New York (9-20-64);** charity show which ended the first American Beatles tour.
G $200   **VG $300**   **NM $400**

○ **1294.** **1964 British Tour (10-9-64 to 11-10-64);** their fifth British tour; Mary Wells was the major backup artist; group pictured in playing cards on cover.
G $100   **VG $150**   **NM $200**

○ **1295.** **Odeon Theatre, Hammersmith (12-24-64 to 1-16-65);** the Beatles last Christmas show; Lennon drawing on the cover.★ *Repro Alert*
G $100   **VG $150**   **NM $200**

○ **1296.** **Empire Pool, Wembley (4-11-65);** N.M.E. 1964-65 Annual Poll-Winners All-Star Concert which also included the Rolling Stones, the Kinks, and the Moody Blues.
G $100   **VG $150**   **NM $200**

○ **1297.** **Plaza de Toros, Madrid (7-2-65);** one of two concerts in Spain, both in bullfight stadiums.
G $175   **VG $250**   **NM $350**

○ **1298.** **1965 North American Tour (8-15-65 to 8-31-65);** a 12" x 12" booklet with a color photo of the group on the cover was sold at all venues; "Beatles (U.S.A.) Ltd." was printed on the top of the cover; the booklet was also available from the fan club.
G $12   **VG $18**   **NM $25**

1293

1294

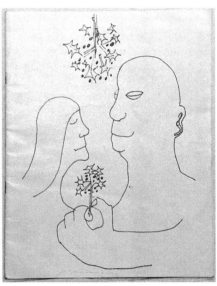

1295

1296

1297

1298

○ **1299.   White Sox Park, Chicago (8-20-65);** "Summer of Stars '65" program with Beatle bios on the first page.
G $15   VG $25   NM $40

○ **1300.   1965 British Tour (12-3-65 to 12-12-65);** their sixth and final tour of Britain; the Moody Blues were also on the bill; Cartoon Beatles on cover.
G $125   VG $175   NM $250

○ **1301.   Music of Lennon and McCartney (12-16 & 12-17-65);** Television broadcast of program taped in October 1965; featured the Beatles and others performing their songs; this booklet is actually more of a publicity book than a concert program.
G $125   VG $190   NM $250

○ **1302.   Empire Pool, Wembley (5-1-66);** N.M.E. 1964-65 Annual Poll-Winners All-Star Concert; this proved to be their last British concert.
G $125   VG $175   NM $225

○ **1303.   Budokan Hall, Tokyo (6-30-66 to 7-2-66);** five shows were performed in three days.
★ *Repro Alert*
G $125   VG $175   NM $250

○ **1304.   Rizal Stadium, Manila (7-4-66);** impressive red, white, and blue Union Jack cover design for their infamous stay in the Philippines.
G $200   VG $300   NM $400

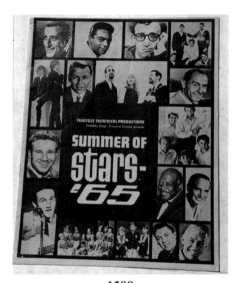

1299

1300

1301

1302

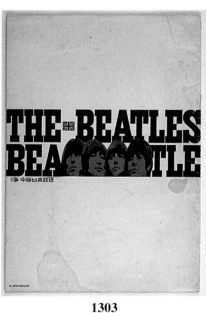

1303

1306

○ **1305.** **1966 North American Tour (8-12-66 to 8-29-66);** 12" x 12" booklet with a color photo of the group on the cover was sold at all venues; "Beatles (U.S.A.) Ltd." was printed at the top of the cover; this booklet was also available through the fan club.

  G $30   **VG $45**   **NM $60**

○ **1306.** **International Amphitheatre, Chicago (8-12-66);** "Summer of Stars '66" concert series program with the Beatles pictured on the first page; the Beatles and other acts from the series are pictured on the cover.

  G $15   **VG $25**   **NM $40**

1305

A Sampling of Concert Posters and Handbills

We have not delved into the area of concert posters and handbills in this book because so few of them exist, and they are not often seen in the collector's marketplace.

We have illustrated several examples, and will reserve further comment for a later time, hopefully, when we have more information on them.

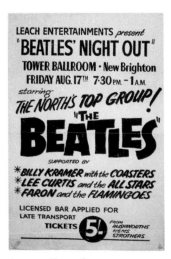

A sampling of concert posters and handbills.

15

Original Ads

As the ads on the next few pages indicate, a Beatles fan in 1964 could buy a truck load of great items for what amounts to a day's wages today. Unfortunately, few of us had the foresight or dollars to buy up these goodies and take care of them. Please don't try to order anything from these companies. They don't have the merchandise anymore—we checked!

YEAH! YEAH! YEAH! HERE THEY ARE
Beatle Dolls

only **1.66** *each*

ALL 4 FOR ONLY 5.99

Paul, Ringo, George, John

Gertz
JAMAICA
FLUSHING
HICKSVILLE
GREAT NECK
BAY SHORE

Yeah, yeah, yeah…it's the
Beatle Phonograph

Only at Gertz on Long Island!

only **29⁹⁵**

ORNAMENTED WITH AUTOGRAPHED PHOTOS OF JOHN, PAUL, GEORGE and RINGO

Beatles stockings

England's BIG HIT!

$1.50
the pair,
postpaid
(12 pairs
for $12)

BEATLE PORTRAITS

YOUR
CHOICE **39ᶜ** *each*

- 12½"x12½" etched chrome coated
- Ideal for pin-ups or for framing!

- **PAUL**
- **RINGO**
- **GEORGE**
- **JOHN**

Complete set
of four (4) _____ **1.39**

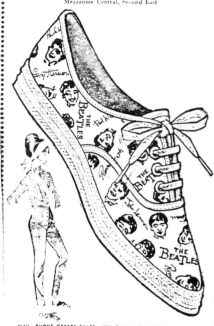

THE BEATLES
LONG EATING LICORICE RECORD
Value 10c ea.

- Scrumptious mouth watering licorice candy
- In shape of a Beatle's record

6 for **25c**
Value 3.60 **1.19** box of 36

MASTRO BEATLES "PIN-UP" GUITAR

Miniature of the popular Mastro Beatles playing guitars. Only 5" with built-in clip. Beatles' likenesses printed on face.

No. P3-DB—
DISPLAY BOX
2 dozen guitars in box.
Packed 6 boxes to carton. 6 lbs.

No. P3-DC—
DISPLAY CARD
1 dozen guitars to a card.
Packed 1 dozen cards to carton. 6 lbs.

FAB!
BEATLES WATCH FROM SMITHS

Hey girls! Here's the latest gear for Beatle Fans—a Beatle brooch watch from Smiths and it's in a sparkling real marcasite-set case shaped like a beetle with cute red eyes! It's the official Beatles Watch—*and* it comes from Smiths with five jewel accuracy, a year's guarantee and a silk and velvet lined presentation case—with *their* photo! **Great value at £5.15.0.** from any Smiths stockist.

CLOCK & WATCH DIVISION
Sectric House, London, NW2.

BEATLES HAIR SPRAY

Value $2

59c ea.

2 for **$1**
plus tax

- Large 13 oz. size
- Crystal clear spray with autographed pictures of Beatles on can

Toiletries Dept

16

Reproductions and Counterfeits

★ *Repro Alert*

The increase in Beatle memorabilia prices has led to an increase in Beatle memorabilia reproductions and counterfeits. For collecting purposes we define reproductions as copies or fakes of original 1960s memorabilia. Reproductions were made in the mid-1970s up to today. An example of a reproduction is the Beatle metal serving tray. The original 1964 edition has "Made in Great Britain" on the front. The reproduction has "Made in England" on the front. Those original items which have known copies are marked with ★ *Repro Alert* following their entry in the guide. A corresponding entry will be found in the list of reproductions. If you see ★ *Repro Alert* when checking the value of an item, be sure to check the list of reproductions for some tips to determine authenticity.

We define counterfeits as items that never had an original counterpart in the 1960s. An example of a counterfeit is a Beatle pocket mirror. None were ever made in the 1960s. Once in awhile the "Beatlefeiter" will improve on a 1960s item. An example is the Help! bandage dispenser. The dispenser is a counterfeit, though a Help! bandage was produced in 1965. These counterfeits have been "created" by imaginative capitalists to cash in on the return of Beatlemania in the mid-1970s to the present. Some of these counterfeits were made in the mid-1970s and are already twenty years old. These items may have been resold at garage sales and show some signs of age. Consequently the person selling these items may believe they were made in the 1960s. A counterfeit is usually dated "1964 NEMS ENT. LTD." or "SELTAEB." (See preface of book for licensing information.) The counterfeit leads purchasers to believe that the item was made in the 1960s. A list of known counterfeits follows the reproduction list.

The demand for Beatle memorabilia has outpaced the ability of many antique, collectibles, and flea market dealers to find original memorabilia. Counterfeit and reproduction producers have bridged this gap. Obviously every dealer may not be an expert on Beatle memorabilia, but when confronted with an ad or catalogue which offers numerous "original" 1964 items for sale in quantities, they should be suspect. These same wholesale ads offer quantities of "original" items on other superstars such as Marilyn Monroe, James Dean, Shirley Temple, Elvis, etc. Most dealers know that original memorabilia on these stars is hard to find, especially in quantity. Some dealers may unknowingly sell a counterfeit or reproduction. Be wary of dealers who do not offer return privileges or can offer no other knowledge of authenticity other than saying "the item is dated 1964." We could offer that same dealer a plastic Abe Lincoln corn cob pipe and respond "well it's dated 1863!" Items which are found in a collection from someone who was a first generation fan in the 1960s are much more likely to be genuine than a group of items from a collector who started collecting in the late 1970s. The items from the 1960s collection have a "pedigree," so to speak.

These unscrupulous manufacturers have been working overtime in the 1980s and are getting more sophisticated and creative. The phony items used to be limited to small items such as pinback buttons, plastic items, or paper items. The ability and incentive for producing higher quality phony items has increased with improved technology, such as color photocopy machines, and escalating prices for original items. Be especially wary when buying flat cardboard display cards and cardboard box items such as the Flasher Buttons display card or the Remco Doll box. A color photocopy of an original when pasted on a plain cardboard box can be convincing when viewed from afar. But close inspection may reveal blemishes, such as creases or marks, which were copied from the original, yet are smooth on the "new" box. Open the box flaps and see if the box is pure white, which may indicate age, or lack thereof. (Though people have been known to age fake concert posters by creasing them, staining them, etc.)

A few years ago a dealer had some original Beatle wigs, but not with the original packaging. The dealer printed up a good copy of the original header card. Admirably he marked on the header card that the wig was original, but that the header card was reprinted in 1983. Unfortunately, years later someone has trimmed the header card to remove the statement off some of them. We have seen dealers selling the wig with the reprinted header card as originals for a hefty price. We do not know who trimmed off the disclaimer—the dealer or the person he bought it from—but in the end the collector ends up paying for it!

While we may not be able to carbon date these items to determine age or authenticity, we can safely say that in a combined sixty years of collecting, buying and selling Beatle items we have never seen an item that suddenly "floods" the market. Occasionally any collector, even the advanced collector, can get "burned" with that "great" piece of memorabilia just acquired. Hopefully this guide will help reduce the number of burns. We have listed known reproductions and counterfeits and their defects, but counterfeiters are constantly producing new items and some may not be listed here. Reproductions can always be improved to eliminate known defects which identify them as fake. For these reasons these lists are not all inclusive.

This chapter is divided into two sections. The first lists reproductions—copies of items actually produced in the 1960s. We try to pinpoint details on these items which will help differentiate the copies from the originals. The second section of this chapter lists counterfeits—items that were never actually produced in the 1960s in the first place.

Reproductions

★ *Repro Alert* items will be found here.

Reproduction/color copy boxes have been made for many memorabilia boxes. To detect a fake, check the outside of the box. Usually it has been copied from a box that has dents, lines, or creases. If you see marks on the box or creases, feel the area. The color photocopy will be smooth where the defect is. The color white on some photocopiers will also appear to be yellowed. The reproduced box is actually a color photocopy that has been glued to a box, so check for folds that don't look like they were made by a machine. Color photocopies sometimes exhibit spotty colors which are not uniform.

Reproduction/color copy display cards have been made for several memorabilia/jewelry/pinback button items. As noted above for boxes, check for imperfections which can be seen on the card, but not felt. The color white on some color photocopies can appear yellowed. The color photocopy will have been glued to cardboard, so check the edges. Original display cards usually have machine cut holes to hang or to attach items. Repros may have these holes done manually and therefore may not be uniform in appearance. Some repro cards may lack the company name or printing which appears on the back of some display cards.

Chapter 1, General Memorabilia

RA3   **Arcade Cards;** repros generally do not have printed information on the back of the card; the photo on the repros can be fuzzy with lack of detail; originals usually are somewhat yellowed with age, while repros will be white on the back.

RA22   **Bedsheets (Detroit);** original is on paper while the repro is on a card stock; original paper is parchment-type which is a creme color, the repro is on white color stock; printing is fuzzy on the repro.

RA46   **Book Cover;** original is on high-gloss shiny paper; photo on the original is clear; repros are normally seen for sale individually.

RA50   **Bowl;** (see information on the Plate, Biscuit #RA312).

RA53   **Paul Bubble Bath;** repro is made of a resin material, while original is blue colored plastic; the resin material is white and ready to be painted; the repro does not have a cap, instead the head has threads inside it; the repro body does not have a hole on the top of the body that the cap would go on.

RA54   **Ringo Bubble Bath;** same as above; original is red colored plastic.

RA58   **Cake Decorations;** 4" tall nodders; these have flooded the market in the late 1980s; check the bottom of the base; the originals have "MADE IN HONG KONG" in raised letters on the bottom of the base; on the George and Ringo repros the "MADE IN HONG KONG" is blurry; on the John and Paul repros the "MADE IN HONG KONG" marking usually has a smear through "HONG KONG"; the repros have a streaky brown-colored hair which can look reddish; originals either have a dark brown hair or a dull lighter brown hair.

RA61   **Calendar;** the "Make a Date With The Beatles" idea has been applied to a bank.

RA85   **Clutch Purse;** repros usually lack strap handle; repros are marked with "NEMS ENT LTD 64" while the originals do not have this info printed on them.

RA89 **Coin Holder;** original is made of very thick plastic and is rounded at the bottom corners; repro is flimsy and has squared edges; the repro has a metal closer under the vinyl covering to snap the holder closed.

RA97 **Comb;** repro has less flexible teeth and weighs less than the original; original combs have "Jumbo Comb" molded into back of comb.

RA105 **Cup;** (see the information on the Plate, Biscuit #RA312).

RA121 **Bobbin' Head Dolls;** one set of repros do not have autographs at bottom; another very good set of repros has a number on the back of each head, the originals do not have a number on the back of the head; repros vary in weight from one another, the originals all weighed about the same; the detail on the faces is not as good on the repros (check the ears and hands); on the repros the Carmascot sticker on the bottom has letters that are not even and tend to run together. (Take care, we've seen where people have broken off the back of the heads to hide the fact that the repro doll had a number on the back of the head.)

RA128 **Remco Doll Box;** repro is a color photocopy glued to box; graphics are fuzzy-looking; check outside of box for imperfections such as creases or marks which were copied from the original, even though these marks are on the repro box, they will be smooth; open the box lid and look at the construction of the box to see if it looks like it was made by a machine or hand glued or folded.

RA184 **Guitar;** picture quality is poor; repro guitar is missing Selcol markings.

RA196 **Hairbrush;** the original had the Beatles' faces in raised plastic on the brush; the original brush was a solid color, the print and faces were the same color as the brush; repro has the Beatles' faces printed onto the brush; the repros have the print and faces in different colors than the brush itself.

RA199 **Hair Pomade Box;** repro is a color photocopy affixed to a box.

RA200 **Hair Spray;** repro has a color photocopy label; watch for imperfections such as tears, missing pictures or autographs, which were copied from a damaged label; the original has "SDA 1419" or similar numbers printed on the bottom of can, which is concave.

RA260 **Megaphone;** original has "Yell-A-Phone" embossed on the inside; original has a metal mouthpiece; repro has a plastic mouthpiece.

RA261 to 264 **Models;** repro models have flashing, extra thin plastic, hanging from many of the pieces; see description for repro boxes at the beginning of the listings.

RA268 **Mug;** repro has a circular-type handle; original has an almost rectangular-type handle.

RA295 **Pencil;** original has all four Beatles on one pencil; repros have one Beatle on each pencil.

RA300 **Pencil Case;** original is 4" x 7" and has no NEMS markings; repro can be a different size and is marked "NEMS ENT LTD. 1964"; original vinyl is somewhat textured; repro vinyl is smooth.

RA311 **Plate;** (see the information on the Plate, Biscuit #RA312).

RA312 **Plate, Biscuit;** repros are translucent while the originals are opaque when held up to the light; any marked "fine china" or having gold rims are repros. (This applies to any of the Washington Pottery items such as RA50-Bowl, RA105-Cup, RA311-Plate, or RA356-Saucer, except for the Candy Dishes, item #111-114. The original candy dishes do have gold rims.)

RA314 **Playing Cards;** the repro cards have photo in black and white while the originals were in color.

RA315 **Playing Cards;** the repro cards have photo in black and white while the originals were in color.

RA356 **Saucer;** (see the information on the Plate, Biscuit #RA312).

RA358 **Scarf;** repro does not have fringe; original has fringe and has a white background; the repro can also be found with a different color background.

RA396 **Tablecloth;** the repro measures 26" square, while the original is 36".

RA417 **Tray;** repro is marked "Made in England" on the front at the bottom; original is marked "Made in Great Britain" on the front; the original is heavier than the repro.

RA418 **Tumbler;** original has a white plastic lip that measures $5/8$" high; the repro lip is smaller.

RA442 **Wig;** on the repros "Mfd. by Lowell..." is printed on the rear of the cards; this printing runs into the white block letters of "Wig," on the originals it does not; repro header card had a disclaimer on the back which stated that the wig was original, but the header card was reprinted in 1983; this statement sometimes has been trimmed from the header card; watch for an uneven bottom edge, which may indicate that the card was trimmed.

Chapter 2, Yellow Submarine Items

RA443   **Alarm Clock;** original has "Beatles Yellow Submarine" on face, repro has "Beatles Yellow Submarine LOVE" on face; original has psychedelic designs on sides of clock, repro is brass colored on the sides.

RA444   **Banks;** repro is heavier and the paint shades are not the same as on an original, you would need to compare it to a known original; originals had two stickers on the bottom; original has a $1/4$" recess on the bottom, while the repro has a flat bottom (except for the hole).

RA445   **Bank;** (see Bank #RA444).

RA446   **Bank;** (see Bank #RA444).

RA447   **Bank;** (see Bank #RA444).

RA464   **Buttons;** lots of these have flooded the market, but we have not been able to determine a difference.

RA508   **Model;** the kit is a resin material which is not yellow, original is made of white plastic; see description for repro boxes at beginning of listings.

RA543   **Cereal Box;** on the original, colors on the back of the box should be vivid and uniform, colors on the repro are dull and have dots of color; repro boxes were cut by hand and flaps were not uniformly cut; check all white areas for browning or yellowing, which appears on the repros; white areas include some lettering and the background of the rub-ons on the box's front, the background on the box's side panel, and the background on the box's rear panel.

RA555   **Submarine;** reissued by Corgi in 1997 in a different box; new toy held together by screws not rivets; original box has been copied, see description of copied boxes at beginning of listings; the blue/green plastic sea insert has not been copied.

RA570   **Wrist Watch;** original has painted face, repro is a paper insert with printed face; original has a colorful decorated wrist band.

Chapter 3, Jewelry

RA592   **Brooch;** the original guitar brooch has a color paper photo insert placed under a clear plastic lens inset into the guitar, repro has a silver photo attached on the outside of the guitar (this can look like a button attached to the outside of the guitar); the repro has "The Beatles" raised in the neck strings and is marked "NEMS 64" on the head of the guitar; other repros have same color pictures as originals, but the pictures are slightly fuzzy and they lack the plastic lens over the photo; the repro backing card has straight edges while the original card has scalloped (zigzag) edges.

RA619   **Necklace;** repro is usually found as a brooch; repro measures $2^3/_8$" with a $1^3/_4$" photo disk, while the original necklace is $1^3/_8$" with $7/_8$" photo disk; the repro photo disk has a less clear photo and the disk is thinner.

RA653   **Rings;** original rings were a silver- or gold-plated plastic, repros are usually found in blue or other color plastic.

RA654   **Rings Display Card;** see description for repro display cards which appears at the beginning of these listings.

RA658   **Tac;** original B&W backing card which pictures a single Beatle has perforation dots running vertically to the edges of the card, repro card has dots which end before reaching the edge of the card; the original photo on the B&W card has definition, single strands of hair can be seen, on the repro card, the hair can look like a clump of black, especially on John, Paul, and Ringo; the color repro card has a fuzzy photo which lacks clarity and the colors look washed out.

Chapter 4, Pinback Buttons

Since pinback buttons are very cheap to produce, many have been reproduced since the 1960s. Check for clarity of photo. We have listed almost all known 1960s pins. If it is not on our list then it may be a repro or counterfeit.

RA662   **1" Buttons by the Green Duck Co.;** these have been heavily reproduced; buttons that have pins that extend beyond the outer rim should be suspect; pins which lack the company info along edge are repros.

RA676   Flip Button Display Card; see description for repro display cards at the beginning of the listings.

RA711   Button Display Poster; color photocopies exist.

Chapter 5, Pennants and Posters

RA746   Pennant; repro marked "NEMS ENT 1964" while the original did not have any markings.

RA748   Pennant; repro marked "NEMS ENT 1964" in lower left corner while the original did not have any markings.

RA751   Poster; the original has "Litho by Louis F. Dow Co. USA" printed in the center of the bottom margin of the poster, repros do not have this statement.

Chapter 6, Books

RA816   *A Cellarful of Noise* paperback; original has yellow pages (as viewed from the side) and the photo pages are on glossy paper; repro book has white pages and the photos are printed on the same type of white paper.

Chapter 7, Magazines

RA877   *The Beatles in America*, 1986 reprint has a blurry cover photo and record store ads on inside cover and centerfold; the original does not have any advertising inside.

RA916   *Paul McCartney Dead—The Great Hoax*; 1978 reprint has a $1.95 cover price, original issue from 1969 has a 60-cent cover price.

RA939   *Rolling Stone* #1; the reprint is marked as a reprint on the cover or inside the first page.

Chapter 9, Movie Items

RA996   *A Hard Day's Night* Lobby Cards; repros have a dot in the corners (dot was caused because the originals which were copied had tac holes in the corners); the colors look "washed out" on the repro and the colors tend to bleed onto white edge; on repros "The Beatles" at the bottom is printed in light red whereas it should be in bright red on originals.

RA997   *A Hard Day's Night* Poster; repros lack movie number stamping of title and movie number on the back of the poster; some repros are smaller than 27" x 42"; colors on repros can look splotchy and uneven; black color on repros does not look dark black, kind of a light black or grey; copies are on glossy-type paper while originals are on a "flat" paper.

RA1017   *Help!* Poster; see description for RA997; glossy original posters for *Help!* do exist.

RA1029   *Yellow Submarine* Poster; see description for RA997; glossy original posters for *Yellow Submarine* do exist.

Chapter 10, Record Promotion Items

RA1085   "Meet The Beatles" standee; some repros do not have easel backs; Repros lack clarity in the photos, especially on the "I Want to Hold Your Hand" picture sleeve.

RA1108   "Yesterday & Today" Butcher poster; Capitol logos are jet black on the original, Capitol logos on the repro look brown and are not jet black; on originals Paul's knees are dark brown and the Capitol logo below them should black, on the repros Paul's knees and the Capitol logo are the same color; repro has a red lightning-like line through the "Dr. Robert" song title above the album title.

RA1110 "Revolver" Poster; original has a chalky texture on the front and the back is uncoated, repro has a glossy back and the front is smooth.

Chapter 12, Fan Club Items

RA1176 Christmas Album (U.S.); known repro has blurry photos on front; check the second photo from the left at the bottom on the front cover; the words "Theatre Royal" should be visible on originals above John's head.

RA1184 Christmas Album (U.K.); label on original should be a dark green Apple label and the "A" side, one known repro has a white label, another known repro has a light green Apple label; known repro's cover has prominent black specks on the yellow background of the 1963 Christmas single sleeve which is shown on the cover.

Chapter 13, Trading Cards

The black and white 4th, 5th and 6th series cards were not made in the 1960s. The original B&W cards were numbered 1 through 165 only.

Chapter 14, Concert Tickets, Programs and Related items

Paper items are always at risk of being reproduced. If the ticket has a photo then check it for clarity. In many repros their hair will look like a solid mass. Check tickets for clarity in printing. Small logos or union marks should be clear. In some cases the repro will show perforation lines, that are printed on, but not actually perforated. If multiple tickets are available, check to make sure they are different seats! Be wary when buying a framed ticket, because it makes it hard to check the ticket to see if it a color photocopy. Most original tickets are printed with the same color paper on both sides. Many repros only have color on one side. We have seen repros made from tickets in our last book. Check to make sure the ticket doesn't have the same seat location as one that has appeared in this or previous books. Most original tickets measure from 1" x $3^1/_2$" (Dallas) to $2^1/_2$" x $5^3/_4$" (Candlestick Park), with most larger than the Dallas ticket. If the ticket is smaller, then beware.

RA1274 Astoria Cinema, London (12-24-63 to 1-4-64) program; repro is missing NEMS credits and phone number which were located below Tony Barrow's name on bottom of the first page on the originals; on centerfold of repros the word "interval" is printed in a blue box, while on the original the box is white.

RA1295 Odeon Theatre, Hammersmith (12-24-64 to 1-16-65) program; on originals at the bottom of the first page, credits are printed for lighting, scenery, costumes, etc., on repros these credits are missing.

RA1303 Budokan Hall Program; originals have a staple on the spine 4" from the top and a second staple $3^3/_4$" from the bottom, repros have the top staple starting 3" from the top and the bottom staple starts $2^1/_4$" from the bottom, the photo of the Beatles on the cover of the original program is a sepia tint, on the repro the Beatles have a gray tint; inside the front cover of the original "presents" is spelled with a small "p," on the repros "Presents" is spelled with a capitol "P"; the third page in the program is a one-third page blue color paper tab with "The Beatles" written in large letters, on originals the printing of "The Beatles" is in gray, on repros "The Beatles" is printed in black.

List of known Counterfeits

Many are marked "NEMS ENT LTD 1964."

Bandage Dispenser

Bank; round plastic Ludwig drum with painted images.

Bank; Make a Date with the Beatles.

Bubbles; plastic bottle with paper label.

Cartoon Beatle Pinbacks; as the characters from the cartoon show.

Chewing Gum

Coloring Set; B&W picture to color with crayons.

Eraser

Fan; cardboard with wooden handle.

Guitar Fob from Candlestick Park concert

Guitar Keychain

Gumball Machine Label

Help! **Pinback Button**

Help! **Whistle**

Key Ring; fan club.

Knife; pocket or folding.

KYA Keychain

Marbles

Paperweight

Pen and Holder Desk Set

Pendant; heart-shaped metal with B&W group photo; raised signatures on the back; $2^{1}/_{2}$" x 2".

Pinback Buttons; originals usually are 1", $2^{1}/_{2}$" (flasher), or $3^{1}/_{2}$" (slogan) diameter in size.

Pocket Mirror

Puzzle, Jigsaw; B&W picture; "Official Beatle Fan Club" printed on it.

Ring; gold with raised faces.

Ruler

Slide Puzzle; marked as fan club item.

Spoons

Tape Measure

Thermometer; metal; marked as fan club item.

Thimbles

TWA Flight Bag; red vinyl with shoulder strap.

Wallet Dollar; small plastic fold-open wallet with B&W picture of Beatle on one side and Beatle dollars inside.

Wooden Nickels

Wristwatch

Various counterfeits and reproductions.

GLOSSARY

B&W: Black and white. In most cases this refers to a photo.

BBC: British Broadcasting Corporation

Counterfeit: An item purporting to have been made in the 1960s, but actually made in the 1970s up to today. An item that never had an original counterpart in the 1960s.

Date: Listed as Month-Date-Year (9-8-63 is September 8, 1963)

Die-cut: A process by which an item is cut into a particular shape or to outline a specific image.

Flasher: An insert (usually found on a pinback button or ring) which has an illustration or words on it. The illustration or words change when viewed at different angles.

Flexi disc: A record which is pressed on a flimsy sound sheet.

(G): Good condition. (See guidelines in Introduction and at the beginning of certain chapters.)

Header card: Cardboard card with product name, artwork, etc. which is placed on top of a plastic or cellophane bag containing the product. Many header cards had a hole punched in them, enabling the package to hang from a rack in a store.

Mfd.: Manufactured

Motion display: A display item which has moving parts powered by a motor.

(NM): Near mint condition. (See guidelines in Introduction or at the beginning of certain chapters.)

NME: *New Musical Express*. Weekly British music newspaper.

OP: Original packaging.

Picture sleeve: Paper or cardboard jacket which is issued for a 7" record. (This sleeve usually has a photo of the group or artwork on it.)

Pinback button: An ornamental badge with pin attachment on back made to be worn on clothing.

Pub.: Published

Rack pack: Three pack of trading cards that has a header card and is made to hang on a rack. Term can also be used for other items which have a header card and were made to hang on a rack in a store.

Reproduction: Copies or fakes of original 1960s pieces of memorabilia. Reproductions were made in the mid-1970s up to today.

Shrink wrap: Clear plastic covering placed over a product and exposed to heat sealing the product in plastic.

U.K.: United Kingdom, Britain

U.S.: The United States

(VG): Very good condition. (See guidelines in Introduction or at beginning of certain chapters.)